ARTISANS, PEASANTS & PROLETARIANS
—1760-1860—

Essays presented to Gwyn A. Williams

Edited by

CLIVE EMSLEY and JAMES WALVIN

CROOM HELM
London • Sydney • Dover, New Hampshire

© 1985 Clive Emsley, James Walvin and contributors
Croom Helm Ltd, Provident House, Burrell Row,
Beckenham, Kent BR3 1AT

Croom Helm Australia Pty Ltd, Suite 4, 6th Floor,
64-76 Kippax Street, Surry Hills, NSW 2010, Australia

British Library Cataloguing in Publication Data

Artisans, peasants and proletarians, 1760-1860:
   essays presented to Gwyn A. Williams.
   1. Social history — Modern, 1500-
   I. Emsley, Clive   II. Walvin, James
   III. Williams, Gwyn A.
   370.19'3   HN13

ISBN 0-7099-3635-4

Croom Helm Ltd, 51 Washington Street,
Dover, New Hampshire 03820, USA

Library of Congress Cataloging in Publication Data

Main entry under title:

Artisans, peasants, and proletarians, 1760-1860.

   Bibliography: P.
   Includes index.
   1. Great Britain—social conditions—addresses,
essays, lectures. 2. Europe—social conditions—
addresses, essays, lectures. 3. Labor and laboring
classes—Great Britain—history—addresses, essays,
lectures. 4. Labor and laboring classes—Europe—
addresses, essays, lectures. 5. Williams, Gwyn A.
I. Williams, Gwyn A. II. Emsley, Clive. III. Walvin
James.
HN388.A78   1985   305.5'62'094   85-17498
ISBN 0-7099-3635-4

Typeset by Leaper & Gard Limited, Bristol, England
Printed and bound in Great Britain
by Billing & Sons Limited, Worcester.

CONTENTS

I Gwyn,
Hanesydd ei werin,
Hanesydd y werin.

INTRODUCTION

Editors of any *Festschrift* are inevitably faced by a variety of often conflicting problems. Their basic ambition — to pay homage to their chosen scholar — is rarely reason for the publication in a single volume of essays which all too often have little in common. In this instance we feel that we have assembled a collection with a broad internal coherence: each essay explores an aspect of the historical experience of the plebeian classes during the turbulent era of 'the dual revolution'. Our regret is that the collection, varied and even diffuse as some readers may find it, scarcely scratches the surface of the extraordinary range of interests — and the remarkably varied influence — of Gwyn A. Williams. Indeed, it is one of his unusual claims to abiding fame that Gwyn Williams' scholarship, teaching and general intellectual influence have spilled into a variety of historical areas (and even into other disciplines and literary forms). In an academic profession which takes its greatest pride in specialisation (often to a restrictive degree) it is perhaps Gwyn's *range* of historical interests which has marked him out as a distinctive and even unique British scholar. Moreover this range of interest cannot be accused of being merely general historical interest. Whatever he has published has been characterised by exacting scholarship, a distinction and originality, in conception, execution and expression, which has substantially reformed the study of these various fields.

It is worth, at this point, reminding ourselves of Gwyn Williams' written historical achievements, if only to illustrate his remarkable range. His early career, as lecturer in Welsh History at Aberystwyth was punctuated by a series of superb articles in that field. But in English historical circles — where Celtic scholars and their journals were often considered marginal — the general significance of many of those early articles remained unappreciated outside the boundaries of Welsh history. Later, when the substance of those pieces came to be incorporated in the re-assessment of British history, it became apparent to an ever-widening circle that Gwyn Williams' articles of the early 1960s were not merely innovative in themselves but continued to be a turning-point in the historiography of modern Britain. To a marked degree, the cul-

1

mination of this early work can be seen in his five books on Wales — published between 1978 and 1985 — which develop and incorporate his work of two decades earlier and which are similarly characterised, in mature form, by a unique combination of perception and insight, qualities which have always marked out Gwyn Williams from the great majority of his historical colleagues. In a sense Gwyn's historical work came full circle when, in the mid-1980s he ended his university career with a book *When Was Wales?*, which returned to some of the issues explored a generation earlier — the historical forging of the Welsh people. But, like these earlier articles, the importance of *When Was Wales?* transcends the national limits of the study.

The symmetry of Gwyn Williams' publishing career to date, originating and culminating in Welsh history, can mask the range of his work. His first major scholarly impact was his study *Medieval London*, and while he is perhaps best known as a modern historian, his work as a medievalist produced a book which remains a classic more than 20 years after publication. Moreover, it was for his work on medieval London that Gwyn Williams was awarded the prestigous Alexander Prize in 1960. All of these achievements were effected from the Universities of Wales and London in his capacity as teacher and researcher. But it was Gwyn Williams' move to the new University of York in 1963 which heralded a new direction to his teaching and writing.

The challenge of helping to establish a new department of history and of creating new courses provided the foundation for Gwyn Williams' new interests. From his teaching on late eighteenth and early nineteenth-century western history, there emerged a book of comparative history, *Artisans and Sansculottes* (1968), which is a masterpiece of concise and perceptive analysis. This study of Britain and France in the revolutionary decade of the 1790s was a major contribution to that new wave of historiography effectively set in motion by E.P. Thompson's *Making of the English Working Class* (1963). Furthermore it was Gwyn's teaching in this field that persuaded a number of undergraduates and graduate students to work in this expanding field of historical research — a fact more than amply reflected among contributors to this volume. At York, as earlier at Aberystwyth, Gwyn established an immediate and continuing reputation as a teacher and lecturer of rare brilliance. Classes and lectures, always full to overflowing, were the vehicle not only for the exposition of a remarkable historical range of interests but also the means of enthusing successive waves of students with history. Studying history became a rare and memorable excitement in a fashion which is hard to convey to those unlucky enough never to have been exposed to his unique style of teaching. Term after term, the highlight of the university's varied offerings were Gwyn's lectures, often crowded and presented for a wider, non-historical audience. From one of these lectures on Goya, there emerged eventually a brilliant study of *Goya* (1976; paperback edition, 1984). Other lecture series — notably one on the 1968 'Days of May' — remained unpublished, but none the less proved inspirational to the hundreds of students and staff who crowded the halls to listen to them.

It was in the mid-1960s that the work of Antonio Gramsci began to attract interest among growing numbers of western scholars. Although Gwyn Williams' own teaching and scholarly work began to reflect this interest, it is often forgotten that his work on Gramsci long pre-dated the popular upsurge in Gramscian studies. Indeed his article on hegemony, 'The concept of *Egemonia* in the thought of Antonio Gramsci', (1960), was a pioneering study which, characteristically, paved the way for the work of many subsequent scholars in the field. Thus not only did Gwyn range far beyond the normally restrictive boundaries of specialised academic history, but he set his own seal of innovation and originality on those areas he studied. His was, and remains, a remarkable and riveting brilliance which was never dimmed nor been deflected by being applied to an unusually wide range of topics. Conversely, each topic he worked on was fundamentally enlivened and revised by Gwyn Williams' scholarly and literary impact.

Gwyn Williams' return to the University of Wales in 1975 to a Chair in Cardiff witnessed a return not only to his home region, but a positive explosion of historical output. Within a decade, he published five books on Welsh history, each foreshadowed by earlier work, but each an important (and accumulating) contribution to Welsh history. Although independent and autonomous, the first four of these books (*The Merthyr Rising, The Search for Beulah Land, Madoc* and *The Welsh in their History*) were stepping-stones (although it could not have been obvious at the time) toward the book *When Was Wales?* The importance of this last book has still to be fully digested. But even at this early date it is possible to see *When Was Wales?* as a major achievement, not merely in terms of Welsh history but, more subtly, for the wider study of British history. Historians of England can find in that book a series of fascinating insights and subtle reappraisals of English no less than Welsh history. Indeed it seems to the editors that *When Was Wales?* has a major historiographical significance for the study of modern British history on a par with Edward Thompson's *Making*... 20 years earlier. The book is unquestionably a superb example of a master craftsman at the peak of his very considerable powers. Yet there is always a danger in such a *Festschrift*, of writing an appreciation which reads more like an obituary than an introduction. Now that Gwyn has retired from active university life we can look forward to more publications.

This volume is designed to mark Gwyn Williams' retirement from university work and to celebrate his sixtieth birthday. Yet it is surely ironic that British universities are losing one of *the* great teachers of his generation, in large measure as a result of the economies forced on universities in the early 1980s. In different times, or different societies, a man of such attainment — an historian of major eminence and a uniquely gifted teacher — would be cherished and encouraged to enhance the intellectual life of his institution. The loss of senior academics of such quality is little short of a tragedy for the intellectual well-being of British universities.

It would be wrong however to suggest that Gwyn Williams' attainments and influence have been restricted to academic life. Few who have experienced his public oratory can be in any doubt of his brilliance as a public speaker. He has, in addition, been a highly successful broadcaster on radio and television and has had his own plays performed in public and on radio.

It is, naturally enough, impossible to do justice to the full range of Gwyn Williams' interests in a volume of this kind. Indeed it would be impossible to try to represent the diversity of his historical interests in a single volume. We have therefore opted for a collection of essays which cluster around one of Gwyn's prime and abiding interests — an interest which is, we feel, summed up in the title *Artisans, Peasants and Proletarians*. The next difficulty faced by the editors was to decide on the team of contributors; there are numerous historians — former pupils, graduate students and colleagues — who were willing and keen to contribute. The eventual list of contributors was chosen to give some flavour of Gwyn's abiding influence in a reasonably narrow historical period and yet to create a book which was also autonomous and coherent. This is a book which can stand on its own as an independent volume whose essays are designed to cohere into a significant collection. Moreover each specific essay follows a particular line of inquiry — an idea, a suggestion — first raised by Gwyn himself. In one capacity or another all the essayists were taught by Gwyn; some were subsequently colleagues. But all bear the imprint of his historical influence.

It seems unlikely that our collective endeavours will even remotely mirror those unique qualities of Gwyn Williams — qualities which first excited us and persuaded us to embark on historical careers. Equally his own intellectual and literary achievements will continue to influence an expansive and appreciative audience and readership. Our modest ambition is to make our own contribution in areas already marked by his own work. At a more personal level, this book is conceived as an act of individual and collective *pietàs* to a man of extraordinary talents.

Clive Emsley
James Walvin

1 TRANSATLANTIC PATRIOTISM: POLITICAL EXILES AND AMERICA IN THE AGE OF REVOLUTIONS

Michael Durey

I

On 7 September 1784 Mathew Carey, the young but lame Roman Catholic editor and proprietor of the fiercely patriotic Dublin *Volunteer's Journal*, limped up the gangway of the *America*, Captain Keiler, bound for that asylum of liberty, the United States. Dressed in female clothing, with £25 in his pocket, he had evaded the clutches of the Dublin magistrates who sought him to answer a charge of criminal libel against John Foster, Speaker of the Irish House of Commons. Carey landed in Philadelphia seven weeks later, poorer but wiser for losing half of his money to a gang of sharpers.[1]

For the next 15 years he literally struggled: against the possible financial failures of his printing ventures and bookselling business; against rival editors (in 1785 he was wounded in a duel with the anti-federalist and anti-Irish republican Eleazer Oswald, who later left his wife and children 'in order to struggle under the banner of liberty' in France, commanded a regiment under Dumouriez at Jemappes, and acted as a French agent to the United Irishmen);[2] and, more circumspectly, in the 1790s against the monarchist and aristocratic pretensions of Federalism. A moderate republican during Jefferson's administrations, in the war of 1812 Carey abandoned all political parties and took the high ground of political conciliation and American nationalism.[3] When he died in 1839, renowned as the largest bookseller in the United States and the father of American cultural and economic nationalism, his funeral procession was the second largest ever seen in Philadelphia.

Nearly nine years after Carey's flight, early in January 1793, as the Lord Advocate Robert Dundas was ordering the arrest of Thomas Muir in Edinburgh, the outlawed messenger-at-arms and writer James Thomson Callender took flight to London, from

where he too escaped to America. The author of two pamphlets
critical of Dr Samuel Johnson in the early 1780s,[4] and a member
of a circle of aspiring writers surrounding the eccentric judge, Lord
Gardenstone (who kept a pig in his bedroom over which he draped
his breeches to keep it warm), Callender in July 1792 had
published *The Political Progress of Britain*, in which he attacked
the royal family and Westminster's political control of Scotland,
and in December had represented the Canongate No.1 Friends of
the People at the first Scottish Convention.[5] In America, like
Carey, Callender in the 1790s became a strong supporter of the
Jeffersonian Democratic Republicans, and again like Carey
clashed violently in print with the irascible Tory William Cobbett,
who immortalised the Scotsman as 'NEWGATE Callender'.[6]
Always close to or below the poverty line in Philadelphia (he had a
wife, four children and a drinking habit to support),[7] Callender
gained notoriety first for forcing Alexander Hamilton publicly to
admit to an extramarital affair which had led to blackmail, then for
his farce of a trial before the 'Braxfield' of the American courts,
Judge Chase, at which he was convicted and imprisoned for libel-
ling President John Adams, and finally, having received no reward
for his martyrdom, for turning on his mentor Thomas Jefferson
and publicising his supposed relationship with his black slave,
Monticello Sally. Frustrated, friendless (except for some erstwhile
Federalist enemies), his wife dead of yellow fever, and only
recently reunited with two of his children whom he could not support, 'nearly putrid in his own filth', Callender was found dead in
three feet of water in the James river in Virginia in July 1803. The
verdict of the coroner's jury was accidental drowning while intoxi-
cated, but for Meriwether Jones, Callender's rival Republican
editor in Richmond, it was a clear case of suicide, 'putting a miserable end to a miserable life'.[8]

These sketches of the careers of Carey and of Callender represent the outer limits of a spectrum of experiences undergone by
those British and Irish patriots who, in the late eighteenth century,
were forced into exile across the Atlantic, victims of their own zeal
for a libertarian society based on a rational polity, and of the
repressive policies of the British government under William Pitt.
The exact number of people who became refugees because of their
political beliefs and activities will never be known, but so far,
omitting from consideration those Welsh settlers of Beula and on
the Ohio whom Gwyn Williams has brought so vividly to life,[9] I

have collected information, of varying extent, on 66 men who were active in British opposition politics between the American Revolution and the Irish Rebellion of 1798, and who for political reasons decided to emigrate to the United States.

Some of these 'foreign intriguers', 'wild Irishmen' and 'anglo-democratic outlaws'[10] have been the subject of previous research. Their careers before they fled to America can sometimes be pieced together from a number of works focusing on the popular political movements in Britain and Ireland in the 1790s[11] although to date there has been no consideration of them as a group with common characteristics. Arthur Sheps has explored the idea of America as a haven of liberty for political radicals in the late eighteenth century. Imbued with the Old Whig or Commonwealth ideas of Harrington, Sidney and Locke, he claims, these radicals viewed America as 'a retreat from oppression and a place where the greatest extent of natural liberties ... might be enjoyed.' Apparently, however, America was 'an asylum many contemplated but few sought'.[12]

Some of the refugees have also featured in works concerned with particular aspects of American politics in the 1790s, such as James Morton Smith's *Freedom's Fetters* on the alien and sedition laws, Joyce Appleby's *Capitalism and a New Social Order* in which their political impact is underestimated, William F. Brown Jr's thesis on John Adams and the American press, and Donald H. Stewart's book on the Republican press in the 1790s.[13] Smith views the most politically active of the refugees as victims of Federalist repression; Appleby combines the same activists with men who emigrated from Britain or Ireland long before the 1790s (the common denominator being their political activism in America, not in Britain or Ireland); and Brown and Stewart again concentrate on the same half-dozen refugees who are involved with the Republican press. The names of Cooper, Priestley, Callender, Duane and Paine continually recur. It is somewhat similar with articles and books on individual refugees: there is Malone's life of Cooper, and two pieces on Priestley's, and two on Paine's declining years in America.[14] Callender has been resurrected as the debate on Jefferson and Monticello Sally has become rekindled.[15]

The one major exception to this narrow focus on a handful of political refugees is Richard Twomey's impressive thesis on Anglo–American radicalism in the United States between 1790 and 1820.[16] Twomey not only considers a broader range of refugees than most (he is particularly interested in the United Irish immigration at the end of the century), but he also examines issues other than the battle against Federalism during Adams' presidency. In particular, he explores the changing nature of 'Jacobin' ideology, especially with reference to the question of class relations in the early nineteenth century. Nevertheless, despite his wider focus, Twomey still concentrates primarily on the 'twenty or more' prominent leaders who emigrated between 1794 and 1806, and on their political activities.[17]

It is the purpose of this paper to demonstrate that by broadening the approach to the political refugees, and by considering the 66 on whom there is some information, a clearer understanding of their role in America can be achieved. This requires an examination of the refugees' common social characteristics. I shall concentrate on their social status and on their religious beliefs, which together made them essentially *marginal* to the dominant culture in Britain and Ireland. In addition, I shall examine their political beliefs in the light of their marginality and shall argue that underpinning their political stance was a quasi-millennial world view, predicated on a belief in the unlimited progress of man in a market society, where talent, unhindered by prescriptive status norms, would be given full freedom of expression.

Finally, I shall examine the impact of the inflow of meritocratic ideas and agitators on American life, and will show that their influence was not confined merely to the political process, but was also exerted in the fields of political economy and of culture. I do not intend to reduce the importance of the refugees' political role in America: indeed, I hope to show that it has been underestimated. To the surprise and chagrin of many of the exiles, their beliefs in the virtues of merit and of talent had to be fought for in the United States. The war was waged through the Democratic Republican Party, and the exiles played a significant part in the ultimate defeat of the Federalists, those

> traitors, who have the assurance to preach *royalty*, who not satisfied to make their fortunes at the expense of Americans, set themselves up as judges of government and regulatories of states, always giving the *preference* to British institutions, and treacherously infusing the *royal poison* into weak minds.[18]

What was at stake in America was the possibility of an open, ascriptive society, where all fields of endeavour were open to the talented. It was a libertarian vision which the exiles had nurtured and fought for in the popular societies in Britain and Ireland in the 1790s.

II

Thousands of people emigrated to America from Britain and Ireland in the 1790s. As Callender noted in 1795, 'Of emigrants who intend to settle in the United States, at least nineteen parts out of twenty arrive from Britain and Ireland. Of these, a numerous majority remove, not in search of a republic, but of bread.'[19] Most of these immigrants were from Ireland. In 1791 Mathew Carey informed John Chambers, a Dublin United Irish printer who subsequently migrated to America, that between 3000 and 4000 Irish immigrants had reached Philadelphia that summer alone. On average, about 3000 Irish arrived annually in America over the next 10 years (400 'men of '98' arrived in just one ship in Norfolk, Virginia in the early 1800s).[20]

The 66 political refugees amongst this mass migration may appear only a trivial proportion, and it is undoubtedly true that the number of emigrants who moved because of their political activities was considerably higher. Callender's distinction between immigrants seeking a republic and those seeking bread, which effectively separates the perceptions of America as an asylum of liberty and as a land of opportunity, ignores the fact that many anonymous immigrants viewed America in both ways. Rank-and-file members of the popular societies, especially the Irish who carried the stigma of insurrection but who were not part of the United Irish leadership, made up a part of the mass migration. They brought with them attitudes shaped by their experiences in the popular societies, even if on arrival they scattered themselves across America and did not play a major role in American political affairs.

Very occasionally glimpses of these anonymous exiles can be seen: Morgan John Rhees on his journey through the southern states met in Savannah 'Citizen S., an English republican refugee from Manchester' (possibly one Smith, a member of the plebeian Manchester Reformation Society who had fled in 1794); and in 1809 an unnamed Scotsman, who had been involved in the Watt

conspiracy of 1794, was found working on one of the new steam-
boats on the Delaware river: 'He is here a very useful man, and
there is no danger of his setting the Delaware on fire.'[21]
Thus for most, America was a place to retreat into anonymity.
Considering their experiences in Britain, this desire can be readily
understood, as the case of the Belfast tailor, Joseph Cuthbert,
affirms. He was pilloried and imprisoned in 1793 for trying to
corrupt a soldier by giving him an extract of one of Thomas
Cooper's pamphlets (probably his anti-war leaflet signed 'Sydney',
which circulated so widely in Scotland also in late 1792). In
November 1796 Cuthbert was one of four arrested on the oaths of
a sergeant of invalids and a prostitute and charged with conspiracy
to murder. None was convicted, but Cuthbert was immediately re-
arrested on a charge of high treason. He was never brought to trial,
but with the United Irish leaders became a state prisoner and was
transferred to Fort St George, Scotland, only arriving in New York
in 1802.[22] Altogether he was in prison for seven years, easily long
enough to be ruined financially (and probably spiritually) for his
political convictions. A new, anonymous life across the Atlantic
had its attractions.

Nevertheless, even though there is this hidden element to the
political migrations from Britain and Ireland, it is those whose
careers can be documented who are most important for an understanding of the impact of British ideas across the Atlantic. Of the
66 known refugees, 33 were Irish, 22 English and 11 Scottish. In
their social composition the political exiles differed fundamentally
from the majority of the immigrants. Fewer than one-third of the
patriots can be classified within the journeyman/lowly artisan
stratum of society, the uneasy class living precariously only one
step away from the abyss of poverty. Most of these came from
England (13 of the 22); only two of the Scots and five of the Irish
were of the artisan trades. These artisans, unlike their anonymous
peers, have left some record of their activities in Britain and of
their removal to America primarily through their connections with
notable middle-class patriots. Nearly one-half of the English
artisans, for instance, are known because of their involvement in
Thomas Cooper's emigration scheme from Manchester in 1794.
Similarly, Richard Davison, the journeyman printer and secretary
of the Sheffield Constitutional Society, left for America in 1794
with his master, Joseph Gales. Once in the United States, unless
they took up the printing and publishing trades, as did Davison in

Warrenton, North Carolina, John Miller in Charleston, and Patrick Byrne in Philadelphia, they too sank into obscurity.[23]

More than 70 per cent of the political exiles were from middle-class backgrounds, or were in the process — before their political activities intervened — of attempting to rise into the solid middle ranks of society. William Duane, although born in upstate New York, grew up in Ireland, and was one of a number of future patriots whose families were part of a small but growing Roman Catholic middle class in Ireland. The father of Mathew and James Carey was a prosperous baker in Dublin who had made good by supplying the British navy. Patrick Byrne, Dublin printer and bookseller, whose shop was a meeting-house for United Irishmen, was one of the first three Roman Catholics to be admitted as full members into the Guild of Booksellers. The father of William James MacNeven, physician, chemist and United Irishman, was a Roman Catholic country gentleman who lived on his own country estate in County Galway.[24]

Also amongst the Irish refugees were Thomas Addis Emmet, qualified in both medicine and law, whose father was State Physician in Dublin; Edward Hudson, whose father was a captain; William Sampson, the son of a Presbyterian minister; and Harman Blennerhassett, whose family were of independent means.[25] Even John Binns, who is normally referred to as a plumber or plumber's mate (he worked for his brother Benjamin in London),[26] was the son of a prosperous ironmonger, and relatives on both sides of his family were involved in Irish politics.[27] From Scotland, James Tytler's father was a clergyman; Callender was the son of a tobacco factor; and John Craig Millar's father was Professor of Civil Law at Glasgow University.[28] Even amongst the English 'artisans', Daniel Isaac Eaton, whose father was also a printer and publisher, received a good secondary education which included studying in France; and Joseph Gales came from a long line of country school-teachers.[30]

The same respectable middle-class nature of the political exiles is inescapable when their occupations are considered. At least seven were qualified in medicine; Callender had attended some of the medical lectures at the University of Edinburgh; Hudson was a dentist; and John Edmonds Stock was a medical student at the time he became embroiled in the Watt conspiracy in Edinburgh.[31] Millar, Sampson, Blennerhassett and Emmet were lawyers or barristers. Thomas Ledlie Birch was a Presbyterian minister, David

Baillie Warden, James Hull and John Miles were probationer Presbyterian ministers, Denis Driscol had been a clergyman before taking up the pen, and Joseph Priestley was an eminent, if controversial, divine.[32] Thomas Cooper was, before the collapse of his business in 1793, a prosperous manufacturer, and the United Irishman Henry Jackson was a wealthy ironfounder (he owned a country house called Fort Paine).[33] At least four of the refugees were to hold professorships at American institutes of higher learning: Cooper, MacNeven, the Scotsman John Maclean, who became Professor of Chemistry and Natural History at Princeton on his arrival in America in 1795, and the United Irishman Daniel McCurtin, who taught at Washington College in Maryland.[34] In addition, Warden was offered a professorship at Union College, Schenectady, but became for a while principal tutor at the Columbia Academy in New York; and John Wood, the Scotsman, was tutor to Aaron Burr's accomplished daughter.[35] At least 18 of the exiles had attended university, although by no means all took a formal degree.

Finally, nearly one-half of the 66 exiles were involved at one time or another in journalism and pamphleteering, 15 of whom made the media their career. They ranged from the hack writers Callender and James 'Balloon' Tytler, and the unsuccessful newspaper owners and editors such as James Carey and John Mason Williams (Carey published eight different and short-lived newspapers in America between 1792 and 1800), to the successful newspaper barons such as William Duane, John Binns (in America) and Joseph Gales.[36] These professional media men led the fight against Federalism, and although they were harried, assaulted and maligned (they gave as good as they got), the subsequent reputation of the patriot refugees is based primarily on their activities.

The most obvious point to emerge from this occupational analysis is the fact that the majority of political refugees were part of what today we would call the liberal professions: the law, the Church, medicine, education and journalism. Only two of the exiles were involved in industrial or mercantile enterprises: Henry Jackson and Thomas Cooper (and even the latter was a trained lawyer). Thus it is probably true to say that the political refugees were unrepresentative of patriot politics in Britain in two ways: in the small number of known emigré artisans, compared with the undoubted majority of such trades in the membership of the popular societies; and in the almost complete absence of mercantile or manufacturing representatives, such groups being of some consequence in popular politics at least until 1794. In other words, it appears that 'men of moveable property', as John Brewer calls them,[37] were not themselves particularly mobile; when they abandoned popular politics, they either could not, or would not, pack up their property and head across the Atlantic.[38]

On the other hand, the exiles *were* representative of the leadership cadres of the popular movements in Britain and Ireland, and as such they reflect one of the major characteristics of the patriot leaders — their marginality. The concept of the marginal man is of long standing in sociology, being used first by Robert Park in 1927. He defined the marginal man as one who moves in more than one social world but who is not completely at home in any. Schermerhorn's definition is more precise, a marginal man being

any individual who is simultaneously a member (by ascription, self-reference or achievement) of two or more groups whose social definitions and cultural norms are distinct from each other.[39]

The members of the liberal professions in the late eighteenth century were classically caught between two worlds; one response to that situation was to work towards changing the dominant world, the one of privilege, interest and influence, to open it up so that individual marginalism could be reduced and merit given its true reward. For the professional classes, this was precisely the appeal of the cry for liberty.

The liberal professions in the eighteenth century did not have, except at the very highest echelons, the social status and esteem which they have today. None of the basic tenets of professionalism — a single portal of entry into a profession, an enforceable code of professional conduct, *esprit de corps*, an ideal of community service — existed, except in the most rudimentary fashion. The power, authority and status within the professions were confined to small oligarchies who jealously defended their privileges. The majority of professionals could not, on merit, improve their position within their chosen fields, nor could they attain social respectability and status within the community unless they showed suitable deference to the local élites. In a hierarchical society, where patronage made the wheels turn smoothly, the skills of

ingratiation, dependency and fealty were necessary for the journalist mindful of readership figures and advertising volume, for the
medical man building up his practice, and for the lawyer with his
eye on the profits from estate agencies. Called 'the forgotten
middle class' by Harold Perkin, doctors, lawyers and pedagogues
had an ambiguous identity, caught betwixt and between in a
society where prescription remained paramount. This is not to say
that there were strong moves for reform of the professions in the
1790s; rather, amongst individuals in the professions, those in particular who were socially aspiring but hostile to deferential modes
of living, who were not necessarily the most brilliant (they would
be taken up by the élites and shown off like toy poodles)[40] but of
considerable, if untapped, abilities, there was a powerful sense that
their talents were under-used, and that it was the structure of
society, based on an unreformed political system, which manufactured their marginality.[41]

The feeling of being outsiders and second-class citizens was
reinforced for many patriots in the 1790s by their religious disabilities.[42] The Test and Corporation Acts and, in Ireland, the anti-
Roman Catholic Penal Laws, although not strictly enforced,
encoded social discrimination against those with heterodox
religious beliefs. Although in the late eighteenth century Protestant
dissenters made up only about 7 per cent of the population of
England, they were grossly over-represented in the movements for
political reform. In Isaac Kramnick's view, 'They were the boldest
voices attacking the traditional order; they were the secular pro-
phets, the vanguard, of a new social order.'[43] It was out of the
unsuccessful campaign to repeal the Test and Corporation Acts
between 1787 and 1790 that the Radical Dissenters' movement for
political reform emerged, led by Priestley in Birmingham, Thomas
Walker and Thomas Cooper in Manchester, and, until his death in
1790, Richard Price in London.[44] In the ideology of Dissent,
religious freedom and political liberty — both seen as inalienable
natural rights — were hard to distinguish.[45] Richard Dinmore of
Norwich, who was ostracised for refusing to sign the conservative
Associators' petition against subversive ideas in 1792 and who
later emigrated to America, placed first on his list of 40 'Democratic Aphorisms' summing up patriot principles, the opinion that
'Man requires no moral mediator between himself and God'.
'Jacobinism' was attractive because 'they are of all religions; their
question is — How does a man act? Not, how does he think? Many

years later, in 1824, the Unitarian Joseph Gales was still echoing these sentiments. Diversity of religious opinion was not a lamentable evil; 'All that is necessary to produce happiness ... is that men should think charitably of each other, and agree to differ, believing that everyone who professes himself to be guided by the principles of the Gospel, and leads a good life, is sincere in his profession.'[46] However, from 1794 the loyalist reaction to the political clamour scared away most of the middle-class dissenters, leaving leaders such as Walker and Cooper uncomfortably exposed.[47]

There were two main phases of patriot emigration: between 1794 and 1796, and from 1798 to the early 1800s. It is not surprising to find that in both periods most of the refugees were dissenters. In the first phase, when the English emigration was at its height, the refugees reflected the defeat of the Radical Dissenters; many of those heading for America were either Unitarians or Deists, the former primarily from that circle of rational religion which encompassed the leadership of the Manchester Constitutional Society and the Gravel Pit chapel in Hackney. Their departure was a grievous blow to English Unitarianism, which collapsed as a political force and became loyalist and quietist. For Anna Barbauld, the East Anglian bluestocking, Cooper, Priestley, Toulmin and Gales took with them to America the very essence of European civilisation.[48] A major part of America's appeal was the absence (outside of New England) of an established church; it was well known that 'every man has as good a right as another, to enjoy his religious opinions in the United States'.[49] Thus, at a stroke, by emigration the marginal position of the dissenting refugees would be reduced.

The next major phase of patriot emigration, after 1798, consisted primarily of United Irish leaders, although James Cheetham, of the Manchester Constitutional Society and the United Englishmen, the apothecary Richard Dinmore, the Deist and blasphemer John Wood, and John Binns of the London Corresponding Society and the United Englishmen did not leave until this period. The United Irish leaders were unique in Ireland for their non-sectarianism and included Church of Ireland members such as Thomas Emmet and John Chambers, Ulster Presbyterians such as Samuel Neilson and Thomas Ledlie Birch, and Roman Catholics such as William MacNeven and Patrick Byrne.

The Roman Catholics were the most socially disadvantaged. Although given some measure of relief in 1792 and 1793, they were still debarred from becoming Members of Parliament and King's Counsel, and they remained liable to pay the tithe to support the Church of Ireland; Presbyterian disabilities were less severe. Nevertheless, both groups remained outsiders, their chances of advancement slim, and their influence on the Irish Ascendancy miniscule.[50] In addition, their sense of being marginal was reinforced by their growing anti-colonial and nationalist mentality. By 1796 United Irish policy included republicanism and independence, their methods secret and revolutionary. As MacNeven told the Secret Committee of the House of Lords in 1798, independence 'certainly became our object, when we were convinced that liberty was not otherwise obtainable.'[51]

Those who emigrated to America, then, were a particular type of patriot. They tended to be from the professional classes, of middle-class origin, and with dissenting religious opinions. It is in the light of the political refugees' marginal position created by these social characteristics that we should view their political ideology. The most common ideological thread linking the exiles was a desire for a meritocratic society, where careers were open to the talented and where all had full civil liberties. American society had just this reputation, so it was there that these patriots, disgusted with their prospects in Britain and disillusioned with the course of the Revolution in France, headed. From Dublin in April 1792 John Chambers told Mathew Carey that the American constitution was increasingly admired in Europe, and 'even that of France shrinks from a contrast.' Carey, although having second thoughts on Federalist policy by 1792, agreed. He had informed his father in 1789 that 'From one of the weakest and most contemptible governments in the world, America has now one of the best; indeed ... it is the best form of government in the world.'[52] For Thomas Cooper in 1794, there was 'little fault to find with the government of America, either in principle or in practice; we have very few taxes to pay ... we have no animosities about religion; it is a subject about which no questions are asked.'[53] For Joseph Gales, preferring 'Freedom to Despotism' and 'Republicanism to Monarchy', America became the obvious country in which to settle.[54] And for John Campbell White, a member of the United Irish Executive, America was 'a young country where political and religious liberty are enjoyed to the utmost extent and where no more taxes [than necessary] are levied on the citizen.'[55]

Equality of opportunity acted as the linchpin in the refugees' social and political thought. Richard Dinmore, in his consideration of patriot principles in 1796, wrote that,

> The first grand principle, from which 'all others flow', is equality; without which ... there can be no liberty; but I must beg the favour of you not to confound this principle with a desire, forcibly to equalize all property. The jacobins entertain no such absurd notions; the equality they contend for is, that every many should possess an equal right to the honours and to the justice of his country: they are of course enemies to all hereditary claims; ... every man is equally ... entitled to the profits of his own industry, and to the disposal of it. ... They oppose all laws which cramp industry. With them every man has a right to get his bread wherever he pleases, and by whatever honest means; consequently, they are hostile to corporations and all chartered rights.[56]

'We do not seek an equality of wealth and possessions, but an equality of rights,' wrote Walker, so that all 'may have a fair opportunity of exerting to advantage any talents he may possess.'[57] Tom Paine's toast when he returned to Baltimore in November 1802 was, 'The three guarantees of a Republic: may rights be equal; opinions free; and the majority govern, as they would be governed.'[58]

It is clear, therefore, that the political refugees were not proponents of Civic Humanist or Commonwealth ideology. Their vision was not of a resurrected society of civic virtue, where citizens put the interests of the state before their own self-interest;[59] nor did they look back with nostalgia to a mythical Golden Age. As Callender argued, history showed that British freedom and liberty had never existed:

> At what era this *freedom* and *virtue* existed, nobody could ever tell. ... British annals ... [are] full of calamity and disgrace. ... Some people talk of restoring the constitution to its *primitive* purity. They would do well to inform us what that purity was and where its traces are to be found.[60]

The exiles wholeheartedly accepted the idea of progress, which they saw being fulfilled by the development of market relations within a commercial society. John Locke and Adam Smith, rather than Machiavelli and Bolinbroke, were their mentors; the recognition of natural rights and an unregulated economy were their objectives. For them virtue was not, as for the Commonwealth men, the ideals of citizenship and the common good, but was to be found in economic productivity and hard work. Corruption too was redefined, becoming the corruption of 'jobs and places going to undeserving, untalented men of birth'.[61] It is true that, like the Commonwealth men, the political refugees attacked the government funding and financial system; the public funds were seen as 'a stupendous mass of fraud, profligacy, imposture and extortion'.[62] However, they opposed it not in defence of an agrarian polity, but because of the uses towards which the funds were put — to fund wars in defence of the interests of oligarchic corporations, and to support idle, unproductive, untalented men who reduced the opportunities of the meritorious: 'The civil list is a gulf yawning to absorb the whole property of the British empire. We look back without satisfaction, and forward without hope.'[63]

Parliamentary reform was a necessary first step towards breaking the monopoly on opportunities for advancement which the parliamentary élites kept to themselves through corruption. A wide franchise would ensure the proper representation of the middle classes' interests in Parliament, and the emancipation of their talents. As Denis Driscol claimed,[64]

> The history of mankind, as well as our own experience, shows us, that riches do not command all the virtues and all the talents in the world — on the contrary, by far the greater and purer share of virtue, honour and integrity is to be found in the middling spheres of life, and it is from this class of free and independent citizens, that we wish to see our representatives chosen. It is men of this description in general, who feel a pride in preserving liberty and equality — they are not intoxicated with prosperity and they feel no ambition from the wheel of fortune, to become a *privileged caste*, superior to the *herd of mankind.*

Viewing the patriots' political ideology from this vantage point helps to explain why they could continue to believe (to the consternation of some modern historians) that political rather than social change was the first priority. Their priorities are only wrongheaded if one sees them as forerunners of modern socialism. But this, of course, they were not; they were the first generation of 'bourgeois radicals', and they demanded political reform 'in order to destroy for ever the aristocratic world of ascribed status'.[64] Their vision of the future encompassed a competitive struggle in a market society, where hard work, thrift and self-interest brought their merited rewards. 'Superior talents, superior knowledge and superior industry, ought, on the plainest principles of justice and equity, to enjoy superior advantages,' wrote Cooper.[65] Mathew Carey was to explain his ultimate success in terms of 'indefatigable industry, the most rigid punctuality, and frugality';[66] Gales viewed 'industry, frugal habits and a good system of general education' to be 'the surest means of promoting and securing individual and national prosperity and happiness'.[67]

III

... May this free Country evermore
Prove to the oppress'd a friendly shore:
An ASYLUM from TYRANNY
And DIRE RELIGIOUS BIGOTRY:
May they from Hants to Georgia find
A Welcome Hearty, warm, and kind;
May servitude abolished be,
As well as negro-slavery,
To make *one* Land of Liberty.[68]

Mathew Carey's optimism was not well founded. The political refugees, especially those who arrived in the 1790s, quickly found that America was not always as hospitable as they had expected. Priestley received on his arrival in New York welcoming addresses from the Democratic Society, the Tammany Society and the Republican Natives of Great Britain and Ireland, but he was also the subject of a venomous pamphlet from William Cobbett, in which he was denounced as a dangerous revolutionary and his Unitarianism seen as part of a plot for a revolution 'on the French plan'.[69] Wolfe Tone, during his short sojourn in Philadelphia in 1795, found that 'the country is beautiful, but it is like a beautiful scene in a theatre; the effect at a proper distance is admirable, but it will not bear a minute inspection.' The Americans were unfriendly and selfish and 'they do fleece us emigrés at a most unmerciful rate'.[70] Tom Paine was to be pilloried by the Federalist press when he returned in 1802, and Grant Thorburn, the ex-nailmaker and member of the Edinburgh Friends of the People, was dismissed from his Baptist ministry in New York in 1803 for shaking Paine's hand.[71] Furthermore, of course, waves of nativist sentiment pounded the immigrants, the high tide coming between 1798 and 1801 following the passing of the Alien and Sedition Acts. The refugees were confounded by the sight of a supposedly republican American society moving swiftly, under Federalist direction, towards the British system of corruption. Not only, from 1794, was the American government pro-British and anti-French in its foreign policy, but under Hamilton's economic programme the infrastructure necessary for an 'aristocratic' social system (a national bank, a national debt which seemed capable of sustaining a placeman system, high taxation, stockjobbing and speculation) was being created.[72] It is hardly surprising to find that, at least, in the 1790s, virtually every refugee supported the Jeffersonian Republicans.

The 1790s was a crucial decade in the United States, as yet again Americans underwent the trauma of interpreting the meaning of republicanism and considering the future of their society. At one extreme on a continuum of options was the Federalist view of a hierarchical and deferential society, resting on a capitalist, commercial system through which America was enmeshed in a transatlantic market economy. Hamilton's objective was to create a stable but powerful economic foundation to support the new constitution and its government. To achieve this he embarked on a policy favouring a finance-capitalist class in order to harness their self-interest to a strong central government.[73] At the other extreme was a Jeffersonian vision of an egalitarian society looking westwards for its inspiration, based on the moral rectitude and independence of small farmers.

Neither of these extreme positions was capable of appealing to all sections of society. Hamilton's policies, which included encouraging imports (to be taxed to fund the national debt), alienated the urban artisans, who opposed competitive imports and wanted government encouragement of domestic manufactures. The policy of high taxation also alienated the agricultural interests. On the other hand, Jefferson's ideal agrarian republic was of little appeal to the commercial interests and to the urban middling classes. Nor did it take into account the undoubted fact that by the 1790s, even amongst the farmers in the eastern states, a market-oriented mentality was very strong, and that America was already far along the road towards becoming a commercial society. It was Jefferson's reluctant recognition of this fact, and his admission that government policy ought to 'let things take their natural course without help or impediment', which ultimately helped the Democratic Republicans to victory in 1800.[74]

The successful Jeffersonian republicanism of 1800 was an egalitarian, non-deferential doctrine based on equal rights, which recognised and accepted the power of market forces in a *laissez-faire* economy. It appealed to 'enterprising and ambitious elements struggling for recognition and power' against an entrenched Federalist élite.[75] Although all the constituent parts of this republican philosophy existed in American political theory before the political refugees arrived, the emigrés made a significant contribution towards its dissemination and acceptance. They quickly appreciated that the solution to the problem of Federalist élitism was the same solution they had urged in Britain when faced with the strength of hierarchical notions and the power of corruption. Their opposition to the Bank of the United States and to the excise laws, and their strong support for domestic manufactures, was due not to hostility to commercial society and market relations, but to the Federalist economic programme which curtailed individual opportunities in favour of a system of corruption on behalf of a few.[76] The political refugees were important in expounding the commercial aspects of Jeffersonianism and for publicising a political economy which saw no contradiction in the possibility of an egalitarian but commercial society. The acceptance of such a political economy amongst large sections of the American community was instrumental in the victory of Jeffersonianism.

The political refugees were influential in three main ways in the 1790s. Above all, it was in their role as propagandists that they left their mark. Of the most influential Jeffersonian newspaper editors, who were greatly outnumbered by their Federalist opponents before 1800, only Philip Freneau and Benjamin Franklin Bache could claim the same devotion to the cause of Jeffersonianism and to have taken the same risks as the emigré editors William Duane, James Carey, John Daly Burk, Joseph Gales, James Thomson Callender, Denis Driscol and James Cheetham. James Carey was almost alone in standing up to the brilliant newspaper activities of William Cobbett in Philadelphia. John Daly Burk even had the effrontery to publish a strongly Republican newspaper in Boston, the heartland of Federalism.[77] From New England to Georgia Republican newspapers, edited by British and Irish emigrés, were published in the 1790s, although most were concentrated in the politically sensitive middle states.[78] In pamphlets as well as newspapers the emigrés got the Republican message across. Callender, who after Bache's death in 1798 saw himself as Jefferson's main propagandist, promoted — along with very effective if sometimes scurrilous personal invective — the ideas of the Democratic Republicans at considerable personal sacrifice.[79] Appleby has shown how influential Cooper's *Political Arithmetic* was in the election of 1800.[80] Indeed, Appleby's own very strong reliance on Cooper, Cheetham and Paine to explain the ideology of Jeffersonianism, but on which she fails to comment, effectively demonstrates the crucially significant role of the propagandists in Jefferson's success.

Stemming from their propagandist activities, the emigrés were influential as a conduit linking the Jeffersonians to a mass constituency. Early in the 1790s the urban middling classes strongly supported Federalism, and although Federalist policies themselves helped to erode that support, it was the refugees' continual emphasis on the egalitarian and commercial aspects of Republicanism which helped to create and sustain a powerful Jeffersonian rank and file. Moreover, the work of, amongst others, Mathew Carey and James Reynolds in Philadelphia and James Cheetham in New York, ensured the preference of new Irish immigrants for the Republican party.[81]

Finally, although it may appear paradoxical to associate this with men who were internationalists and individualists in outlook, the refugees were important for strengthening the sense of the United States as a national unit. Their perception of America was formed at a distance across the Atlantic and they did not at first possess the strong local ties or sectional attitudes which were common in America. Faced with the threat from an intrusive British commercial policy, and from the Federalists' attempts to sustain an élitist social structure, sectional rivalries appeared trivial, especially as the emigrés were promoting a political economy which was predicated on class harmony and which recognised the uniformity of interests between the agrarian, mercantile and manufacturing sectors of the economy in a Republican polity. The refugees' emphasis on the unity of the many in opposition to the few was fuelled by a strong feeling of desperation, which flowed from their experiences in Britain and Ireland. They *knew* what the Federalist system, if successfully implemented, would be like, for they had lived under it before. Their desire to prevent the history of Britain after 1688 repeating itself in the United States ensured that the political refugees were some of Jefferson's major lieutenants in the 1790s.

IV

Approximately a half of the political refugees were involved in political affairs in America after they had fled from Britain and Ireland. The careers of many of the others demonstrated convincingly that, in a society where talent was not artificially restrained, they had the abilities to go far. In one sense the successes of the refugees in America are more condemnatory of the political system under Pitt than even the repressive measures which were necessary to retain control in Britain during and after the French wars. In the fields of science, medicine, and the arts the refugees were to leave their mark on American society.

The connection between patriot principles, Dissent and a commitment to natural knowledge, strong in late eighteenth-century Britain, was paralleled in the careers of some of the refugees. Apart from Priestley, whose most fruitful research was completed before emigration, at least six other refugees were involved in the development of American science. William MacNeven, for example, became Professor of Midwifery at the New York College of Physicians and Surgeons in 1808, exchanged this Chair for that of Chemistry in 1811, and in 1816 added Materia Medica to Chemistry. His chemistry laboratory was said to be the first in New York. Between 1826 and 1830 he lectured at the new Duane Street Medical School. MacNeven published several scientific works, the best known being his *Exposition of the Atomic Theory of Chemystry* (1819), and co-edited the *New York Medical and Philosophical Journal and Review*.[82]

Thomas Cooper's career as Professor of Chemistry and Law at the future University of Virginia, and his professorship and presidency of the future University of South Carolina are well known.[83] Less well known is the American career of Alexander Wilson, the Scottish weaver-poet, who emigrated following imprisonment for publishing a bitter satire in 1794. Largely self-taught in the classical artisan mode, Wilson's eight-volume *American Ornithology* made him the 'pioneer writer of the bird essay' and one of the pioneers of American nature literature. Before his death in 1813 he had been elected to the Columbian Society of Artists, the American Philosophical Society and the Academy of Natural Sciences of Philadelphia.[84]

Wilson was unusual amongst the scientifically-minded refugees in at least two ways. He alone had little formal education —

MacNeven, Maclean, Cooper, Hudson, Vaughan and Tytler had all attended universities. Moreover, only Wilson can be said to have made major contributions or discoveries to his chosen field. Hudson, for example, made no technical advance in the art of dentistry, but was one of the first to use a gold foil root-filling technique in America.[85] In his retirement in Maine, Benjamin Vaughan carried out numerous agricultural experiments, which he communicated to the Massachusetts Agricultural Society, but none of them carried agricultural science very far forward.[86] As with their counterparts in political life, they were 'philosophical borrowers', proselytisers for advanced thought rather than innovators in their own right. To call them second-rate would be a grave injustice; but they were of the second level, men of considerable talents although not originators. In the open society of Jeffersonian America, their abilities blossomed in a way which could not have happened in Pitt's Britain.[87]

The same conclusions can be reached for those emigrés who became involved in American culture and literature. Mathew Carey's self-appointed role was to encourage the development of an indigenous American literature, which he accomplished through his publishing business, although he was himself a clever and effective writer and fearsome literary opponent. On Carey's publication list were the works of Mrs Rowson, Noah Webster, Freneau, Irving, Weems and Cooper, as well as a host of lesser authors. Indeed, 'no other publishing firm, even in proportion to its size, published so many works of native production between 1787 and 1824.[88] He was a promoter rather than instigator of American literature, and was instrumental in reducing the 'cultural cringe' which many Americans still possessed when confronting European culture. It was a position which harmonised with his own views on the American economy and with the political refugees' sense of American unity.[89]

Neither Carey nor his fellow exiles were of course isolationists; their internationalism was too strong for that. Through a series of book-swapping deals with European booksellers, Carey attempted to increase European awareness and understanding of America and its society. Another refugee was influential in this manner also. David Bailie Warden returned to Europe in 1804 as private secretary to General John Armstrong, the American minister to France. He was to remain there for the rest of his long life, acting as a cultural linkman for Americans visiting Europe. In addition, he published a number of works on America, the most notable being *A Statistical, Political and Historical Account of the United States in North America* (3 vols., 1819), in which he sought to 'defend the democratic experiment by presenting the facts to speak for themselves'.[90] In one sense this was precisely what the careers of many of the political refugees helped to do.

It would be wrong, however, to leave the impression that for all of the political refugees emigration to the United States was a resounding success. Callender was not the only emigré to drown while drunk; his fellow Scotsman James Tytler, having scraped a bare subsistence in Salem from 1795 to 1804, drowned in a drunken stupor late one January night while on a mission to borrow a candle;[91] Harman Blennerhassett lost a considerable part of his fortune financing Aaron Burr's western imperial schemes in 1806;[92] John Craig Millar and the poet Robert Merry died soon after they arrived in America;[93] and James Carey, who once told his brother Mathew that as Irishmen they were 'heirs to disappointment', left only $425 when he died in 1801.[94] Others obviously regarded America purely as a temporary refuge: Wolfe Tone and James Napper Tandy stayed only a short while before returning to France and involvement in the disastrous Irish rebellion; the United Irishman Archibald Hamilton Rowan was eventually allowed to return to Ireland; and the LCS printers Richard Lee and Daniel Isaac Eaton returned to England when the hue and cry had died down.[95] So too, eventually, did Richard Dinmore and the printer of the *Manchester Herald*, Matthew Falkner.[96]

Nevertheless, for the majority of the refugees, America was indeed a land of opportunity, a palimpsest to put their ideas into practice and to exercise their talents to the full. Beating a retreat from the animosity of people frightened by the implications of the French Revolution and deeply suspicious of unorthodox thinkers, the exiles found that, with those very qualities which they had defined as virtue, it was possible to demonstrate that superior abilities did lead to superior advantages. What was Britain's loss was very much America's gain.[97]

Notes

1. 'The Autobiography of Mathew Carey', *New England Magazine*, July 1833, 412.
2. Joseph J. St Mark, 'The Red Shamrock: United Irishmen and Revolution, 1795-1803', Ph.D. thesis, Georgetown University 1974, 17-19.

3. Carey, 'Autobiography', *passim*: Edward C. Carter II, 'The Political Activities of Mathew Carey, Nationalist, 1760-1814', Ph.D. thesis, Bryn Mawr 1962.

4. [J.T. Callender], *Deformities of Dr. Samuel Johnson*, (London 1782); idem; *A Critical Review of the Works of Dr. Samuel Johnson*, (Edinburgh; 1783).

5. J.T. Callender, *The Political Progress of Britain* Part 1, 2nd edn (Philadelphia: 1974), 3; PRO H0102/7, William Scot-Robert Dundas, Edinburgh, 3 January 1793.

6. Peter Porcupine [William Cobbett], *A Bone to Gnaw for the Democrate*, Part 2 (Philadelphia; 1795), 4.

7. James Carey — Mathew Carey, Philadelphia, 8 July 1797, Lea and Febiger Collection, Letter Book VI, 1st Series, Historical Society of Pennsylvania (hereafter HSP).

8. J.T. Callender, *The History of the United States for 1796: including a variety of interesting particulars relative to the federal government previous to that period* (Philadelphia 1797), Chs. 5 & 6; J. Callender — Thomas Jefferson, Philadelphia, 28 September 1797, in W.C. Ford (ed.), 'Thomas Jefferson and James Thomson Callender', *New England Historical and Genealogical Register*, vols. LI-LII (1896-97), 8; Francis Wharton (ed.), *State Trials of the United States during the Administrations of Washington and Adams*, (New York 1854), 688-721; Fawn M. Brodie, *Thomas Jefferson: An Intimate History*, (New York, 1974), 373-4.

9. Gwyn A. Williams, *The Search for Beulah Land* (London, 1980).

10. Stephen Higginson — Timothy Pickering, 29 August 1795, quoted in John R. Howe Jr, 'Republican Thought and Political Violence of the 1790s', *American Quarterly* 19 (1967), 150; Walter F. Brown Jr, 'John Adams and the American Press, 1797-1801: The First Full-Scale Confrontation between the Executive and the Media', Ph.D. thesis, Notre Dame University 1974, 45 (quoting Harrison J. Otis); Richard J. Twomey, 'Jacobins and Jeffersonians: Anglo-American Radicalism in the United States, 1790-1820', Ph.D. thesis, Northern Illinois University 1974, 79.

11. E.P. Thompson, *The Making of the English Working Class* (London, 1963); G.A. Williams, *Artisans and Sans-Culottes* (London, 1968); Albert Goodwin, *The Friends of Liberty* (London: 1979); Marianne Elliott, *Partners in Revolution: The United Irishmen and France* (London, 1982).

12. Arthur Sheps, 'Ideological Immigrants in Revolutionary America', in P. Fritz and D. Williams (eds.), *City and Society in the Eighteenth Century* (Toronto, 1973), 231-46. See also C. Bonwick, *English Radicals and the American Revolution* (Chapel Hill, 1977).

13. Smith, *Freedom's Fetters: The Alien and Sedition Laws and American Civil Liberties* (New York, 1956); Appleby, *Capitalism and a New Social Order: The Republican Vision of the 1790s* (New York, 1984); Stewart, *The Opposition Press of the Federalist Period* (Albany, 1969).

14. Dumas Malone, *The Public Life of Thomas Cooper* (New Haven: 1926); Caroline Robbins, 'Honest Heretic: Joseph Priestley in America, 1794-1804', *Proceedings of the American Philosophical Society*, 106 (1962), 60-76; Colin Bonwick, 'Joseph Priestley: Emigrant and Jeffersonian', *Enlightenment and Dissent*, 2 (1983), 3-2; Eric Foner, *Tom Paine and Revolutionary America*, (New York, 1976); Jerry W. Knudson, 'The Rage Around Tom Paine: Newspaper Reaction To His Homecoming in 1802', *New York Historical Society Quarterly*, 53 (1969), 34-63; Kim T. Phillips, 'William Duane, Revolutionary Editor', Ph.D. thesis, University of California, Berkeley 1968.

15. Douglass Adair, 'The Jefferson Scandals', in T. Colbourn (ed.), *Fame and the Founding Fathers: Essays by Douglass Adair*, (New York, 1974), 160-91; Brodie, *Jefferson*; Virginius Dabney, *The Jefferson Scandals: A Rebuttal* (New York, 1981).

16. Twomey, 'Jacobins and Jeffersonians'. See also his 'Jacobins and Jeffersonians: Anglo-American Radical Ideology', in M. and J. Jacob (eds.), *The Origins of Anglo-American Radicalism* (London, 1984), 284-99.

17. Ibid., 284.

18. [Baltimore] *American Patriot*, 25 September 1802 (editorial of Denis Driscol, who left Ireland in 1799).

19. J.T. Callender, *A Short History of the Nature and Consequences of the Excise Laws* (Philadelphia, 1795), 45.

20. Edward C. Carter II, 'A "Wild Irishman" Under Every Federalist's Bed: Naturalisation in Philadelphia, 1789-1806', *Pennsylvania Magazine of History and Biography*, 94 (1970), 332-3; *American Patriot*, 17 February 1803.

21. Williams, *Search for Beulah Land*, 86; A. Hook, *Scotland and America: A Study of Cultural Relations* (Glasgow, 1975), 240.

22. *American Patriot*, 16 October 1802; R.B. McDowell, *Ireland in the Age of Imperialism and Revolution. 1760-1801* (Oxford; 1979), 484.

23. Twomey, 'Jacobins and Jeffersonians', 68; D.H. Gilpatrick, 'The English Background of John Miller', *The Furman Bulletin*, 20 (1938), 14-20; T. Wall, *The Sign of Dr. Hay's Head* (Dublin, 1958), 38-9.

24. Phillips, 'Duane', 4-5; Carter, 'Carey', 2; *Dictionary of National Biography* (hereafter *DNB*), XII, 153-4; R.R. Madden, 'Memoir of William James MacNeven', *The United Irishmen* (London, 1846), 3-4.

25. *Dictionary of American Biography* (hereafter *DAB*), III, 145-6; J.O. Baylen and N.J. Gossman (eds.), *Biographical Dictionary of Modern British Radicals*, vol. 1 (Hassocks, 1979), 153-5; *DAB*, V,337; Ibid., VIII, 321; Ibid., I, 367-8.

26. Thompson, *Making of the English Working Class*, 153; Twomey, 'Jacobins and Jeffersonians', 24-5.

27. Baylen and Gossman, *Dictionary*, 44-8.

28. Sir James Fergusson, *Balloon Tytler* (London, 1972), 17-18; Hook, *Scotland and America*, 25.

29. Malone, *Cooper*, 4; G.S. Rowell. 'Benjamin Vaughan — Patriot Scholar, Diplomat', *The Magazine of History* 22 (1916), 43-57.

30. Baylen and Gossman, *Dictionary*, 140; W.G. Briggs, 'Joseph Gales, Editor of Raleigh's First Newspaper', *The North Carolina Booklet*, 7 (1907), 105.

31. Ford, 'Callender and Jefferson', 34; R.G. Gallin, 'Scottish Radicalism, 1792-4', Ph.D. thesis, Columbia University 1979, 223.

32. *DNB*, V, 70; W.T. Latimer, 'David Bailie Warden, Patriot 1798', *Ulster Journal of Archeology*, 23 (1907), 29-38; A. Aspinall, *Politics and the Press, 1780-1850*, (London, 1949), 62; Twomey, 'Jacobins and Jeffersonians', 33-34.

33. Malone, *Cooper*, 6; McDowell, *Ireland in the Age of Imperialism*, 480-1.

34. Hook, *Scotland and America*, 241; Carter, 'Carey', 244.

35. *American Patriot*, 13 January 1803.

36. James Carey's newspapers were: *Virginia Gazette and Richmond Daily Advertiser* (1792); [Charleston] *Star* (1793); [Savannah] *Georgia Journal* (1793-94); [Charleston] *Daily Evening Gazette* (1795); [Philadelphia] *Daily Advertiser* (1797); [Philadelphia] *Carey's United States Recorder* (1798); and [Philadelphia] *The Constitutional Dairy and Philadelphia Evening Advertiser* (1799-1800).

37. J. Brewer, 'English Radicalism in the Age of George III', in J.G.A. Pocock (ed.), *Three British Revolutions: 1641, 1688, 1776* (Princeton, N.J., 1980), 323-67.

38. For one who did emigrate, see J.H. Moore, 'Theophilus Harris' Thoughts on Emigrating to America in 1793', *William and Mary Quarterly*, 36 (1979),602-14.

39. Quoted in I. Inkster, 'Studies in the Social History of Science in England during the Industrial Revolution', Ph.D. thesis, University of Sheffield 1977, 2.

40. See, for example, M. Berman, *Social Change and Scientific Organisation: The Royal Institution 1799-1844* (London, 1978); Paul Saunders, *Edward Jenner: The Cheltenham Years 1795-1823*, (Hanover, 1982).

41. H. Perkin, *The Origins of Modern English Society 1780-1880*, (London, 1969), 252; A. Thackray, 'Natural Knowledge in Cultural Context: The Manchester Model', *American Historical Review*, 79 (1974), 672-709.

42. Goodwin, *Friends of Liberty*, Chs. 3 and 5; Bonwick, *English Radicals*, 12.

43. I. Kramnick, 'Religion and Radicalism: English Political Theory in the Age of Revolution', *Political Theory*, 5 (1977), 506.

44. Goodwin, *Friends of Liberty*, Ch. 3; F. Knight, *The Strange Case of Thomas Walker* (London, 1957).

45. G.I. Gallop, 'Politics, Property and Progress: British Radical Thought, 1760-1815', D.Phil. thesis, Oxford University 1983, 43.

46. R. Dinmore, *An Exposition of the Principles of the English Jacobins*, 2nd edn (Norwich, 1797), 10-11; T. Walker, *Review of the Political Events in Manchester* (London, 1794), 29; Briggs, 'Joseph Gales', 127-8.

47. Knight, *Thomas Walker*, 173.

48. I. Sellers, 'Unitarians and Social Change', *Hibbert Journal*, 61 (1962), 16.

49. *American Patriot*, 25 September 1802.

50. McDowell, *Ireland in the Age of Imperialism*, 414; Roger Wells, *Insurrection: The British Experience, 1795-1803* (Gloucester 1983), 7.

51. W.J. MacNeven, *Pieces of Irish History* (New York, 1807), 233.

52. John Chambers — Mathew Carey, Dublin, 12 April 1792, Lea Febiger Collection, HSP; Mathew Carey — Christopher Carey, Philadelphia, 23 May 1789, Lea and Febiger Letter Book, 1788-1794, Ledger D, HSP.

53. T. Cooper, *Some Information Respecting America* (London, 1794) 54-4.

54. *Raleigh Register*, 10 December 1804.

55. McDowell, *Ireland in the Age of Imperialism*, 135.

56. Dinmore, *English Jacobins*, 7-8.

57. Walker, *Review of Political Events*, 46.

58. *American Patriot*, 13 November 1802.

59. Kramnick, 'Religion and Radicalism', 519: Gallop, 'Politics', 24.

60. J.T. Callender, *The Political Progress of Britain*, Part 2 (Philadelphia, 1795), 55-6.

61. I. Kramnick, 'Republican Revisionism Revisited', *American Historical Review*, 87 (1982), 661.

62. Callender, *Political Progress*, Part 1, 12.

63. Ibid., 72-3.

64. *American Patriot*, 11 January 1803.

65. Kramnick, 'Religion and Radicalism', 519-21; Gallop, 'Politics', 57.

66. Carey, 'Autobiography', 404.

67. Briggs, 'Joseph Gales', 129.

68. Quoted in Carter, 'Mathew Carey', 148.

69. William Cobbett, *Observations on the Emigration of Dr. Joseph Priestley*, (Philadelphia, 1794), 3-6.

70. St Mark, 'Red Shamrock', 154.

71. Knudson, 'Tom Paine', 60.

72. J.M. Murrin, 'The Great Inversion, or Court versus Country: A Comparison of the Revolution Settlements in England (1688-1721) and America (1776-1816)', in Pocock (ed.), *Three British Revolutions*, 409-10; Drew McCoy, *The Elusive Republic: Political Economy in Jeffersonian America* (Chapel Hill, 1980), 153.

73. Appleby, *Capitalism and a New Social Order*, 3; William M. Gavre, 'Republicanism in the American Revolution: the Collapse of the Classical Ideal', Ph.D. thesis, University of California, Los Angeles 1978, 543.

74. Joyce Appleby, 'Commercial Farming and the "Agrarian Myth" in the Early Republic', *The Journal of American History*, 68 (1982), 833-49; Gavre, 'Collapse of Classical Ideal', 587.

75. Appleby, *Capitalism and a New Social Order*, 48-9. It is worth noting that one of Jefferson's first acts as Governor of Virginia in 1780 was to dismiss the clerics at William and Mary College and replace them with lay professors.

76. J.T. Callender, *Sketches of the History of America* (Philadelphia, 1798), 181-2, 185-7; J.T. Callender, *Sedgwick & Co; or, A Key to the Six Per Cent Cabinet* (Philadelphia, 1798), 87; Twomey, 'Jacobins and Jeffersonians', 146-70.

77. Joseph I. Shulim, 'John Daly Burk: Irish Revolutionist and American Patriot', *Transactions of the American Philosophical Society*, 54 (1964), 5-60. John Mason Williams also briefly edited a Boston newspaper, the *Democrat*, in 1804.

78. About 20 newspapers were edited by the emigrés before Jefferson's victory in 1800.

79. Callender — Jefferson, Raspberry Plain, 26 October 1798, in Ford (ed.), 'Callender and Jefferson', 11.

80. Appleby, *Capitalism and a New Social Order*, 88-9.

81. Carter, 'Mathew Carey', 120; Twomey, 'Jacobins and Jeffersonians', 219-23; J.T. Callender, *The Prospect Before Us*, vol. 1 (Richmond, 1800), 37; Jerome Mushkat, *Tammany: The Evolution of a Political Machine, 1789-1865* (Syracuse, N.Y., 1971), 37-8; *Carey's United States' Recorder*, 19 May 1798.

82. Madden, 'Memoir of William J. MacNeven, 54-5; *DAB*, VI, 153-4; *DNB*, XII, 696-7.

83. Malone, *Cooper*, chs. 7, 8, 11.

84. *DAB*, X, 317-19; *DAB*, XXI, 546-7.

85. *DAB*, V, 337.

86. Rowell, 'Benjamin Vaughan', 55-7.

87. Morton White, *The Philosophy of the American Revolution* (New York, 1978), 4.

88. Earl L. Bradsher, *Mathew Carey, Editor, Author and Publisher: A Study in American Literary Development* (New York, 1966), 54.

89. Mathew Carey, *The Olive Branch: or, Faults on Both Sides*, 1st edn (Philadelphia, 1814).

90. *DAB*, X, 443.

91. Fergusson, *Balloon Tytler*, 145-6.

92. *DAB*, I, 367-8.

93. Hook, *Scotland and America*, 241; J.G. Alger, 'The British Colony in Paris, 1792-3', *English Historical Review*, 13 (1898), 686.

94. James Carey — Mathew Carey, Richmond, 22 September 1792, Lea and Febiger Collection, HSP; Letters of Administration, Philadelphia City Hall Archives, James Carey, No. 18, 1801, K. 64.

95. F. MacDermott, *Theobald Wolfe Tone and his Times* (Dublin, 1980), 142-58; Madden, *United Irishmen*, vol. 2, 2, 86-9; PRO TS11/957/3502, S. Hamilton — E. Nepean, Dublin Castle, 2 May 1794; *Porcupine's Gazette*, 25 March 1797; Twomey, 'Jacobins and Jeffersonians', 67, 75: Baylen and Gossman, *Dictionary*, 142.

96. G.W. Janson *The Stranger in America, 1793-1806* (New York, 1807, 1971), 421-3; Knight, *Walker*, 176.

97. I wish to express my gratitude to my colleague, Geoffrey Gallop, for his advice and support (although he will not agree with all I've written here), and to the library staff of Murdoch University, without whose assistance in obtaining obscure references this paper could not have been written, and to Murdoch University's Board of Research and Postgraduate Studies, for their financial assistance in the past three years.

2 ABOLISHING THE SLAVE TRADE: ANTI-SLAVERY AND POPULAR RADICALISM, 1776-1807

James Walvin

On the eve of the American War of Independence, Britain had established herself as the western world's leading slave-trading nation. The West Indian islands and their slave-grown produce fed the voracious British appetite for tropical luxuries and essentials. It was widely assumed that these islands were among the jewels in the British imperial crown; as such, they were watched enviously by other European nations notably the French. The whole edifice of plantation society was kept in place by a complex web of naval and mercantile legislation, all buttressed by supporting laws from London and the colonial capitals. The slave empires, furthermore, went largely unquestioned; their nature unchallenged on economic or moral grounds. And yet, within a very brief period (1787–1838) slavery and the slave trade were subjected to a fierce, and ultimately successful, political onslaught. The abolitionist campaign in those years was perhaps the most remarkable, most popular, vociferous and influential, of any contemporary pressure group; it was also the most successful.[1]

Long before the flowering of organised abolition activity against the slave trade there had existed an important intellectual critique of slavery which, by its very nature, remained the preserve of contemporary intelligentsia. It was a debate of genuinely international proportions drawing on the arguments and experiences of men in Britain and France as well as the North American and Caribbean colonies. There was in a sense an accumulating critique of slavery, primarily from men of the French and Scottish Enlightenment, which slowly but effectively began to erode the previously unchallenged assumptions and arguments supporting slavery. Best known and certainly most influential was *L'Esprit des Lois* published by Montesquieu in 1748. Most famous for the advocacy of liberty (inspired in large measure by studying the English Constitution) *L'Esprit* also and perhaps inevitably embraced a critique of slavery.[2] Montesquieu's contribution to anti-slavery sentiment was crucial, and it proved a seminal work among a host of British writers, few more famous than Burke, who translated the work into English. Montesquieu was the intellectual force which propelled Burke towards reform in colonial policy, notably in India and in the slave islands. As early as 1780, Burke drafted a plan for the amelioration of slave conditions. Twelve years later, in 1792, he submitted his 'Sketch of a Negro Code' to the Home Secretary, Dundas. The 'Sketch' was a remarkably advanced and comprehensive blueprint designed to ease the transmutation of Britain's slaves into free people.[3] But the point to be made here is that there is a clear, direct and unbroken line of descent from anti-slavery as an abstract intellectual issue (in *L'Esprit*), to anti-slavery as a substantive issue of practical politics and reform.

It would be quite wrong, then, to imagine that the apparently obscure arguments of eminent philosophers remained the monopoly of an intellectual élite, for, very quickly, these ideas were transmuted into the stuff and argument of everyday political argument.

Montesquieu was especially influential among a new generation of British Enlightenment writers: Adam Ferguson, James Beattie, George Wallace, William Paley and Adam Smith all drew upon Montesquieu's work, incorporating a number of his ideas into their own writing. In their turn, these men proved influential in theological, political and legal debate in late eighteenth-century Britain, and never more persuasively or swiftly than on the question of slavery. Of course this British (primarily Scottish) tradition ran parallel to (and was, of course, deeply influenced by) the better-known French Enlightenment writers, notably Rousseau, the Encyclopaedists, Raynal, Diderot, d'Holbach and Voltaire.[4]

We need also to recall that educated European society was readily conversant and linguistically at ease with contemporary French publications. Indeed, French culture of the eighteenth century was of an unsurpassed importance and influence throughout the western world; a factor which goes some way to explain the seismic influence of revolutionary ideology after 1789. But even before that dramatic impact, French ideas — expressed in their original form and sometimes in translation — had made a major critical impact throughout Europe and North America. Before the impact of the ideas of the 'Rights of Man', few French ideas had more disruptive and critical an effect than the cumulative pinpricks against slavery and the slave trade. Furthermore, the development of a late eighteenth-century mentality which was increasingly sceptical of long unquestioned values and institutions was paralleled by transformations in theology.

Scholars have identified two major theological changes in the course of the eighteenth century which served, ultimately, though often indirectly, to challenge the acceptance of black slavery. First, the idea of benevolence became progressively more influential, with far-reaching consequences for the promotion of brotherly love. Secondly, the concept of Providence enshrined the idea of progress, an idea which in its turn naturally led to institutional change. Certain changes — progress — were seen 'as the manifestation of a great providential design'.[5] While it may be thought that theologians who addressed themselves to these issues were operating in the inaccessible realms of metaphysics, their hefty and expensive tomes available only to an intellectual élite, in fact their message percolated down to a wider audience than might initially be expected via tracts and, especially, sermons. One result was the widespread belief in divine retribution for sin and evil. When, late in the century, slavery began to incur moral condemnation it was relatively easy — and certainly convincing — to argue that divine punishment would fall on the heads of slaving peoples and nations. Before the launch of abolitionism it would be wrong to suggest that contemporary religion had begun to turn against slavery. But it is abundantly clear that these theological shifts, long in train, were eventually transmuted into powerful anti-slavery sentiment.

The roots of abolition can also be traced to the wider literate world where, in a host of literary sources, anti-slavery had begun to make its mark early in the eighteenth century. Again, the genesis of anti-slavery was more directly a concern of contemporary English liberties — a continuation, in 'modernised' form, of the debate about rights and liberties so characteristic of the seventeenth-century revolution and its aftermath. But there was also a widely advertised and supported vogue for secular philanthropy, the operation of charity towards the less fortunate. Indeed, it was the accepted obligation of philanthropy which provided the essential lubricant for the workings of eighteenth-century English society. Late in the century, the combined problem of population and urban growth, in conjunction with the dislocations of economic change, rapidly rendered traditional philanthropy incapable of maintaining social tranquility. In fact, the inability of philanthropy adequately to cope with the changing problems of want was effectively demonstrated in 1787 when attempts to relieve the black poor collapsed under the sheer weight of the numbers involved. The literary emphasis on philanthropy — on doing good to one's neighbour — was commonly emphasised in eighteenth-century literature. Increasingly, too, there was a literary genre which cast the black in the role of the noble savage — a person deserving of sympathetic, humane consideration and treatment. A number of successful books, poems and plays gave prominence to the primitive noble black: at a time of heightened discussion about liberties and humanity this served to illustrate the contrary condition of black slavery. Thus contemporary literary fashions served to focus literate attention (itself more widespread and 'popular' than the modern observer might imagine) securely on the problems and conditions of slaves and slavery. And all this was in addition to whatever personal experience existed from contact with blacks in Britain or from working in and around the nation's major slaving ports. There was, quite simply, a growing awareness of the existence, nature and problems of black slavery. Moreover, it seems equally clear that there was little corresponding literary support for slavery, though this was to change dramatically from the 1780s, when the abolitionist onslaught prompted a major literary defence of the slaving system by its supporters and their hired scribes.

It may well be countered that the origins of abolition mentioned so far in philosophy, theology and literature belong more appropriately to the realm of intellectual abstractions. In part, this is true. But it is equally clear that at certain crucial junctures ideas from these particular disciplines spilled over, often in transmuted form, into a wider, more politicised arena. Furthermore, there were powerful catalysts at work encouraging the pollination of anti-slavery sentiment throughout British (indeed western) society. Foremost were the Quakers.

By the mid-eighteenth century, the Quakers had evolved into a sizeable and influential community on both sides of the Atlantic; and from the late seventeenth century onwards, Quakers in the New World had complained about slavery. By the mid-eighteenth century this complaint had evolved into a major transatlantic onslaught against both slavery and slave-trading, led most notably by John Woolman and Anthony Benezet.[6] Philadelphia, the intellectual heart of the North American colonies, from whence there flowed a stream of articulate, literate and ultimately reforming sensibility, was also the centre of Quaker anti-slavery, with notable anti-slavery measures demanded of all Friends in 1755 and 1776. From these purely sectarian beginnings there followed a broader campaign to persuade local (American) legislatures to turn against slave trading. But it was towards the slave trade that the pioneering American Quaker abolitionists turned their attacks. Anthony Benezet was especially influential, and his words were sympathetically received in London.

British Quakers rallied to the cause in the 1760s, but the most influential antagonist of the slave trade — the close and influential correspondent of Benezet — was Granville Sharp. Although not a Quaker, Sharp was won over to anti-slavery by the fortuitous accident of confronting slavery in London. The 1770s saw a sympathetic correspondence between Benezet and Sharp and a proliferation of contacts between men of abolitionist sentiment — Quakers and non-Quaker — on both sides of the Atlantic. Thus, on the eve of American Independence, there existed a network of abolitionist correspondents and Friends spanning the English-speaking world — a network readily transformed in later years into the massive political organisation which gave abolition such irresistible strength in the years between 1787 and 1807.

During the American War of Independence, the issues of slavery and the slave trade were partly swamped by the consuming issues of political representation and of warfare. But Quakers kept to their self-appointed abolitionist task and by the summer of 1783 there had come into being a British Quaker committee to supervise abolitionist petitioning of the British Parliament. By the following year a national organisation of some 150 sympathisers throughout the country had been built, the basic structure inspired, to a marked degree, by the encouragement and promptings of American Quakers.

But it was equally bolstered by the increasing prominence given to British slave cases, notably the 1772 Somerset and the 1783 Zong cases. Thus there was an important convergence, before and during the American War, of the more abstract (largely theological) opposition inspired by American Quakers, and the uniquely 'domestic' question of slavery in England, Scotland and on board British slave ships. Moreover the problems of black society in England were compounded by the arrival in Britain of substantial numbers of former slaves (loyalists) fleeing from North America. Their plight — and that of the broader black community, culminating in the 1787 Sierra Leone scheme — served among other things, to give human substance to the humanitarian, philosophical and theological issues already discussed in a broadening community throughout Britain. By the mid-1780s all had been firmly placed on the nation's political agenda.

It was also important that John Wesley had come out publicly against slavery. Wesley had had first-hand experience of slavery when living in Georgia, and made a point of baptising blacks in Britain whenever the opportunity arose. But it was the work of Benezet which persuaded him. In February 1772 Wesley recorded in his journal:

> I read a very different book, published by an honest Quaker, on that execrable sum of all villanies, commonly called the Slave Trade. I read nothing like it in the heathen World, whether ancient or modern.[7]

Two years later, Wesley published his own attack, *Thought on the Slave Trade* (1774), a tract which was to prove instrumental in swinging Methodist organisations in Britain and America against the slave trade. When Methodism increased dramatically, it was to bring extraordinarily large numbers — and an insistent ideological objection — to the campaign for black freedom.[8]

Methodists, like the Quakers, came to view black slavery as wickedly-unchristian — a fact to be explained by the broader shifts in theological thought. But they were crucial in bringing their *institutional* strength to bear, on both sides of the Atlantic, as a vocal, highly-organised pressure-group opposed to the slave trade and, later, slavery itself. Long before the end of slavery, the British Methodists numbered more than a third of a million. By comparison, the Quakers were miniscule (19,500 in 1800) but their influence was to be counted more in their role as pioneers.[9] Long before organised abolition adopted the motto 'Am I not a man and a brother?', Benezet had asserted the same egalitarian point. This was a principle of fundamental — and ultimately irrefutable — logic and strength; one moreover which was to gain in power by the support it gained from the parallel development of secular rights of man after 1789. But it was to acquire a quite unpredictable twist by the early nineteenth century, when the pioneering missionaries (mainly Baptist and Methodist) converted growing numbers of black slaves in the British West Indies. Henceforth the black was not only a brother — a fellow human — but often also a member of the same Church. Thus the sufferings and persecutions of the early nineteenth-century slaves served to accentuate both the secular and religious outrage felt by particular religious communities in Britain. And those communities were often to be found at the heart of the changing urban (and sometimes industrial) communities. By the 1820s and 1830s the voice of anti-slavery was primarily an *urban* voice.

The crucial years in the transformation of abolition from a minority (however voluble) sentiment into wide public debate were the 1780s. The Zong affair, the origins of bitter tract warfare (planters versus their British opponents) and the protracted argument about the black poor and the Sierra Leone scheme all cumulatively focused attention on blacks in Britain and on the ultimate source of their misery — slavery and the slave trade. Throughout, there was an accelerating effort by that small — as yet unorganised — nucleus of abolitionists to bring their viewpoint and their writings to the attention of the influential, the prominent and the potentially powerful. Granville Sharp persistently pestered ministers, politicians and clerics with his thoughts on slavery.[10] Concerned clerics denounced black slavery from their pulpits, and pamphleteers begun to seek public attention through their tracts and letters to the London press. Magazines and newspapers began to give serious consideration — and space — to the troublesome question of slavery; they also began to give editorial judgements *pro* and *con*.[11] Alarmed at the hostile press attention paid to the slave empires, planters and traders — already well-organised for their own economic and political interests — began to defend themselves in print, and by political influence.[12] Planters and slave traders had long had an effective political organisation, the West India Committee. By the mid-1780s, it was clear to many that the loose federation of friends of the blacks were in even greater need of a comparable organisation. Once more, the Quakers provided the initiative.

Shortly after three Royal Navy ships left Plymouth in April 1787, with more than 400 blacks from London, bound for Sierra Leone, Granville Sharp met with a group of sympathisers, the bulk of whom were Quakers, and formed the Society for the Abolition of the Slave Trade.[13] In fact, the core of this committee had been a Quaker gathering as early as 1783. The new committee was joined by Thomas Clarkson, whose earlier tract, *An Essay on the Slavery and Commerce of the Human Species, particularly the*

African, had initially been written as a Cambridge prize essay. More important still, the inspiration for that tract had been Benezet's *Historical Account of Guinea*. Clarkson flung himself into the anti-slave trade crusade with a singleminded and indefatigable zeal, becoming what Coleridge described as 'the moral steam-engine ... the giant with one idea'.[14] Like others before him Clarkson began to pester and badger the famous and the powerful. He turned to William Wilberforce, MP for Yorkshire and close friend of the Prime Minister, William Pitt. Clarkson noted that on their first meeting

> Wilberforce stated frankly that the subject had often employed his thoughts, and that it was near to his heart. He seemed earnest about it, and also very desirous of taking the trouble of inquiring further into it.[15]

From that day forward, Wilberforce entered the abolitionist campaign, his role primarily that of parliamentary spokesman and pricker of the official (and fashionable) conscience. Wilberforce had been unhappy about the slave trade from his schooldays. Henceforth his prime role was to be within Parliament where he could help the cause most. In the words of Granville Sharp, 'The respectability of his position as member for the largest county, the great influence of his personal connexions, added to an amiable and unblemished character, secure every advantage to the case.'[16] Indeed, Wilberforce has come to personify the abolitionist campaign; the one man remembered by millions — black and white — as the prime agent in destroying black slavery in the British Empire. It was in no way to diminish Wilberforce's stature or uniqueness to suggest that his importance in abolition is less vaunted (and effective) than is generally imagined. But the traditional attention paid to him in abolition has served to diminish the work of others, and has deflected attention from the broader socio-historical context within which abolitionism thrived and ultimately succeeded. Few serious scholars would now claim that abolition succeeded because of — or even primarily through — Wilberforce. But this is far from claiming that abolition would have followed the same pattern (run the same parliamentary course, for the same duration and with the same consequences) *without* Wilberforce. There is, for instance, a serious case to be made that in the hands of a better parliamentarian, the abolition of the slave trade might have been brought about *sooner*. Yet whatever the qualifications we need to consider, there can be no denying the fact of Wilberforce's association with anti-slavery in the public mind, both in his lifetime and afterwards.

When the initial abolition meetings took place, in 1787-88, the sole ambition was to end, not slavery, but the slave trade. According to Clarkson,

> Now the question was, which of the two evils the committee should select as that, to which they should direct their attention with a view of the removal of it; or whether with the same view, it should direct its attention to both of them.
>
> It appeared soon to be the sense of the committee, that to aim at the removal of both would be to aim at too much, and that by doing this we might lose all.

The decision to attack the slave trade made logical sense. It was felt, for example, that planters, unable to buy new slaves, 'must treat those better, whom they might then have'. Abolishing the slave trade would lay 'the axe at the very root' ánd the abolitionists would deflect the criticism 'that they were meddling with the property of the planters'. It was, moreover, an infinitely more manageable, practical and less complex problem.[17] Despite the chorus of abuse from planters and traders, the Abolition Committee publicly declared that freeing the slaves 'never formed any part of the plan of this Society'.[18]

This decision taken, clearly, with an eye to the practicalities of contemporary politics, was also influenced by certain preconceptions of the nature of black slavery in the colonies. It seems to have been widely assumed that many of the human outrages witnessed in the West Indies were consequences of the slave trade itself, compounded by the inhumanities of planters who sought to extract the maximum effort from their slaves with no consideration for pain or social justice. There were, however, distinctive problems created by the peculiar demographic structures of slave life which served to confirm (and confuse) contemporary assessments of black slavery. And this confusion could only be altered by firm statistical data about the slave population, which abolitionists did not have in 1787-88. But in the short term, the small band of abolitionists sought to persuade Parliament of the justice — and practicality — of their ambition. And to this end it was thought important to tap public antipathy to the slave trade, and direct its flow to Parliament. Not even the most optimistic of abolitionists could have foreseen the extent, passion and influence of the public feeling which rapidly expressed itself on the issue.

To rally opinion, the small band of London abolitionists needed contacts with sympathisers throughout the country, to promote abolitionism in the localities, and to direct provincial feeling to the centre of political decision-making in London. Initially, however, they resolved to win support by publishing cheap literature. Abolitionist pamphlets (most notably Benezet's) had already established a remarkable influence: in opting for a major publishing venture, the early abolitionists were merely following a well-trodden path. Reformers and radicals of various hues had, since the mid-eighteenth century, made effective use of cheap (or free) tract literature. The Wilkes movement, the Yorkshire Association, the Society for Constitutional Information — all in addition to a myriad of less formal, often individual efforts — had strewn their printed arguments across the face of Britain, though concentrating primarily on friends and associates in the major urban areas, especially (and naturally) in London.

Tracts, reprints and abridgements by prominent abolitionists were published in their thousands, a fact which inevitably encouraged other sympathisers to write supporting pieces in newspapers and magazines.[19] Understandably, the West Indies lobby doubled its efforts, thus accentuating the war of words about slavery and the slave trade which had effectively begun during the Somerset case of 1772, but which substantially increased in the 1780s. Indeed, slavery and the slave trade became something of a literary genre, attracting the most talented (and talentless) of late eighteenth-century poets and novelists.[20] For the next half-century, slavery and all its ramifications were to generate an unprecedented volume of printed material: books, tracts, verses, cartoons, periodicals and newspaper columns. It is, naturally enough, virtually impossible to quantify the output, but it is important to stress that in a British society in which literacy was itself becoming more significant and widespread — a society, indeed, in which literacy was to be a crucial component in contemporary social and economic fortunes — abolitionist literature was produced and consumed on an unprecedented scale.

In addition to these published arguments, the pioneering abolitionists also needed a national organisation. There already existed a sympathetic network of Quakers throughout Britain, who in their turn, were able to recruit local non-Quaker sympathisers. In London and the provinces men found themselves won over or drawn to abolition — men often (though by no means always) experienced in earlier reforming organisations. Not all reformers were abolitionists, and not all abolitionists were reformers. None the less, enough of them shared a common political ground to enable us to suggest that abolition was able to appeal to men of a reforming sensibility despite distinctions between them on the nature of reform. Nonconformists, (themselves keen to see their own disabilities removed), men of letters and science (often prominent in local critical inquiries into moral and scientific issues), intellectuals (won over by the rising cerebral objections to slavery) and the 'new men' of business, commerce and industry (unsympathetic to the old economic doctrines basic to the survival of the old protected slave system) — all of these and more were, by inclination and interest, wooed over to abolition. Such men formed the nucleus for the nationwide proliferation of abolitionist organisations and pressure from 1787 onwards.

To persuade Parliament of the emergent national antipathy towards the slave trade it was decided to petition Parliament. Petitioning Parliament or monarch was an ancient method of expressing grievances or seeking redress and it had been used extensively and with some effect in the reforming campaign of the earlier 1780s. The suggestion to petition originated in Manchester where local reformers, meeting Thomas Clarkson in May 1788, informed him of

> the spirit which was then beginning to show itself, among the people of Manchester and other places, on the subject of the slave trade, and which would unquestionably manifest itself further by breaking out into petitions to parliament for its abolition.

Clarkson was surprised: 'The news, however, as it astonished, so it almost overpowered me with joy.'[21] Further surprises were in store, for the decision to call for petitions elicited a quite staggering — and totally unforeseen — level of abolitionist sentiment. By the end of May 1788 Parliament had received more than 100 petitions. The original petition from Manchester attracted an extraordinary 10,639 signatures; that from Bristol, the heart of the slaving empire, 'was signed by a great number'. Eventually the table of the House of Commons 'was loaded with petitions from every part of the kingdom'.[22] The decision to launch the petitions was fortuitous and abolition's unexpected strength and success instantly established petitioning as a basic and standard tactic of abolitionist politics. Like the printed word, the petition was to remain fundamental to the abolitionist cause for half a century, the best, most effective, flexible and manageable means of expressing public opinion to Parliament despite the changes in political representation. Furthermore, the demographic changes, particularly the concentration of the British population in urban centres, were to make the act of widespread petitioning easier while swelling the armies of names which were so readily recruited in vast numbers. More than that, the petitions were, from the first, politically influential. Their numbers and backing ensured that Parliament could not ignore them. On the contrary, the petitions were thought to carry irresistible political clout. Speaking on the slave trade in 1788, the Prime Minister remarked that the trade was

> a subject which, it was evident from the great number and variety of petitions presented to that House respecting it, had engaged the public attention to a very considerable extent and *consequently deserved the most serious notice of that House.*

Burke went even further: 'If that House neglected the petition from its constituents, that House must be abolished, and the privy council substituted in its stead.'[23]

The petitions in the spring of 1788 were to coincide with parliamentary scrutiny of the slave trade, set in train by Pitt, himself persuaded by Wilberforce and other abolitionists of the iniquities of the trade. The ensuing Privy Council investigation accumulated a massive body of data on the trade, calling witnesses experienced in the trade and from among its opponents. But the Council's proceedings were, naturally enough, detailed, painstaking and lengthy; it did not report until the spring of 1789. It was then decided that further evidence must be heard at the Bar of the Commons, a tactic which delayed until April 1791 a vote on abolition. That was defeated by 163 to 88.[24']

The intervening period had been filled with activity; widespread and persistent lobbying and the continuing programme of building up a factual dossier about the slave trade. In this, the lion's share of activity and achievement belongs to Thomas Clarkson whose seven nationwide journeys between 1787 and 1794 covered 35,000 miles, yielding (often at great personal cost and hardship) an unparalleled volume of information on all aspects of the slave trade — not least important of which was the evidence about the horrific death rates among *white* sailors. Clarkson also unearthed a series of important witnesses whose testimony before Parliament was to have a decisive impact in establishing beyond partisan doubt the full horrors created by the slave trade. Throughout, the London Committee steadily built up its network of corresponding sympathisers — churches, local abolitionist organisations and individuals — all of whom turned their energies into abolitionist agitation and propaganda in their own localities.[25]

However depressing the Commons defeat of April 1791, there was no doubt that by that date abolition had been staggeringly successful in accumulating widespread public backing. But it seems, by all accounts (and quite naturally) to have been supported primarily from the propertied class. In the early 1790s, however, a crucial — and again unforeseen (and to a degree unwelcome) — transformation took place as abolition began to spill beyond the pale of traditional, propertied politics and to embrace 'the people'. This was primarily a result of the French Revolution.

It is tempting to think of the impact of the Revolution in terms of the convulsion of popular and loyalist politics which so bitterly divided Britain after 1792. But in the early stages of the Revolution, events in France had a muted effect. Initially, few shared Burke's instant and abiding hatred of the Revolution, preferring instead to view 1789 as the eclipse of a royal authoritarianism which (so it was felt) the English had dispensed with a century before. To many (including the Prime Minister) it seemed that the French were taking a step towards the constitutional stability achieved by the British. Many, of course, positively rejoiced in the French changes, few more strenuously and openly than the small band of reformers — the SCI, the Revolution Society (formed to celebrate 1688) and the early Romantics. And among their ranks were to be numbered many of the pioneering abolitionists. But events in France — progressively more extreme, volatile and ultimately violent — gradually began to alienate propertied British opinion which had begun to coalesce informally around the standard of opposition raised by Burke in his *Reflections on the*

Revolution in France, published in November 1790. On the other side of the ideological fence, men who had been active in the SCI and anti-slavery came together to form local reforming organisations (often named Constitutional Societies). Meanwhile Burke's old associate and erstwhile friend, Tom Paine, back in England after his influential sojourn in America, where he had taken an abolitionist stance in the constitutional argument which heralded American independence, published his epochal answer to Burke. *The Rights of Man* proved to be one of the major landmarks in modern radical politics and thought. The book gave a remarkable boost to flagging radical fortunes, aided late in 1791 by a downturn in the economy.

Paine's book derived much of its ideological inspiration from the fundamental rights already asserted by the Revolutions of 1776 and 1789. Men began to talk about their 'natural rights'. A Cambridge group argued that : 'Every individual of mankind is born with a natural right to life, liberty and property.'[26] Like the Declaration of Rights of Man in France, so bold an assertion could not, by definition, be hedged in by qualifications. It must of necessity apply to all young and old, male and female, black and white. In the words of that doughty female enemy of radicalism, Hannah More,

> It follows, according to the actual progression of human beings, that the next influx of that irradiation which our enlighteners are pouring on us, will illuminate the world with the grave descants on the rights of youth, the rights of children, the rights of babies.[27]

No less important, these rights were clearly applicable to non-white people. Thomas Hardy, the Scottish shoemaker who founded the working men's London Corresponding Society (LCS) (1792) expressed the point simply. 'The rights of man are not confined to this small island but are extended to the whole human race, black and white, high or low, rich or poor.'[28] Trying to build up contacts with reformers in the provinces, Hardy was told of an abolitionist, the Rev. Bryant in Sheffield, and 'inferred from that that you was [sic] a friend of freedom on the broad basis of the Rights of Man.'[29] The links were, as we have seen, much more complex than Hardy imagined. In the short term, however, there is no doubt that the popular societies led by the LCS, which proliferated throughout Britain in 1792 and which consisted overwhelmingly of working men, inspired by Paine and seeking political reform, were abolitionist. There was a universal identification between men who viewed themselves as dispossessed — the victims of an unrepresentative and oppressive system — and black slaves, stripped of all their rights and consigned to inhuman bondage by the same political and economic system. Indeed from 1792 through to the 1840s, the language and imagery of slavery were infused into British radical and working-class politics (not always fairly, it has to be said); it strengthened an argument to compare the problems of Britons with those of contemporary slaves.

The most powerful provincial radical society was the Sheffield Constitutional Society, rooted among the artisans in the local cutlery trades. At their largest public meeting in 1794, they resolved, among other issues, to end the slave trade: 'wishing to be rid of the weight of oppression under which we groan, we are induced to compassionate those who groan also ...'. But they went much further, arguing that 'no compromise can be made between Freedom and Tyranny' and, accordingly, there should be a 'total Emancipation of the Negro Slaves'.[30] This was well in advance of formal abolition which, although embracing some individuals committed to emancipation, had specifically limited their collective ambition to ending the slave trade.

More important perhaps than the keen attachment to abolition shown by plebeian radicals in the early 1790s was the fact that their national network of links and organisations lent the strength of their unprecedented numbers to the campaign for abolition. When in 1792 the abolitionists called for renewed petitioning, the corresponding societies were able to assist. In the spring of that year abolitionist petitions rained on Parliament in unparalleled numbers; eventually there was a total of 519. The following parliamentary debate was, again, unsuccessful but the balance between the two sides was very fine indeed. Wilberforce had wooed over more members to his side and the outcome of parliamentary votes had clearly become haphazard and unpredictable:[31] illness, absence, laziness, or poor parliamentary management — each of these could tip the vote on the slave trade one way or the other.[32] Furthermore, Wilberforce's dogged insistence on total (as opposed to gradual) abolition alienated parliamentary wavers. Had he moderated his position, the slave trade could quite easily have been voted into extinction as early as 1793.[33] Nevertheless, by early 1792 abolition had firmly lodged itself within Parliament.

This was due primarily to the massive public campaign of recent years and to Wilberforce's singleminded nagging of Ministers and MPs at Westminster.

In a sense, abolition no longer needed the public pressure, save only to complement parliamentary debates. But what *was* needed, by 1792, was astute parliamentary management (never a possibility under the unpredictable leadership of Wilberforce) or a major change in governing circles. Pitt, for all his sympathy, could not commit his Cabinet to abolition as a government measure. Moreover, a number of factors by 1792 had begun to alienate ministers and MPs from the abolitionist cause. First, the success of the corresponding societies alarmed the propertied class who, siding with Burke, sought to distance themselves from popular pressure and from any associated hint of reform (of Parliament or the slave trade). Secondly, events in France were veering further and further towards violence, extremism and, eventually republicanism (though this did not, initially at least, repel the corresponding societies who continued to look to France for ideological leadership). But the most cataclysmic repercussion of the Revolution was in the French colony of St Dominque (Haiti) where the initial political skirmishing (on the model of 1789) was, within a few years, to herald communal racial violence, full-scale war (including the destruction of a British army), the eventual end of local slavery, and the collapse of the prospering economy of the island. Haiti was to be a fearful example used by all sides in contemporary and subsequent debates about abolition and emancipation.

The slave lobby viewed the Haitian revolt as proof of the folly of tampering with so volatile a substance as slavery; the abolitionists regarded Haiti as an appalling illustration of what happens when no effort is made to ameliorate the conditions of slavery. Among slave-holders throughout the Americas, Haiti was a nightmare, an example of slave vengeance and the dormant potential, in all slave communities, for savage revolt. It is now possible to see the Haitian revolution as unique, a distinct set of conditions unrepeatable in the same form anywhere else. At the time, however, Haiti inspired a fear of the uncontrollable contagion of black revolt. Reports from the British islands suggested that the slaves had formed their own (dangerous) conclusions about the events in Haiti. A letter of November 1791 to the Colonial Office remarked, of the Jamaican slaves:

I am convinced the ideas of liberty have sunk so deep in the minds of *all* Negroes, that wherever the greatest precautions are not taken they will rise.[34]

Moreover there was clear evidence to show that British abolition — no less than the more immediate lessons from Haiti — had begun to affect British slaves. It was reported in November 1791 that large crowds of slaves had gathered in Western Jamaica to celebrate the birthday of Wilberforce. In all this, however, we need to remind ourselves of the apprehension — at times the simple terror — of the whites in the islands, where traditional nightmares of slave insurrection had been amply fulfilled, and on a scale which even the planters had scarcely imagined. In the words of the cartoonist George Cruikshank, in a caricature of plantocratic life,

The planter's dream both plainly seem
To point a moral deep
If you choose to whack a nigger's back
You should never go to sleep.[35]

By 1792 it was quite impossible to disentangle the story of Haiti from the British arguments about the slave trade.

The Haitian revolt compounded the doubts, first sewn by the Revolution in France, about the wisdom of conceding change in times of unpredictable international upheavals. Thus, those men who agitated for political reforms — notably abolition of the slave trade and the reform of Parliament — came to be lumped together; to be condemned as different forms of the same subversive group. Reformers and abolitionists became to be labelled 'Jacobins', a process given greater political strength after the outbreak of war between France and Britain in February 1793. A few months later, the Earl of Abingdon remarked in Parliament that

The idea of abolishing the slave trade is connected with the levelling system and the rights of man; his lordship asked who would controvert such a proposition. For the very definition of the terms themselves, as descriptive of the thing, what does the abolition of the slave trade mean more or less, than liberty and equality? What more or less than the rights of man? And what are the rights of man, but the foolish principles of this new philosophy. If proofs are wanting, look at the colony of St Dominque and see what the rights of man have done here.[36]

As if to prove Abingdon's point, within the month the corresponding societies — now pursuing the abolitionists' tactics — despatched their reform petitions to Parliament. Indeed, it was noted that Parliament had been elected by *fewer* people than had signed the petitions.[37]

The petitions revealed a remarkable demand for reform, They came from throughout urban Britain and attracted tens of thousands of names — that from Sheffield had 8,000 names (compared to a mere 800 in 1789), 3,700 from Norwich, while that from Edinburgh stretched 'the whole length of the floor of the House'. The London Corresponding Society petition took half an hour to read; some 10,000 names were attached to it.[38] This manifestation of unprecedented popular radicalism — closely monitored from its inception by the intrusion of government spies — was but one reason for increasing government alarm about the state of internal security and peace. Faced by a hostile revolutionary France across the channel and by a thriving radical movement in British cities (which also openly expressed sympathy for France and its continuing changes), men of property inside government and out began to spurn the ideals of reform. Even those men including Pitt who had once favoured a variety of reforms began to renounce their former sympathies and to resist demands from those outside the political fold. There was indeed a generalised dismissal of all forms of reform, whether parliamentary change or abolition of the slave trade. There was, quite simply, a growing fear that concessions would encourage the political upheavals which had inundated France since 1789. Pitt and the Home Secretary therefore began to plan how best to curb the rising passion of public mass politics.[39]

It was ironic that at the very moment abolition had become unprecedentedly popular, the basis for its popularity came under political attack. According to Wilberforce, 'People connect democratical principles with the Abolition of the Slave Trade and will not hear mention of it.'[40] Absurd — but none the less damaging — accusations were levelled in print against 'the JACOBINS OF ENGLAND, the Wilberforces, the Coopers, the Paines and the Clarksons',[41] this despite Wilberforce's vigorous anti-radical stance. One man complained to Wilberforce, 'I do not imagine that we could meet with 20 persons in Hull at present who would sign a petition, that are not republicans.'[42] Parliamentary abolitionists and their public enemies agreed that there was a growing popular confusion of abolition with French principles: 'I am justified', wrote one hostile critic, 'in classing the promoters of Abolition and Republicans together.'[43] Such an accusation was politically effective, especially when a British army was, at that precise moment, being drawn into a fatal conflict in Haiti.[44] But the key question is, how valid is the accusation? There is no doubt that many of the prominent popular radicals were abolitionists and some were openly sympathetic to the Revolution in France. John Thelwall, the most prominent lecturer within the LCS in 1793-95, proclaimed himself 'the only avowed *sans-culottes* in the metropolis', 'in plain truth I am a Republican, a downright *sans-culottes.*' Thelwall also spoke out against the slave trade and slavery (though unhappy at the way the slave trade had, by the mid-1790s, come to monopolise the national conscience).[45] For Thelwall and his fellow radicals, the political sway exercised by the West Indies lobby in London was further proof of the corruption of slavery. Ending slavery would have the added political advantage of overthrowing West Indian political power in London. Conversely, a reform of Parliament would destroy the West Indians' metropolitan power base, a base they clearly needed for a successful defence of their slaving interests.

While Thelwall became the popular radicals' most prominent spokesman, their most effective organiser and, in effect, founder was Thomas Hardy, the Scottish shoemaker who lived in Piccadilly. There, his house-guest was Olaudah Equiano, the African ex-slave, who became the accepted leader of London's black community and whose autobiography was revised in Hardy's home. Equiano also joined the LCS and provided Hardy with useful correspondents in the provinces whom Equiano had already met as abolitionists.[46] One provincial corresponding society, in Melbourne, Derbyshire, adopted as its motif a picture of Africans being enslaved;[47] and whenever corresponding societies asserted their principles, they often paralleled demands for parliamentary reform with an insistence on abolition. The popular radicals were openly in favour of abolition and, even (more fundamentally) of black equality, and it was perfectly correct for opponents of abolition to suggest that there was a close association between the two issues. It was, however, quite wrong to impute to reformers (and abolitionists in general) the principles of French Jacobinism. British radicals were steeped in the tradition and vocabulary of British reform, but their ideals were transmuted by the lengthening shadows from France into Jacobinism, at least in the eyes of their opponents. Wilberforce himself came to denounce them, his anger doubtless sharpened by the apparent damage caused by the association between radicalism and abolition. He claimed that radicals had created

a contempt for the British Constitution and an attachment to those false principles of liberty which had produced such extensive mischief in a neighbouring country; nor was it only French politics which they imported into this country, but French philosophy also; in the numerous publications by which their opinions were disseminated, there was a marked contempt for everything sacred, an avowed opposition to the religion, as well as the constitution of Great Britain.[48]

By the time of the two Acts, late in 1795, banning most aspects of the popular radical movement, the radicals had come to be denounced even by those whose own principles the radicals supported. Propertied reformers had shied away from them, and abolitionists disliked them. Yet in a sense it did not matter because by then Wilberforce and friends had built up a sufficiently solid parliamentary base to promote abolition within Parliament itself. The popularity of abolition had been instrumental in lodging the cause firmly in Parliament. By the mid-1790s, parliamentary abolitionists no longer needed such extra-parliamentary pressure; indeed, in the changed political climate their cause could actually be damaged by popular backing. What was needed henceforth was astute parliamentary management, and ministerial help (or changes) to transmute public support into tangible votes of change. Henceforth abolition was prone to the capricious circumstances of parliamentary life and exposed to the unpredictable lobbying of Wilberforce in Parliament.

The campaign for the abolition of the slave trade had been able to demonstrate its remarkable national support by using distinctive and effective political tactics. In 1795, however, the foundations of public agitation were, at a stroke, demolished by the two Acts which, though aimed primarily at the corresponding societies were equally destructive of other forms of open and public agitation. It was a process completed by further repressive legislation in 1799. Thereafter, popular and public politics were under the ban, with savage punishments for those desperate enough to continue with the long-established traditions of popular campaigns. For popular radicalism, the Acts of 1795 and 1799 were a death blow, driving most activists into a truculent and begrudging silence, and others (a small minority) into desperate and sometimes violent insurrection.[49]

The ban was less serious for abolition. The campaign to abolish the slave trade was, henceforth, essentially a parliamentary struggle, focused on the motion, periodically moved by Wilberforce, for immediate abolition. In the decade between the two Acts and the passing of abolition, the arguments about abolition remained fundamentally the same; a recitation of the *pros* and *cons* well rehearsed since 1788. But for once, it was without that descant of public opposition which had been the hallmark of abolition up to the mid-1790s. The Parliament returned in 1796 was, as a body, collectively influenced by the fear of 'French principles', and abolitionist motions failed in 1797, 1798, 1799 and 1802, though sometimes by the narrowest of margins. Throughout, the powerful West Indies lobby of MPs waged an effective defence of the slave trade, though a small number began in the late 1790s seriously to consider concessions to the abolitionists, particularly by offering appropriate amelioration among the slaves themselves. Equally, the parliamentary abolitionists were able to steer through Parliament a number of revisionary Bills which served to modify (and improve) conditions for slaves on the Middle Passage.[50]

New conquests in the Caribbean, notably Trinidad, apparently compounded the abolitionist difficulties by offering new and relatively untapped land for further exploitation by slave labour. But by a strange twist of fate, the new possessions were to prove grist to the abolitionist mill. With the possession of Trinidad confirmed by the Peace of Amiens, abolitionists were, ironically, presented with the major chance of a breakthrough for their ambitions. Pitt was now out of office, and his successor, Addington, was soon subjected to Wilberforce's personal pressures. But it was the motion of Canning in 1802, seeking to prevent further slave importations into Trinidad, which obliged Addington's government to pledge caution (and parliamentary approval) on the future development of that island. Furthermore, the continuing recalcitrance of the West Indies planters had, by the turn of the century, begun to alienate more and more MPs.[51]

It was paradoxical that with anti-slavery firmly wedged in Parliament, the British slaving system was enjoying unparalleled success. The slave populations of the British islands were more buoyant than ever before; the slave populations greatly outnumbered their nearest rivals, the greatest of which, Haiti, now lay in ruins. Moreover, the economic strength of the British Caribbean remained undiminished, its tropical staples being consumed in increasing volume by metropolitan society.[52] Furthermore, its expansive economic and geographic frontiers (in Jamaica, Guiana and Trinidad) provided little but continuing growth and its associated prosperity. The military victories in the wars of the 1790s and the territorial acquisitions — none of which could have been predicted (indeed the British military disaster in Haiti provided a cautionary tale of a possible alternative scenario) — had given an unexpected filip to the British slave trade and slavery. The end result, by the end of the century, was a revitalised British slave trade, pouring ever more Africans into the Caribbean and threatening to overwhelm all the earlier successes of metropolitan abolitionists by the sheer momentum of the slaving interest. Indeed, the slaving interest was bigger and stronger at the dawn of the nineteenth century than it had been when abolitionism had been launched in 1787. Yet within a few years, the slave trade had been ended.

The key to success lay in the realisation (initially by James Stephen, Wilberforce's most effective ally) that an embargo on *foreign* slave trading would cripple a substantial part of the slaving system.[53] Submitted in 1806, in the early months of a new administration, the Foreign Slave Bill provoked little of the fierce opposition and controversy which had overshadowed earlier abolitionist measures. Few pro-slave parliamentarians seemed to have realised that the Bill, though far from the old demand for general and immediate abolition, would in fact destroy between three-quarters and two-thirds of the British slave trade.[54] By the early summer of 1806 Parliament had abolished the great bulk of the British slave trade, and abolitionists immediately began to plan to complete the attack. The Foreign Act also wore down opposition, for it had the effect of convincing large numbers of people that abolition was effectively in operation; there seemed little reason to fight the inevitable completion of the process. The initial Act had been promoted in the national economic interest — a blow against real and potential competitors of slave-grown produce. Thereafter it was possible to appeal, once more, to the familiar themes of humanity and justice. When the Abolition Bill was debated in February-

March 1807 it made remarkable and successful progress, and received the Royal Assent on 25 March. In the short term, it was the result of astute lobbying and open pressure from the new Prime Minister, Grenville. Canning remarked that 'the decision of the slave trade shows what a Government *can* do if it pleases.'[55] Both Acts were the result overwhelmingly of parliamentary tactics and ploys. The pressures and arguments, the deals and threats, the rhetoric and the evidence, took place, not in public but within Parliament, government and within the close circle of the politically influential who were the brokers and dealers of the main political activists. When abolition succeeded, it was widely *assumed* that it had public support and that it was, indeed, a victory both for morality and outraged public feeling. Yet for the past decade, public feeling had not been permitted to express itself on this or other matters. In retrospect, however, it is possible to see that it was not needed. Public support for abolition had, however, been crucial in the broader abolitionist campaign for it had been the agency which had transmuted the intellectual and religious criticisms of slavery (by definition a minority preoccupation) into the substance of mass politics. And the tactics and arguments of popular abolition had served to lodge the issue securely within Parliament itself. When fear of 'French principles' persuaded the government to undermine popular politics (including abolition) the parliamentary base for abolition was secure. Thereafter the fight was essentially parliamentarian. The *Edinburgh Review*, remarked, 'This is not, we apprehend, one of the cases where the wisdom of government has gone before the voice of the people. ... The sense of the nation has pressed abolition upon our rulers.'[56]

The Abolition Acts of 1806 and 1807 were substantially aided by contingent and fortuitous circumstances, though this is not to diminish the abolitionists' tactical achievements which lay behind them. The public abolitionist voice had long been silenced, but this should not deceive us into minimising its earlier influence. And yet, for all the unquestionable significance of abolition, there remained hundreds of thousands of black slaves in the British Caribbean. The logic of abolitionism was to embark on a new crusade; to bring freedom to Britain's enslaved Caribbean people.

Notes

1. See James Walvin, *England, Slaves and freedom, 1776-1838* (London, forthcoming).
2. Roger Anstey, *The Atlantic Slave Trade and British Abolition, 1760-1810* (London, 1975), pp. 102-3.
3. Edmund Burke, 'Sketch of a Negro Code' (1792), in *The Works of the Rt Hon. Edmund Burke* (London, 1826), 16 vols IX.
4. Anstey, *op. cit.*, pp. 119-23; David Brion Davis, *The Problem of Slavery in Western Culture* (Ithaca, New York, 1966), pp. 415-17.
5. Anstey, *op. cit.*, p. 133.
6. Ibid., Ch. 9.
7. *John Wesley's Journal*, abridged by P.L. Parker (London, 1902) p. 370.
8. R. Davies and G. Rupp (eds.), *A History of the Methodist Church* (1965), vol. I, p. 66.
9. A.D. Gilbert, *Religion and Society in Industrial England* (London, 1976), pp. 31, 40
10. Granville Sharp, *Letter Book* (Minister Library, York).
11. F. Shyllon, *James Ramsay: The Unknown Abolitionist* (Edinburgh, 1977), Ch. 2.
12. Douglas Hall, *A Brief History of the West India Committee* (Barbados, 1971); L.J. Ragatz, *The Fall of the Planter Class* (London, 1928).
13. James Walvin, *Black and White. The Negro and English Society, 1555-1945,* (London, 1973), pp. 150-1; Shyllon, *Ramsay*, p. 85.
14. Quoted Ibid., p. 84.
15. Thomas Clarkson, *History of the Rise, Progress and Accomplishment of the Abolition of the African Slave Trade . . .* (London, 1808), 2 vols., I, p. 241.
16. R.A. and S. Wilberforce, *The Life of William Wilberforce* (London, 1838), 5 vols., I, p. 53.
17. Clarkson, *History*, I, pp. 283-9.
18. Add. Ms. 21, 255, f.50.
19. Anstey, *op. cit.*, p. 257.
20. W. Sypher, *Guinea's Captive Kings* (Chapel Hill, 1942).
21. Clarkson, *History*, I, pp. 415-16.
22. *The Manchester Directory*, 2 vols. (1788), II, pp. 152, 171-2 (Manchester Central Library); *Annual Register* (1788), p. 134; *Gentleman's Magazine* (1788), p. 1079; *The Diaries of William Dyers, 1744-1801*, vol. II, p. 244. (Bristol Central Library).
23. *Hansard's Debates*, 1066-1918, vol. XXVII (1788-89), pp. 495, 501.
24. Anstey, *op. cit.*, pp. 271-3.
25. Clarkson, *History*, I, Chs. XIV-XIX.
26. C. Wyvill (ed.), *Political Papers*, 6 vols. (York, 1804), I, pp. 135-7.
27. Hannah More, *Strictures on the Modern System of Female Education* (1799; 1801 edn), I, 172-3.
28. Add. Ms. 27, 811, f.9.
29. LCS, *Minute Book* (1791-93); Add. Ms. 27,811, f. 4, 9.
30. *Proceedings of the Public Meeting held at Sheffield, April 7th 1794* (n.d.), pp. 22-5.
31. Anstey, *op. cit.*, p. 275; *The Times*, March 12 1792, pp. 20, 28, 31.
32. *Life of Wilberforce*, I, 349.
33. Fiona Spiers, 'William Wilberforce', in Jack Hayward, *Out of Slavery* (London, forthcoming).
34. Anon., 18 November 1791, C.U. 137/89.

35. George Cruickshank, *The Comic Almanack, 1834-43* (London, n.d.), p. 185.

36. *Annual Register* (1793), p. 90; *Hansard's Debates* (1792-94), pp. 632-59.

37. *Annual Register* (1793), p. 157.

38. Ibid., pp. 148-50; *Gentleman's Magazine* (1789), p. 1167; M. Thale (ed), *Selections from the Papers of the London Corresponding Society 1792-1799* (Cambridge, 1983), p. 64, n. 93.

39. *Pitt Papers* (Nov.-Dec. 1792), William L. Clements Library, University of Michigan, Ann Arbor.

40. *Life of Wilberforce*, II, p. 18.

41. Anon., *A Very New PAMPHLET indeed!* . . . (London, 1792), pp. 3-4.

42. Quoted in E.M. Howse, *Saints in Politics* (London, 1972 edn), p. 44.

43. *A Very new PAMPHLET indeed!*, pp. 3-5.

44. David Geggus, *Slavery, War and Revolution* (Oxford, 1981).

45. John Thelwall, *Speech to the L.C.S.* (26 October 1795), p. 10; *The Rights of Nature* (1796, p. 20; Letters, 13 February 1794, in T.S. 11.959.3505 (i); Mrs Thelwall, *The Life of John Thelwall* (London, 1837) p. 115; John Thelwall, 'Slaves to Common People', *The Tribune* (1795), p. 167.

46. Peter Fryer, *Staying Power* (London, 1984), pp. 106-7

47. Melbourne Corresponding Society, P.C. 1/3514.

48. A. Cobban, *Debate on the French Revolution* (London, 1950), p. 289.

49. Edward Royle and James Walvin, *English Radicals and Reformers, 1760-1848,* (Brighton, 1982), Chs. 5 & 6.

50. Anstey, *op. cit.*, pp. 321-6, 330-1.

51. Dale Porter, *The Abolition of the Slave Trade in England, 1784-1807,* (Hamden, Conn., 1970), pp. 103-7

52. Seymour Drescher, *Econocide. British Slavery in the Era of Abolition,* (Pittsburg, 1977), Ch. 5

53. Ibid., pp. 122-3.

54. Anstey, *op. cit.*, p. 275.

55. Ibid., pp. 388, 397-9.

56. *Edinburgh Review* (1807), vol. X, pp. 205-6.

3 THE IMPACT OF WAR AND MILITARY PARTICIPATION ON BRITAIN AND FRANCE 1792-1815[1]

Clive Emsley

When Bonaparte, and Nelson too,
And Wellington at Waterloo,
Were fighting both by land and sea,
The poor man gained these victories!

The labouring man will plough the deep,
Till the ground and sow the wheat,
Fight the battles when afar
Fear no dangers, or a scar;
But still they're looked upon like thieves,
By them who bide at home at ease

Do what they will, do what they can,
They can't do without the labouring man

(*Ballad of the Labouring Man*, c.1816)

Thirty years ago Stanislas Andreski published *Military Organisation and Society*. A key concept developed in the book is the military participation ratio, by which Andreski argued that there is a systematic relationship between war and changes in the pyramid of social stratification when the technique of warfare and the duration of a particular war lead to change in the proportion of the population called upon to participate militarily. Several queries might be raised about the concept, not least of which would be to challenge the presumption that it is 'almost always those who wield military power who form the supreme stratum of society'[2] — a presumption especially debatable following the decline of feudalism, the rise of economies dominated by market relationships of supply

57

and demand, and the growth of the sovereign state with its monopolistic claims to legitimacy and organised violence.

Yet the notion that participation in war can lead to some kind of benefit has been central to much of the historical study of war and society in the last two decades. With few dissenting voices, historians have seen war functioning as an agent of social change fostering women's suffrage, improved nutrition, Britain's welfare state, and an improved market position for a variety of groups ranging from the British working class to the Black American. In a broad survey of war and social change in the twentieth century, Arthur Marwick proposed a 'four-tier model', subsequently revised to the 'four dimensions' or 'aspects' of war, by which the analysis of war's interrelationship with society might be explored: the destructive and disruptive dimension, the test of a society's institutions, participation, and the psychological impact. The third of these dimensions clearly owes something to Andreski. Marwick has written,

> as wars more and more involve the participation of hitherto underpriviledged groups in the community — and this is a characteristic of total war — those groups tend to benefit from such participation.[3]

Such benefit does not depend entirely on the conscious efforts of governments to buy support or reward such groups; there can be simply 'a strengthened market position, and hence higher material standards, for such groups ... a new sense of status, usually leading to a dropping of former sectional or class barriers.'[4]

The aim of this essay is twofold: Section I broadly contrasts the experience of Britain and France between 1792 and 1815, the two major combatants of what can well be considered as the first 'total war'. Section II seeks to assess the impact of participation on the social groups who supplied the fighting men and produced weapons, equipment and food for the war effort.

I

The Revolutionary and Napoleonic wars have not left any abiding, horrific images of battle and bombing like the world wars of this century; indeed, for long periods of the conflict it was difficult for the principal combatants to get at each other militarily. Yet this must not be allowed to obscure either the efforts or the expense in blood and money. Compared with conflicts in the preceding 100 years, the scale of warfare in Europe between 1792 and 1815 was much bigger and far more destructive as the political and social limitations of warfare were broken first by the Jacobin and then by the Napoleonic state, thus enabling the tactical revolution contemplated during the eighteenth century to be implemented on the battlefield. During the Revolutionary wars battlefield armies appear to have been no larger than their predecessors, but they clashed three times as frequently; the average armies in Napoleonic battles were about three times the size of those which fought during the eighteenth century, and they clashed six times as frequently.[5] A quarter of a million men were involved in the Waterloo campaign; half a million in the second stage of the battle of Leipzig. The *levée en masse* of 1793 proclaimed that every French citizen was involved in the war effort; conscription was introduced in 1793, and more efficiently and lastingly under the draconian Jourdan Law of 1798. By the latter, between March 1804 and April 1815, practically 2 million native-born Frenchmen saw active service.[6]

Britain did not introduce conscription, but her armed forces grew to an unprecedented size. At Minden in 1759, Britain's most significant European land engagement during the Seven Years' War, there were a mere 4,400 British infantry; Sir Arthur Wellesley had 17,000 British infantry at Vimiero in 1808, and, as the Duke of Wellington, he had 21,000 British infantry at Waterloo. During the Seven Years' War the British army averaged some 67,000 regulars and 27,000 militia; in 1801 the numbers were about 150,000 and 104,600 respectively; and in 1810, 199,000 and 72,000. In the summer of 1809 the British population was supporting an armed force of 786,500 men (excluding colonial troops); even allowing for foreign-born soldiers and sailors, roughly one man in every ten of military age in Britain and Ireland was serving in the regular forces of the army, navy or embodied militia; if volunteers and local militia are added, the proportion rises to one in six.[7]

Losses were heavy. Jacques Houdaille has estimated that over 900,000 Frenchmen failed to return home; about half of these were killed, died of wounds or disease; the other half were prisoners who never returned, or men who otherwise went missing. Proportionately it was during the last three years of the empire, beginning with the disastrous Russian campaign, that the French sustained their greatest losses. In the middle of the nineteenth century William Barwick Hodge calculated that 210,000 British soldiers and sailors were killed, died of wounds or disease during the wars; his calculations sought to take account of those men who would have died even if there had been no war. These losses, it was subsequently computed, were proportionately greater than those sustained by British forces during the First World War. In France economic historians have concluded that the loss of so many men in the child-producing cohorts had a long-term impact on French demographic trends. Yet any similar impact is not apparent in Britain where the labour supply continued to grow rapidly.[8]

The British government raised £1,500,000,000 in loans and taxes to fight the war, establishing a new form of taxation, income tax, in the process. Richard Cooper has recently argued that Pitt did not set out to be revolutionary with this tax.[9] But that surely is not the point; for even if income tax was to preserve the old dream of paying off the national debt, it was the new war which jeopardised this dream. After the sale of the *biens nationaux* — essentially a result of the Revolution and beginning in 1789 with the sequestration of Church land — the French did not come up with any startlingly new fiscal measure. The fiscal system of Napoleon was much like that of the old regime, and lasted until the First World War — which did necessitate the adoption of income tax. Napoleon was reluctant to resort to loans, probably fearing the way the Bourbon monarchy had collapsed. But France was able to call on the wealth of defeated and annexed territories. Similarly, she was able to call on the manpower of these territories — more than half of the 600,000 men who began the Moscow campaign were not French-born.

Faced with the dangers of invasion and civil war, the Jacobins resorted to draconian powers to organise France for war between 1792 and 1794. Almost a million men were grafted onto the remnants of the old royal army. Among these were three-quarters of the newly-organised *gendarmerie nationale* who, when brought together in large camps at Chalons, Fontainebleu and Versailles, found that they had many common concerns and complaints about their role as policemen; they threatened not to depart for the front without 'justice'; once that was granted 'ils voleraient à la defense

de la liberté et de l'égalité.'[10] These troops had to be armed and
equipped, which meant the creation of new weapons factories, the
biggest being in Paris with men drafted in from outside the city
(notably the threatened arms centres on the eastern frontiers,
Charleville and Maubeuge) to work in the 258 forges, working 14
hours a day, producing nearly 700 muskets a day, and being paid
at rates determined by an arbitration tribunal on which they had a
majority of the elected representatives. Intensive courses were
organised to train men in the manufacture of gunpowder and
canon. The same intensity was to be found in the seaports, as men
and material were drafted in an attempt to bring the revolutionary
navy up to parity with the British. According to Geoffrey Best, 'in
the history of no other European country is there any comparable
feat of total mobilization for war purposes before the twentieth
century.'[11] This organisation for war did not survive the fall of
Robespierre, though requisitions continued to be made. Under the
Directory, military supply went back into civilian hands. The
fournisseurs made considerable profits from speculating in military
supplies and, of course, the unlucky ones were ruined. Arms and
clothing contractors enjoyed periodic booms also as a result of
military demands right through the Napoleonic period.

Britain had no equivalent of the Jacobin dictatorship. She was
never threatened in quite the same way that France was threatened
in 1792 and 1793, though faced with the possibility of invasion
draconian measures such as martial law were contemplated,[12]
while aliens and British Jacobins were roughly treated. Men might
be requisitioned by a press gang, crimp or corrupt recruiting
sergeant, but skilled men to work in the dockyards were poached
rather than drafted. Pitt contemplated selling off the church tithe
to raise finance for the war in 1798,[13] but property was never
requisitioned. During 1803-1804, for example, timber for warships
was in short supply. The succession of wars during the eighteenth
century had taken its toll of England's woodlands; furthermore the
contractors, who supplied 90 per cent of the navy's timber, found
that they could get better prices for wood from merchant ship-
builders and from those involved in constructing canals, houses
and mills. The problem was compounded by the new dockyard
timber masters who enforced a new and rigorous system of quality
control, and by Earl St Vincent at the Admiralty, who was
determined to make economies in naval expenditure and to hold
merchants to contracts agreed during the Peace of Amiens. St

Vincent was forced to resign in May 1804 (partially because of the problems in naval mobilisation) and market forces were allowed full play once again: the 1802 contracts were cancelled and prices were allowed to rise.[14]

As in France, fortunes were to be made, or lost, in supplying the armed forces. Most regiments negotiated directly with clothiers and equipment suppliers; a colonel whose regiment suffered heavy losses in battle could consequently suffer heavy financial losses. The War Office negotiated some clothing and equipment contracts directly, and, particularly in the second stage of the wars, began a more serious development of its own weapons production plants with a more rigorous vetting of weapons. Again, gunsmiths stood to make money — if they could squeeze it out of the Treasury. The French paid up on time, at least according to a paragraph in the *York Herald* of the 3 September 1808:

> EMBARGO — Notwithstanding all the attempts of Bonaparte, trade still finds its way, and orders for cloth for the *French army* have been executed in the West Riding to the amount of £40,000, and the money paid for it immediately.

But, of course, far fewer men risked their capital in supplying military needs than risked life and limb on the battlefield. On the surface the recruiting systems as administered by local government look very different in France and Britain. In France, local government came within an increasingly centralised system. Ultimately, under Napoleon, a hierarchy ran from the head of state, through the Minister of the Interior, the prefects, the sub-prefects, and ended with the mayors who were screened and selected from local men with sufficient wealth and standing. In Britain, local administration was in the hands of part-time officials, notably the magistrates. In boroughs the magistrates were generally drawn from the self-perpetuating oligarchies of aldermen. In the counties they were those gentlemen of sufficient property and standing to be included in the commision of the peace who were prepared to take out their *dedimus* and to serve as magistrates. Deputy-lieutenants were drawn from the same background and served part-time, if they were prepared to accept office. Men from lower down the social scale served as part-time parish constables, appointed in a variety of ways, and quite often reluctant to serve.

Magistrates, deputy-lieutenants and constables were all involved in recruiting under the Quota Acts and for the various auxiliary forces embodied during the war. The war put enormous new burdens on these officials and probably dissuaded many men from serving as magistrates or deputy-lieutenants — it was already very difficult to get magistrates in some fast growing, populous areas because of the burden of their tasks. Charles Mostyn agreed to serve as deputy-lieutenant in Oxfordshire in 1803, and reckoned he spent one day a week involved in recruiting business. John Carrington, a farmer of Bramfield, Hertfordshire serving as a chief constable, believed that he was spending three days a week during the summer of 1803 on military business.[15] Some local officials began to interpret the law in their own way, or else to ignore the law so as to protect relations and, perhaps, friends. After all, they had to continue living in the community when the exigencies of war were over.

Precisely the same thing happened in France. Prefects and sub-prefects may have sought to enforce the recruiting laws rigorously; but the local man, the mayor, however loyal, sometimes had other ideas. Mayors failed to submit lists of conscripts, lost or destroyed the relevant birth registers, and connived with reluctant conscripts and their parents in a variety of ways. Birth certificates were falsified; men were sent who were too young or too short and who would be rejected by the army.[16] Even gendarmes were accused of coming to understandings with local populations about evading the conscription legislation and leaving deserters alone.[17]

The systems in both Britain and France were grossly inefficient by modern standards, but recruits were secured and the ranks were, by and large, filled. Generally speaking the war did little to alter the traditional practice of local government administration; and probably it did little to alter the long-term tradition of central government administration. Of course the Jacobin dictatorship of 1793-94 cannot be discussed outside of the war context; the Committee of Public Safety and the Committee of General Security acquired enormous powers and established a massive bureaucracy to conduct the war and to preserve their perceptions of the Revolution. Yet the Jacobin Republic was ephemeral; as the war turned in France's favour, so the Jacobins' administrative machine slowed down and was dismantled. Over the long term it can be argued that the Revolution, propelled admittedly by war, provided the opportunity for administrative reorganisation and nationalisation long dreamed of by the monarchy — though, of course, the forms of reorganisation and rationalisation were not those of Bourbon dreams. In Britain some administrative changes were to be found in the Board of Trade and with the creation of an Aliens Office within the Home Office. The Treasury also recruited a larger staff of expert administrators to supervise the new taxes. But none of these changes represented anything like a revolution in government and administrative practice.

On the surface the British and French economies appear to have been greatly influenced by the war. Britain seized the advantage of mastery of the seas to push the products of her new industries across the world; while France suffered. If official trade figures are taken as the guide, then the prolonged disruption of revolution and war might be said to have cost France nearly 40 years of overall growth.[18] Her colonial trade was destroyed. Bordeaux, most notably, stagnated. From a boom in the eighteenth century, its population growth fell below the average of that for France as a whole in the first 30 years of the nineteenth century. Large areas of the city's hinterland, which had been booming in the eighteenth century, were ruralised; parts of Brittany and Normandy similarly. There was a major boost to Alsatian trade as French trade concentrated more and more on Northern Europe. But the question remains: how much of this change was inevitable before the first shots were fired?

In François Crouzet's comparative analysis of the French and British economies during the eighteenth century,[19] he stressed French dependence on St Dominique in the area of overseas trade in contrast with the much more diversified trade of Great Britain. The total exports of Britain included far more manufactured goods than those of France. The British proportionately had a much smaller share of European markets than the French, but French trade within Europe largely involved the re-export of colonial goods. The result was that although directly and indirectly the wars hit both economies, French colonial trade was destroyed. Britain was virtually excluded from Europe by Napoleon's blockade, but sought eagerly — and generally successfully — for markets in a wider world. Of course, conflict with the United States, largely the result of the economic struggle between Britain and France, had a serious, if ephemeral, impact in the early years of the nineteenth century. France, cut off from her colonies and from the Americas, sought under Napoleonic hegemony to restructure the European markets on the principle of 'la France avant tout'. Certain

Alsatian towns profited from this new policy as French trade swung more determinedly towards Northern Europe.[20] But the structure of trade in the pre-war period, the general weakness of French trade, and the contrasting diversity of British trade, do not suggest that the war threw the economies into a totally different direction. Rather, it appears to have accelerated movement in the direction in which foreign trade was already going.

Furthermore, war does not appear to have caused more superficial fluctuations in the pace and content of Britain's industrial revolution.[21] Some industries, such as iron, benefited from the demands of war, and, while it suffered consequently at the end of hostilities, the boost remained significant. Some industries suffered from war; none more so than the small metal trades in Birmingham during the first years of the conflict. Taxation appears to have inhibited the development of the paper and glass industries. Other industries fluctuated. Textiles, for example, benefited from the demand created by full and regular employment brought about by the war; but they were seriously hurt in the second stage of the conflict by the American embargo. Money which could be used for financing industry does not seem to have been sucked into financing the war to any serious degree. The agricultural interest, which did very well out of the war, paid more than its fair share for the war through the new income tax; it appears to have paid twice as much as the mercantile interest.

Much of the French war effort was paid for by countries defeated or occupied by France, directly through French demands on their treasure as tributes, or indirectly by the French army's custom of living off the country. Napoleon was very conservative in his fiscal policies. Besides his reluctance to consider loans he refused, unlike British governments, to consider issuing paper money: the Revolution's disastrous experiments with *assignats* and *mandats* had provided him with an awful warning.

Industrialisation and the capitalisation of industry developed at a different pace in France, but again war appears to have had only a superficial impact. Cotton did well, taking advantage of the absence of British competition to press ahead with its own successful industrialisation process. Yet even sectors which prospered tended to be conservative in comparison with their British counterparts. There was no incentive to invest in agriculture — why bother to invest when profits accumulated regardless? The iron industry behaved similarly, though geographical factors were also significant since iron production in France continued to be centred in regions where ore was to be found, and where forests were plentiful. France's new coal deposits were generally far away. The individualistic nature of revolutionary legislation defeated the attempts by early industrialists like Pierre-François Tubeuf, who had already been confronted with the opposition of 'feudal' landowners, to rationalise and concentrate coal and iron-ore mining. Legislation in 1791 gave landowners the mining rights to any ores found under their property and, in consequence, the number of mines increased while the size of mines decreased; it was 20 years before Napoleonic legislation began to reverse this process.[22]

II

Industrialisation and the capitalisation of industry were probably the most significant developments in British society between 1780 and 1830. But at the time people were probably far less aware of this than they were aware of war, certainly between 1793 and 1815. While few knew that there was an industrial revolution in progress, everyone knew there was a war on. The recruiting sergeant, the press gang, the militia ballots, the weekly parade of volunteers in their fancy uniforms all ensured this; and, less obviously, there were the increases in indirect taxes, and increases in the poor rates to assist the families of servicemen and embodied militiamen. Richard Cobb, with typical impishness, has called the French Revolution 'a magnificent irrelevance' for many Frenchmen;[23] but irrelevant or not, it invaded their homes, and with it came the wars which continued long after most terminal dates which historians put on the Revolution. The French people, like the British, experienced demands for men and money and in addition, in the early stages of the war at least, the peasants faced the demands for draft animals, and the demands for food for the towns often exacted at bayonet-point by the paramilitary *armées révolutionaires.*

What then, did the people of the two countries think about the wars? And, bearing in mind the concept with which I began, what did they get out of it for all the sacrifices in men and money, and for the effort of producing weapons, clothing and equipment for the conflict?

There was no common home-front attitude to the wars in either

Britain or France, and attitudes were influenced by a multitude of variables. Patriotism was apparent when both countries were under serious threat, notably in France in 1792-93, and in Britain in 1803-05. But patriotism could wear thin as the conflict wore on. Three thousand men armed with old guns, pikes and scythes turned out to repel a reported landing of British troops on the coast of the Gironde near La Teste de Buch in May 1793. Five years later a mere 50 assembled to meet another 'invasion'; in 1807, when a British frigate did put a small landing party ashore, the garrison of the fort of La Roquette fled.[24]

Sentiments of loyalty, and fear and hatred of the enemy, were pronounced among some people throughout the duration of the conflict; in both countries prisoners of war or enemy agents were seen behind every disorder. In Messidor, Year VII (the summer of 1799) a *commissaire* in Tarn was reporting his opinion that English agents were reimbursing parents for the expense of a *garnissaire*.[25] After provision riots in 1812 the prefect of Alençon reported 'L'influence de l'Angleterre n'a pu être douteuse'.[26] The *feuilles de travail* of the Prefect of Police in Napoleonic Paris reveal a continuing concern about British agents, and annoyance at the slapdash way in which some provincial officials issued passports to aliens.[27] In Britain there were periodic fears of spies and saboteurs, and there was a continuing fear of French prisoners of war (there were always more French prisoners in Britain than British prisoners in France). At the beginning of the revolutionary war, the French prisoners' new principles led some to see them as potential subverters of good, but simple Britons or allies of the British Jacobins.[28] Some regarded the French as prime instigators of the Luddite disorders.[29]

Yet prisoners of war could be another source of profit. French prisoners on parole, according to one gentleman in Okehampton, filled lodgings and were generally good for local tradesmen — 'the best substitute that could have been devised for the losses resulting from the war.' If French prisoners of war were to be removed from Okehampton in January 1812, he requested that Dutch prisoners recently taken in Java could replace them.[30] Prisoners of war also provided a lucrative sideline for smugglers. Large-scale smuggling continued around Britain's coasts; indeed it was given greater opportunities by the economic blockade. France's land frontiers also witnessed widespread smuggling, again boosted by the war. The removal of the Belgian frontier appears to have spread the

French smuggling bands northwards to Flushing, Middleburgh and Ghent;[31] while the general switching of French trade to eastern Europe, together with embargoes and the blockade, boosted smuggling along the Alsatian frontier. Furthermore, when Napoleon went off on campaigns and needed troops, customs surveillance by troops declined proportionately and smuggling became that much easier.[32]

Loyalty to the state and hatred of the enemy was only one side of the coin. On the other was anger and annoyance at the continuing demand for men and money. Recruiting provoked trouble in both countries. In Britain the practice of pressing men for the navy provoked both riots and strikes in coastal towns throughout the war years. The fear that the Supplementary Militia Act 1796 was a form of conscription occasioned a wave of rioting in parts of rural England. The Scottish Militia Act 1797 had a similar impact.[33] The pressures of the war contributed to much working-class unrest, and were recognised as so doing. In France, where conscription proper was introduced, there were attacks on the gendarmes and officials responsible for implementing the legislation. It was recruiting legislation which sparked off the uprisings in Brittany and in the Vendée, and which boosted Catholic Royalism in the south-east.[34] Under Napoleon the system of recruitment became more efficient, but by no means more popular. An English prisoner of war described how,

> during the drawing of a conscription, the town hall is surrounded by the relations of the youths, and an ignorant spectator would rather suppose they were waiting the sentence of a criminal court, about to award life or death to their friends, than the decision of chance, whether they are to be citizens or soldiers.[35]

Anti-imperial cartoonists had a ready subject with

> L'Ogre Corse sous qui nous sommes
> Cherchant toujours nouveaux exploits
> Mange par an deux cent mille hommes
> Et va partout chiant des Rois.[36]

There was widespread avoidance of conscription by disappearance, desertion, self-mutilation and, since married men were generally exempt, large numbers of young men found wives — often very unlikely wives. In Maucourt, Picardy in 1808, for example, four conscripts aged respectively 20, 21, 21 and 23 married four women aged respectively 74, 72, 77 and 87.[37] At least one young conscript sought a more permanent escape; in the summer of 1807 the Paris police reported that Alexandre Pauchon and his 16-year-old girlfriend had tried to poison themselves on hearing that he had been conscripted.[38] The demands for men, coupled with the enormous tax increases in 1813, probably contributed to the demand for Napoleon's removal.

In the aftermath of the wars people looked back on them with different attitudes. In *The Country Doctor*, Balzac portrayed a peasant veteran describing Napoleon as a godlike figure to villagers assembled in a barn to hear his stories. A romantic cult of military glory was present among some of the young men of post-Napoleonic France, epitomised by Stendhal's Julien Sorel and this was fostered during the July Monarchy. But at the same time, it was possible to find wealthy farmers proud of desertion during the war years; as one farmer of Gevaudan asked in 1844, 'What did the wrangles of the Emperor and the other rulers mean to us?' In eastern France the *Te deums* celebrating Napoleon's victories became *tue-hommes*, and in lower Brittany *tud-eom* (need men).[39]

In the 1830s the 1840s Shropshire miners looked back on the war as the good old days when going down the pit was almost a voluntary activity because of high pay; only three days work a week could provide an adequate wage for a man and his family.[40] Yet during Radical unrest which followed Waterloo it was asked: Why should the workingman fight for Britain when he had no say in its government or its Parliament?[41] This leads back directly to the question of what rewards were handed out to producers and fighters in the war effort.

Servicemen demobilised at the end of a war generally merge back into their communities and consequently it is difficult to estimate whether, as a group, they are better or worse-off as a result of their participation. For some military service was a cheque to be cashed when a man sought a job, or was looking for a way out of trouble:

> I am In hopes [you] Will Excuse my Writing For I am hard of Earring I Never Intended Keeping the Spade. ... I took the Spade to dig Pottatoes ... I placed the Spade Where any one

might See It and It Remained there three hours as thee Moon
Shone Bright If [I] Intended Keeping the Spade or hid It ... I
served to take anything from any malitia and never was known
to take anything from any of my Quarters or to make away any
of the County Stores.[42]

During the Revolutionary and Napoleonic wars some men picked
up new skills in the army which may have been an asset back in
civilian life; literacy and numeracy are the obvious examples. For a
few there was the opportunity of serving as policemen and thus
clinging on to some vestiges of the military life they had enjoyed,
or become used to. On the other hand, passing the best years of
youth in the military with its long periods of idleness and short,
frenetic periods of danger, did not make it easy for a man to return
to a trade, or for a peasant to return to his land to start consoli-
dating his position of building up any independence.

Joseph Chambord was demobilised in Messidor, Year IX (June
1801). He could find no work in his native Creuze so, leaving his
wife and two children, like thousands of others, he sought work in
Paris. In July 1806, working as a *garçon maçon*, he fell from a
building to his death. His brother Michel identified his body to
commissaire Alletz explaining that Joseph had died

> in the greatest indigence ... he lodged for two *sols* a night and
> has left neither possessions nor money in his room ... the little
> money which he earned he sent to his wife who, together with
> his two children, is without bread as a result of his death.[43]

Robert Guillemand, the Frenchman credited with shooting Nelson
at Trafalgar, was conscripted in 1805; after almost 20 years of service he returned to his native Sixfours to find his brother

> solely devoted to the mean labours of agriculture, and [speak-
> ing] a language foreign to my heart; he is quite absorbed by his
> daily habits, and despises a soldier, who cannot sow a field of
> grain. ... Of the group which old friendships had gathered
> round our family, I find that very few remember me at all. ...
> The trade of a soldier is the only one I ever knew; and now I
> can carry it no longer. ... In a word, during the whole of the last
> twenty years, I have been an alien to the affections of my own
> family, and a stranger to the feelings of the farmer, the citizen,

in fact, of everyone of the industrious classes; and, wherever I go, I am out of place.[44]

Louis Canler volunteered at the age of 14 in 1811 so that he would no longer be a burden on his parents. Seven years later he was demobbed and, like the unfortunate Chambord, he went to Paris:

but in order to live there you needed work, a job or a private income. Unfortunately I had neither and, to tell the truth, I did not know either what I could do well.[45]

'T.S.', a native of Edinburgh enlisted in 1806 from similar motives to Canler; he sent £5 from his bounty money to his parents. He returned in 1815 to find his parents dead; not wishing to be a burden on his sister and her husband he disappeared in 1818 leaving a letter:

I wish I was a soldier again. I cannot even get labouring work. ... I will go to South America. Or, I shall go to Spain. ... If I succeed in the South, I will return and lay my bones beside my parents: if not, I will never come back.[46]

John Green, an apprentice carpet-maker, also enlisted in 1806. Nine years later he came back to his native Louth.

I was sorry to find that my old shop-mates were in the same state as I left them, having little more than half employment; so that there was no hope whatever that I could meet with an engagement, at least not until things took a turn.[47]

Of course, no case can be regarded as typical; desperation, misery and unemployment were not the lot of every demobilised serviceman. John Green eventually was able to start his own small business, while Louis Canler became a celebrated detective. Yet, generally speaking, there was no improvement in the economic conditions or the quality of life of the social groups who supplied the fighting men. Indeed, initially, as hundreds of thousands of men were demobilised and as economies had to restructure themselves for peace, the situation of the veteran was bleak, especially given the appalling harvests which followed the summer of Waterloo.

The Highlands of Scotland appear to have provided men on a scale greater in proportion to available manpower than any other area of mainland Britain. Under-employment was endemic in the Highlands and from the mid-eighteenth century military service provided employment opportunities. Military service also brought income into the region with soldiers' bounties and pay. Peace brought a diminution of this income and consequently problems for many of the families in the northern interior glens. The landlord–tenant nexus was also significant in military recruiting during the Revolutionary and Napoleonic Wars as in earlier conflicts. Not enlisting, or enlisting in a regiment not favoured by the chief could lead to eviction of a man, or even of his parents. Some parents traded sons for the promise of more secure tenure or a better holding; but often landlords failed to honour such promises. The involvement of half-pay junior officers in the Highland disturbances of the post-war years may reflect some sympathy between officers and other veterans of the war, and from recruiting practices, though often the junior officers themselves had much to lose from the landlords' resettlement plans.[48]

Some of those who produced for the war effort prospered while the war was being fought and as long as their market position was maintained by the shortage of labour or various commodities: for example, those involved in agricultural production benefited. In Britain corn prices increased; landowners could claim higher rents; while farmers, more and more noticeably, distanced themselves socially from their labourers. Even allowing for inflation, the labourers themselves would appear to have commanded reasonable wages during the war. But peace brought problems. The resulting cuts in taxes and better farming techniques helped farmers over the worst when the wartime boom ended. Overall, however, they probably experienced a cut in living standards. Given the importance of agricultural production to the war effort it is possible to see the 1815 Corn Law as a reflection of the notion of reward accompanying war effort; but such an assessment would underplay the power of the landed élite in Parliament. Agricultural labourers who supplied men for the army and brought in the harvest (sometimes while they were serving as soldiers) had no power, no financial shield, and suffered accordingly when peace came and agriculture was less profitable.

Some workers were able to wring concessions from their employers because of the temporary improvement in their bargaining position brought about by the war. This was the case, for example, in the Royal Dockyards. Yet it was not always possible for workers to hang on to concessions with the restoration of peace, and their spokesmen in industrial disorders were particularly vulnerable. The Navy Board took advantage of Nelson's Copenhagen and Baltic successes to discharge 340 men regarded as ringleaders of the dockyard combinations. The enormous and rapid demobilisation following the defeat of Napoleon brought problems for others who had successfully used their wartime bargaining power. The seamen of the Tyne and Wear agreed to large numbers of their comrades joining the navy while they braved French privateers and storms, as well as press gangs from warships, sailing undermanned vessels on the coal run from the north-east to London. The added dangers and the shortage of men enabled them to force their pay up; but when peace came the men serving in the Royal Navy returned, the shipowners reduced pay and insisted on keeping crews down to the skeleton size employed during wartime. Lord Sidmouth hoped that 'Consideration and Liberality' be shown to the seamen as their 'due', but the inexorable laws of economics and *laissez-faire* rendered intervention impossible.

In France the war provided work opportunities. During the Terror a variety of workers in the militant Faubourg Saint-Antoine — carpenters, coachmakers, joiners, hatmakers, shoemakers, stockingers and tailors, as well as metal workers — found work on military contracts. Two decades later Napoleon deliberately placed orders in the Faubourg to alleviate under-employment. But military requirements also hurt some small employers and workers. In 1795 the owner of a small mine in the forêt d'Abilon protested that the army had taken 15 of his workers in two years. While workers often found themselves in a poor bargaining position because of the vast numbers of deserters and *réfractaires* who had to take whatever work they could get at whatever an employer was prepared to pay.[54] Workers in the naval dockyards received a wage increase shortly before the declaration of war on Britain, but inflation and the government's insistence on paying a proportion of the pay in the shaky *assignats* rapidly cancelled out the increase; the dissatisfaction with pay in *assignats* and the demand for 'real' money contributed to the decision of the arsenal workers of Toulon to throw in their lot with those who yielded the port to the British in 1794. The Jacobin dictatorship professed care and sympathy for the workers as *sans-culottes* and introduced bonus schemes for good work, but it was distrustful the moment that its authority was called in question; its representatives in the dockyards responded to manifestations of discontent, as well as to 'idleness' and the shipwright's insistence on the *copeaux* ('chips'), with ferocity. The *ouvriers de levée* (men conscripted into the yards during the war) were disadvantaged far more than the regular employees; besides missing out on some of the benefits given to the permanent employees, family men conscripted into the yards probably had to maintain two sets of lodgings, and the Jacobin dictatorship refused to allow them the same facility as seamen in transmitting, automatically, a part of their pay to their families in their native ports.[55]

Plans for social welfare provision for soldiers, their widows and orphans, were popular with the National Convention, but they did not really survive Thermidor.[56] At the same time the war undermined the new system of hospitals for the poor and indigent by rapidly filling them with sick and wounded troops.[57] In Britain a few voices urged that those who were doing the fighting should receive some material and social benefits,[58] but proposals for legislation to help the poor came to nothing and the new Malthusian ideas of population growth found a receptive audience amongst propertied men who were having to dig ever deeper into their pockets for war taxes and for poor rates swollen by the departure of so many breadwinners.

In neither country did new legislation favour those social groups who provided the soldiers and sailors, who made the weapons, uniforms and equipment, and who brought in the harvest. The *Code Napoléon* gave the employer superiority over his workforce in law; it also established the workers *livret*, a certificate bearing name, description and place of employment. The *livret* had to be signed by a man's employer and by his local mayor whenever he left a job. The mayor was also supposed to note the name of the town to which the man said he was moving, which made the *livret* a kind of passport or identification card, but carried by one class of individual only. In Britain, the war years saw the introduction of the Combination Laws bringing summary justice to trade disputes. And if the Acts only survived the wars by 10 years it is worth emphasising that the Master and Servant Act 1823 gave the English employer the same sort of legal superiority as his French counterpart.

Andreski argued that an extension of the military participation ratio could be vitiated by improvements in the techniques of state and police repression which might also result from a war.[59] Both countries witnessed repression and an extension of their police systems during the war years, but assessing the effectiveness of policing and of repression is never easy.[60] Fouché does seem to have been efficient at checking threats to the Napoleonic regime; but his successor, the rigid and unimaginative General Savary, manifestly failed in this respect as the near success of General Malet's conspiracy in 1812 testifies. At the same time, the central police offices in Paris — the Prefecture and the Ministry of Police — appear to have become partners in a monumental bureaucratic paper-chase. Outside Paris the effectiveness of policing and repression was not significantly different from the situation in the eighteenth century; there were more gendarmes, but much of their time was taken up with army recruiting problems. There were more *commissaires* established on a national system, though their effectiveness and reliability often left much to be desired. But alongside the 'stick' of repression, the Napoleonic regime also offered the 'carrots' of bread and circuses. It called upon the cereal fields of the empire to alleviate any shortages in France, while military parades and imperial spectacles were carefully planned and orchestrated. In 1795 and 1796 for the first time the British government found it necessary to import foodstuffs to feed its population and thus to quieten popular unrest. The repression of working-class political groups and of economic organisations was largely conducted under existing laws, using traditional methods and existing personnel — magistrates, constables and soldiers. Furthermore, there could be significant limits to the repression of working-class economic organisations because of those organisations' market strength. At the same time as Parliament was discussing the Combination Act 1799, the Navy Board was discussing dockyard pay and regulations with representatives from the workforce in the great naval dockyards.

Did all the effort, all the demands for money, then have no effect? In Britain the war does appear to have contributed to a raising of consciousness among social groups. There were massive working-class demonstrations calling for peace and for parliamentary assistance for trades hit by the economic aspects of the struggle. There was a feeling during the war that the social groups which supplied the fighting men, at least, should get something out of it. Ballad literature in the aftermath of the war suggests a disillusionment after all the sacrifice, and in precisely these terms. The provincial middle class, especially the dissenter elements, also mounted massive campaigns during the war both against the war itself and against its economic aspects. Well before the end of the war the Anglican landed élite which had ruled Britain during the eighteenth century recognised that it must come to terms with this potent new force.

France was different. In France the working class was much smaller, and the provincial middle class lacked the cohesion of that in Britain. Of course, middle-class industrialists protested to the government about the impact of the blockade on their trade, but the protests came from individual towns and cities: Strasbourg, Bordeaux and Marseilles literally did not speak the same language. During the Revolution several significant towns and cities had taken up arms against Paris, but there was no real co-operation within the federalist revolt, and Napoleon never had to face anything like the massive provincial campaign against the Orders in Council. France also had an enormous peasant class quite unlike anything in Britain. Even if Eugen Weber's picture of late nineteenth-century France is not universally viewed as adequate, it remains clear that large numbers of individuals living in Revolutionary and Napoleonic France had only the vaguest idea of what 'France' was. Historians have portrayed the Revolution and the subsequent war as great unifying forces, yet even provincial Jacobin clubs sometimes did not conduct their business in French.[61] Rather than fostering a sense of national unity, as the war went on it seems just as reasonable to argue that the peasant turned inward, more and more to his *pays natal,* becoming more and more hostile to France, the state, which appeared to concern itself only with getting hold of his money through taxes, his animals and produce through requisitions, and his sons through conscription. There was little point in the state's attempting to reward participants who were so hostile to it and who did not even know or care what it constituted.

The evidence of these wars suggests that participation in war, no matter how great, does not automatically secure rewards particularly when the structure of the combatant societies does not provide for participatory groups exerting significant, united pressure on governments not only during but, more to the point, after a conflict. Participation in the Revolutionary and Napoleonic wars by groups like munitions and dockyard workers could, and did, lead to increased bargaining power in the marketplace so long as the wars kept their labour at a premium. Yet any such gains were largely ephemeral and, rather than favouring such groups, the legislative regulations passed in both countries during the wars favoured the employer over his workforce. At the conclusion of the wars the demobilised servicemen, who might be said to have had a strong claim on the state for their participation, were not in a position, in either country, to exert influence either as individuals or collectively to achieve any benefits. The Jacobins' amplification of the socio-economic rights of citizenship did not outlive Thermidor, and the Jacobins always reserved the authority to define these rights and to brand any challenge as counter-revolutionary and unpatriotic. The British government, in contrast, always saw itself as fighting to preserve the existing constitution and existing social relationships; thus, any proposal for reform or any challenge to the *status quo* was viewed warily as smacking of sympathy for the enemy — or worse.

Notes

1. An earlier version of this paper was read at the Social History Society Conference on War and Society, 4-6 January 1984. My thanks to Geoffrey Best, David Englander, Alan Forrest, Gwynne Lewis, Arthur Marwick and Bernard Waites for their invaluable comments on drafts.

2. Stanislav Andreski, *Military Organisation and Society* (2nd edn, 1968), p. 26. The military participation ratio is defined pp. 33-8.

3. Arthur Marwick, 'Problems and Consequences of Organizing Society for Total War', in N.F. Dreiszinger (ed.), *Mobilization for Total War: The Canadian, American and British Experience 1914-1918* (Kingston, Canada, 1981) pp. 3-4.

4. Arthur Marwick, *War and Social Change in the Twentieth Century* (1974), p. 13.

5. R.R. Palmer, 'Frederick the Great, Guibert, Bülow: From Dynastic to National War', in Edward Meade Earle (ed.), *Makers of Modern Strategy: Military Thoughts from Machiavelli to Hitler* (2nd edn, Princeton, N.J., 1971) p. 57.

6. David Chandler, *The Campaigns of Napoleon* (1967), pp. 333-4.

7. This is putting military age at between 18 and 45, the ages between which men were liable for the militia ballot. Clive Emsley, *British Society and the French Wars 1793-1815* (1979), pp. 33, 94, 133, 150.

8. Jacques Houdaille, 'Le problème des pertes de guerre', in *La France à l'époque napoléonienne: Actes du colloque Napoléon*, special number of *Revue d'histoire moderne et contemporaine* (juillet-septembre 1970); Louis Bergeron, *France under Napoleon* (Princeton, N.J., 1981) p. 118; M. Greenwood, 'British Loss of Life in the Wars of 1794-1815 and the 1914-1918', *Journal of the Royal Statistical Society*, cv (1942), pp. 1-16.

9. Richard Cooper, 'William Pitt, Taxation and the Needs of War', *Journal of*

British Studies xxii (Autumn 1982), pp. 94-103.

10. Archives de la Guerre xf4, 'Mémoire sur les Réclamations que font les Gendarmes qui composent la 2ᵉ Division organisée à Versailles pour le service des armées'.

11. Geoffrey Best, *War and Society in Revolutionary Europe 1170-1870* (1982), p. 93. Though it is stretching the word 'European', the exertions of the confederate states in the American civil war may have reached similar proportions as that conflict progressed.

12. H.O.42.40, 'Extract in case of invasion' (n.d., [1797?]); H.O.42.69, John Brown, Deputy Keeper of State Papers to John King, 13 October 1803.

13. Cooper *loc. cit.*, p. 102.

14. Roger Morriss, *The Royal Dockyards during the Revolutionary and Napoleonic Wars* (Leicester, 1983), pp. 78-84, 88-9.

15. Leicestershire R.O. Turville Constable-Maxwell MSS DG 39/1621 Mostyn to Francis Fortescue; Turville, 22 March 1804; W. Branch Johnson (ed.), *Memorandums for ... the diary between 1789 and 1810 of John Carrington* (Chichester, 1973), p. 89.

16. Eric A. Arnold, Jr, *Fouché, Napoleon and the General Police*, (Washington, D.C., 1979) pp. 120-1; Alan Forrest, *The French Revolution and the Poor*, (Oxford 1981), pp. 156-9. Dr Forrest is currently preparing a study of French recruitment during the Revolutionary and Napoleonic periods.

17. Jean-Paul Bertaud, *La révolution Armée: Les soldats-citoyens et la Révolution française* (Paris, 1979), p. 274.

18. Geoffrey Ellis, *Napoleon's Continental Blockade: The Case of Alsace* (Oxford, 1981), p. 200.

19. François Crouzet, 'England and France in the Eighteenth Century: A Comparative Analysis of Two Economic Growths', in R.M. Hartwell (ed.), *The Causes of the Industrial Revolution* (1967).

20. Ellis, *op. cit., passim.*

21. Phyllis Deane, 'War and Industrialisation', in J.M. Winter (ed.), *War and Economic Development* (Cambridge, 1975).

22. I am grateful to Gwynne Lewis, who is currently investigating the coal industry in south-east France during the early nineteenth century, for information on this point.

23. Richard Cobb, *Reactions to the French Revolution* (1972), p. 125.

24. Jacques Ragot, 'Les batteries defendant les passes du bassin d'Archachon (1792-1815)', in *L'Armée et la Société de 1610 à nos jours: Actes du 103ᵉ Congrès national des sociétés savantes* (Paris, 1979), pp. 411-26.

25. A.N. F9 316, administration du Tarn au ministre, 11 messidor an VII. A *garnissaire* was a military garrison set up in a district as a punishment for serious evasion of the conscription laws.

26. A.N.F.11 715, Prefêt au ministre, 24 juillet 1812.

27. A.N.F 7, 3119-42, *passim.*

28. H.O.42. 31, Col. J. Rolle to Dundas [?], 27 June 1794; H.O.42.32, R. Blair to Dundas, 8 July 1794.

29. H.O.42. 120, George Greebe to Ryder [?], 7 February 1812; H.O.42.121, *passim*; H.O.42.125, 'A well wisher' to Sidmouth, 'July' 1812.

30. H.O.42 120, Nicholas Newscombe to Commissioners of Transport Office, 28 January 1812.

31. Richard Cobb, *Paris and its Provinces 1792-1802* (1975), pp. 167-8.

32. Ellis, *op. cit.*, pp. 201-8.

33. Emsley, *op. cit.*, pp. 27-8, 30, 32, 100, 165; John Bohstedt, *Riots and Community Politics in England and Wales, 1790-1810* (Cambridge, Mass., 1983), pp. 173-84; J.R. Western, 'The Formation of the Scottish Militia in 1797', *Scottish*

Historical Review, xxxix (1955)

34. T.J.A. Le Goff, *Vannes and its Region: A Study of Town and Country in Eighteenth-Century France* (Oxford, 1981), pp. 354-7, 360; Donald Sutherland, *The Chouans: The Social Origins of Popular Counter-Revolution in Upper Brittany 1770-1796* (Oxford, 1982) pp. 258-63, 281-2; Charles Tilly, *The Vendée* (1964), pp. 308-20; Gwynne Lewis, 'Political Brigandage and Popular Disaffection in the South-East of France 1795-1804', in Gwynne Lewis and Colin Lucas (eds.), *Beyond the Terror: Essays in French Regional and Social History 1794-1815* (Cambridge, 1983), p. 213.

35. Major General Lord Blayney, *Narrative of a Forced Journey through Spain and France* (2 vols., 1814), i, 493.

36. See also 'La Fête des Innocents'; both cartoons are reproduced in Open University Course A309, *Conflict and Stability in the Development of Modern Europe* (Milton Keynes, 1980), Block 1, p. 45.

37. Forrest, *op. cit.*, pp. 160-1; see also Lewis, *loc. cit.*, pp. 214-15; and Alan Forrest, 'Conscription and crime in rural France during the Directory and Consulate', in Lewis and Lucas (eds.), *op. cit.*

38. Archives Nationales F 7 3845, report of 10 June 1807.

39. Eugen Weber, *Peasants into Frenchmen: The Modernization of Rural France, 1870-1914* (1976), pp. 108-10, 295.

40. B. Trinder, *The Industrial Revolution in Shropshire* (Chichester, 1973), pp. 361-2.

41. William Cobbett, *Advice to Young Men* (1829), para. 338.

42. Bedfordshire Record Office QSR 1.827/321, Petition of Thomas Short [?]; see also petition of George Gould [?], a drummer in the 7th Foot imprisoned in 1818 as he was unable to indemnify the parish of Biggleswade for an illegitimate child: 'I have now been in his Majesties Service 9 years and Upwards and Fought Hord the Battles of My King and Countrey and at No Period in My Life Ware ever Confined upon Aney Othere Ocasion before what soever ...' (Beds R.O. QSR 1818/332); and petition of Thomas Wiles requesting mitigation of punishment: 'Relating to the earlier part of my life. I spent 12 years and 12 days in his Majesty's service and I was in several engagements and received three wounds' (Beds. R.O. QSR 1830/886).

43. Archives de la Préfecture de Police, Aa 213/581-84.

44. Robert Guillemard, *The Adventures of a French Sergeant from 1805 to 1823* (English trans., 1898; first published Paris, 1825) pp. 304, 307-8.

45. *Mémoires de Canler ancien chef du service de sûreté* (Paris, 1968 edn), p. 32.

46. T.S., *Journal of a Soldier of the 71st Regiment from 1806-1815* (Edinburgh, 1828), p. 139.

47. John Green, *The Vicissitudes of a Soldier's Life* (Wakefield, 1973 edn), p. 222.

48. Eric Richards, *A History of the Highland Clearances: Agrarian Transformation and the Evictions 1746-1886* (1982) pp. 147-56; see also Eric Richards, 'Patterns of Highland Discontent 1790-1860', in John Stevenson and Roland Quinault (eds.), *Popular Protest and Public Order: Six Studies in British History 1790-1920* (1974), pp. 86-7.

49. See, *inter alia*, J.D. Chambers and G.E. Mingay, *The Agricultural Revolution 1750-1880* (1966), pp. 117-22.

50. Morriss, *op. cit.*, esp. Ch. 4.

51. Norman McCord, 'The Seamen's Strike of 1815 in North-East England', *Economic History Review*, 2nd series, xxi (1968), pp. 127-43.

52. Raymonde Monnier, *Le Faubourg Saint-Antoine (1789-1815)* (Paris, 1981), pp. 67, 225-7.

53. Lewis, *loc. cit.*, p. 215.

54. Roger Darquenne, *La Conscription dans le départment de Jemappes (1798-1813) Bilan démographique et médico-social* (Mons, 1970), Forrest's current work on conscription bears this out for other areas.

55. Norman Hampson, 'Les ouvriers des arsenaux de la marine au cours de la Révolution française', *Revue d'histoire économique et sociale*, xxxix (1961), pp. 287-329, 442-73.

56. Colin Jones, 'Picking up the Pieces: The Politics and the Personnel of Social Welfare from the Convention to the Consulate', in Lewis and Lucas (eds.), *op, cit.*, pp. 57-9.

57. Forrest, *French Revolution . . .*, esp. Ch. 4.

58. See, for example, C. Hall, *The Effects of Civilization on the People in European States* (1805, reprinted 1850), pp. 130-1.

59. Andreski, *op. cit.*, pp. 35-6. Andreski actually uses the term 'the suppression facility'.

60. For a general survey of policing during the wars, see Clive Emsley, *Policing and its Context 1750-1870* (1983), Ch. 3.

61. Richard Cobb, *The Police and the People: French Popular Protest 1789-1820* (1970), pp. 130, 336.

4 THE WELSH AND CRIME, 1801-1891

David J.V. Jones

Taffy was a Welsh man, Taffy was a thief?

As a young undergraduate, listening to one of Gwyn Williams' marvellous lectures in the Spring of 1960, I was struck by the extent to which Welsh history had been written around myths. Much of our identity had been formed in those creative years of the early nineteenth century. I knew, for instance, because we had been told so by generations of writers and teachers, that the Methodist revival had transformed the personality of our nation. We had become, in the late eighteenth and nineteenth centuries, the most religious, respectable and law-abiding people in Britain. Yet my own background in an isolated part of rural Wales suggested other interpretations, and here, on a lazy afternoon in 1960, Gwyn Williams was telling us that the skin of nonconformist respectability had been paper-thin and that there were places in nineteenth-century Wales — notably his beloved Merthyr — which could hardly be mentioned in religious circles. This alternative world has been much explored in recent years but some of it still remains to be discovered. In this chapter I shall be examining one neglected area, that of Welsh crime and criminal forms of protest.

The historian of nineteenth-century crime is constantly attracted by two contemporary images. The first view of the Welsh can still be found in Queen Victoria's diaries, government correspondence and the Commissions and Select Committees of the period. Whenever Home Secretaries received news of serious outbursts of criminal violence from across Offa's Dyke in the years from 1816 to 1868 their reactions were remarkably uniform. Their instinct was to shake their heads, mutter despairing words about the uncivilised nature of the *gwerin*, and send unwelcome requests for military assistance to the Horse Guards. Lord Melbourne had special reasons for his prejudice against the 'rebellious Welsh': the Merthyr insurrection of 1831 had been, in his opinion, the worst manifestation of disorder in the Reform crisis, whilst the Scotch Cattle, the Newport rising of 1839 and the Rebecca riots a few years later, were the epitome of industrial and rural violence in the early part of Victoria's reign.

What was disconcerting about so many of these troubles was the secrecy behind them. In Ireland one could expect opposition, but the behaviour, attitudes and language of Welsh people made it more difficult to anticipate unrest. The Welsh workman

> is left to live in an underworld of his own, and the march of society goes so completely over his head that he is never heard of, excepting when the strange and abnormal features of a Revival, or a Rebecca or Chartist outbreak, call attention to a phase of society which could produce anything so contrary to all that we elsewhere experience.[1]

One of the purposes of contemporary inquiries into Welsh life was to unravel this 'volcanic mystery'. The notorious Commission on Welsh education concluded that over much of the country the standards of morality, decency and honesty were low; 'Petty thefts, lying, cozening, every species of chicanery, drunkenness, prevail to a great extent among the least educated part of the community'.[2] Several observers claimed that private and public behaviour in rural Wales had not improved since the days of the Rev. Griffith Jones a century earlier, whilst only London could match the industrial districts for personal violence, appalling insobriety and female decadence. Sir Edmund Head, Assistant Poor Law Commissioner, compared the South Wales coalfield in 1839 to a penal colony inhabited by 'bad characters', 'runaway criminals and vagrants'.[3] 'It requires some courage to live amongst such a set of savages' the conclusion of Reginald Blewitt, MP for the Monmouth boroughs summed up the attitude of a generation of industrial capitalists, landowners and ministers.[4]

Even later in the century, Lord Melbourne's impression of Wales was not totally dispelled, as the second Rebecca riots, the ferocious battles over mountain land, the deaths of miners and women in industrial and political demonstrations, and the extended tithe riots of 1886-93 rekindled the annoyance of Westminster politicians. Some of the more outspoken judges on the Welsh assize circuits in these years were also convinced that crime and protest were more common in 'this secret land' than the empty calendars in front of them indicated. Civilisation and the rule of law had yet to be firmly established in the far-flung corners of Victoria's domestic empire.

The other image of Wales was directly set against the one above. It was developed soon after the turn of the century, and was promulgated by, amongst others, Thomas Phillips, the 'hero' of the Newport rising, and later, Thomas Rees, a Swansea minister, and Henry Richard, the first Liberal MP for Merthyr Tydfil. These famous defenders of a nation's honour were supported by newspaper editors, clergymen, magistrates and chief constables. One can identify three popular strands in their argument. First, it was stated that Wales had been, since the Act of Union, and more particularly since the Methodist revival, the most loyal and peaceful part of Britain:

> When compared with the morality of England, Scotland and Ireland, [that of Wales] stands very high. ... No landowner, proprietor of works, nor any other class in the Principality, has cause to fear the dagger of the assassin, the fire of the incendiary or the rude assaults of the infuriated mob.[5]

Official criminal statistics published in the mid-nineteenth century showed that the rate of committals for serious offences in Wales was between one and two times lower than that of England. As they crossed the border at this time judges often praised the Welsh 'freedom from crime', and Lord Aberdare, addressing the National Association for the Promotion of Social Science in 1875, believed that the extent of petty offences in his country made no difference to this favourable balance.[6]

The second claim of Thomas Phillips and his friends will not surprise students of nineteenth-century nationalism: 'Of those criminals who disgrace the Principality,' it was argued, 'nearly one-half are not natives.'[7] Lord Aberdare, chairmen of quarter sessions and chief constables across Wales blamed rises in criminal statistics on immigrants — navvies, vagrants, contractors, Irish travellers, gypsies and all manner of sailors, dockworkers and immigrant miners. The published information on prisoners in Welsh gaols after 1857 was used in support of the claim, for about a third of the inmates had been born in England or Ireland.[8] The Irish were especially criticised for their illegal activities in the 1830s and 1840s, but it was the vagrants in the Principality who were most abused. The Welsh countryside and market towns were favourite places for these wanderers, and much police time and newspaper attention was devoted to this group of people. From the first decades of the century, Poor Law authorities and magistrates sought to turn the vagrant issue into a police matter, and by the 1860s they had largely succeeded. During the 1880s almost every activity of the trampers was outlawed, in the expressed belief that it would make Wales 'almost free of crime'. To justify such a policy the proportion of vagrant criminals was deliberately exaggerated.[9]

The same kind of self-deception was practised in the matter of protest. The defenders of the Welsh character insisted that the people were naturally quiet and deferential, but could be stirred by outsiders or agitators. In 1831, much of the responsibility for trouble was placed at the door of William Twiss, the union leader; whilst the rising of 1839 had been planned in England by leaders such as Feargus O'Connor and Major Beniowski. Even the man who had tried to kill Thomas Phillips at the Westgate Hotel in Newport had been a young Englishman! In the countryside the situation was a little different, but there too much of the blame for unrest lay with the 'insolence and tyranny' of alien landowners, foreign agents, non-resident sporting and fishingmen, and collectors of unwelcome tolls and Church of England tithes.[10] Even then, so it was argued, the protesting Welsh revealed exceptional respect for persons and property.[11]

The third claim of the defenders of Wales was closely related to the first two. Writers, magistrates and policemen maintained that crime — at least of a fairly serious type — was committed by a small deviant class — Sir Edmund Head's 'bad characters'. As Wales was so thinly populated it was comparatively easy to identify such a class, and great efforts were made to tabulate, survey and suppress it. The police and court records for the second half of the century indicate that there were, from a population of over a million people, fewer than 1000 'known thieves' and 'depredators' in the country, though many of these had long lists of previous convictions. The 'criminal class', as it was often called, fell into well-defined categories: members of the 'swell mobs' who appeared at Welsh races, fairs and circuses; some of the vagrants and outsiders mentioned above; notorious 'marginal people' of the countryside like John Jones, 'Coch Bach y Bala'; and the 'Arab population' and prostitutes of the slums and docklands of Cardiff, Swansea and Merthyr.

After the mid-century an increasing amount of attention was given to this last group of 'deviants'. The policemen of the largest towns in Wales were ordered to watch 'suspicious characters' and 'known thieves', and to attend to 'houses of bad character' and 'notorious districts'. By the 1840s these districts had been taken over by prostitutes, bullies, thieves and lodging-house keepers. The very names of 'China', 'Bute Street', and 'the Strand' were enough to send Welsh chapel society into paroxysms of anguish. Over the next 40 years large police stations were built to control the people of such places, and missionary endeavour, and temperance and rescue campaigns matched the sound of slum-clearance work. The intention was clear: in a short period of time it was hoped to decimate the criminal fraternity and to make it, like the over-whelming majority of the Welsh people, 'exceedingly honest' and 'immune from crime'.[12]

It is hardly surprising that these two, almost opposite, contemporary images should have confused historians, and it is probable that a true picture of Welsh crime can no longer be drawn. Yet the literary and statistical evidence can be used to throw some light on the subject. The figures of court cases in the Parliamentary Papers, with all their limitations, reveal that indictable committals in early and mid-nineteenth century Wales were the lowest in Britain. In the counties of Cardigan and Anglesey there was only one person committed for trial at the assizes and quarter sessions per 4-8,000 of the population, confirming Lord Aberdare's analysis that

> Wales is innocent ... because it has the good fortune to enjoy all the [right] conditions ... a sparse population, no towns of vast size, no great accumulation of valuable and unprotected property; and it rejoices in the absence of that [fatal] combined pressure of poverty and temptation.[13]

In fact, the rate of people committed to the higher courts in Wales was to remain lower than that in England until well into the twentieth century.

There were, however, other statistics of crime, although most observers of Welsh society chose to ignore them. In the first half of the century the authorities sometimes provided the government with information on the number of prisoners, whilst in the years after 1857 there are detailed returns of offences determined summarily. 'Not many years ago', declared Judge Bramwell at the Carmarthenshire assizes in 1860, 'the gaol returns [for the three south-western counties] were large and presented crimes of various degrees, many of them of great magnitude.'[14] In a year such as 1834 there were in fact almost 20 times more people in Welsh prisons than stood trial for indictable offences.[15] Most had been apprehended for vagrancy crimes, disobeying bastardy orders, stealing, malicious damage and assault, and two-thirds of these people were dealt with at petty sessions. These, and other less reliable statistics in local Record Offices, indicate that the level of recorded crime in Wales was much higher than most contemporaries suggested, and, when the police court figures became available after 1857, the shortfall between the Welsh and English crime rates was only about 20 per cent. By 1881 the gap had disappeared, and for the rest of the century the rates for the two countries were indistinguishable.

Within these national figures there were some interesting variations. Most of the evidence suggests that the highest rate of offences occurred in the industrial counties, and throughout the century Monmouthshire, Glamorgan and Breconshire headed the lists. In the early nineteenth century Monmouthshire had the unenviable reputation of having about the fastest growing rate of indictable committals in Britain, and, by the mid-Victorian years, at least 1 in 40 people in the coalfield counties appeared in court every year. In the largest towns, notably Cardiff, Swansea and Merthyr, the rate was twice as bad again. Cardiff, at the beginning of its extraordinary growth period in 1861, was already regarded as the criminal capital of Wales, with at least 1 in 15 of its inhabitants facing court proceedings in that year. According to one gloomy report in 1860,

> Cardiff is without a parallel in the number and serious character of offences as compared with population. ... The sad story of the fearful vice of Cardiff, is wafted upon the wings of the wind, and carried by the sailors of every nation to their several countries, until the name of this borough has become a by-word and a reproach all the world over.[16]

There were similar, though less justified, complaints from the counties of Denbigh and Flint, where heavy industry had developed significantly in the first half of the century, but perhaps the most fascinating comments came from Pembrokeshire and Montgomeryshire. In both these counties the rate of recorded crime rose in the Victorian era, and some of the spectacular increases in the early 1880s and 1890s raised questions about the 'honesty and morality of our population'. By contrast, in Anglesey, Merioneth and Cardiganshire no more than 1 in 80 persons annually attended the higher and lower courts, and a considerable number of these were 'outsiders' or 'known offenders'. It was therefore only to be expected that the evidence from these counties was most often used to justify the claim that few Welsh people were 'professionally dishonest'.

Contemporaries rarely addressed themselves to the more interesting questions about the known offences which did not result in court cases, and the crimes which were not even recorded on the occurrence and charge registers of police constables. Only in the 1880s, when the debate on Welsh nationhood was in full swing, did the more informed observers speak publicly on the value of the court returns. 'Gentlemen, I would willingly congratulate you on the non-existence of crime in your several counties IF it did not exist,' commented Lord Justice Brett at Cardigan, 'but as I believe it does exist, though, by some means, it is not brought before me, my congratulations must assume a modified form.'[17] Brett and others believed that the natural course of the law was diverted by magistrates and the police. This attack on the magistrates was an old one. In the eighteenth century it was said that justices were too ready to make private judgments on the outcome of fairly serious cases rather than wait for a full court hearing, and there were complaints, too, that Grand Juries presented an excessive number of 'No True Bills'.[18] It is difficult to establish the truth of these assertions, although there is evidence to show that some magistrates were reluctant to forward cases to quarter sessions and assizes, and in this they were influenced by financial considerations and by the pleas of landowners, clergymen and sometimes the family of the accused. When respectable people were charged with indecent assault, it was suggested that 'Every man of the Grand Jury is seen before [the trial] comes on', and in years such as the 1860s and 1880s, when the gentry of Wales were subjected to bitter criticism, justices were concerned about proceeding with sensitive cases.[19]

As for police policy and efficiency in nineteenth-century Wales, the number of constables was small outside the well-populated districts. Anglesey had only 28 officers in 1881 (1 in 1,836 of the population): Merioneth had 34 but each one was expected to patrol 7,000 acres, and there were many parishes without a local magistrate or lock-up. Constables in such places were sometimes inclined or obliged to deal with offenders in their own way. Big Thomas Roberts of Merioneth used his weight on vagrants, unruly juveniles and suspected poachers; other colleagues handed out cautions. In 1877 the chief constable of Pembrokeshire warned his men about the practice of 'not bringing up more cases than they can possibly avoid'.[20] Unfortunately, we seldom find information on the detection rate for all known crimes, but the rare lists that have survived illustrate the difficulty of securing offenders in cases of burglary, farm thefts and malicious injury in rural areas.[21] The published detection rate for indictable offences, which is based on a small sample, indicates, however, that the Welsh police in general were no less efficient than their English counterparts.

One important factor, notably in the years before a professional police force was established in Wales, was that of prosecution. There are many instances in the early nineteenth century of people withdrawing from prosecution on the grounds of expense or because of the problem of securing witnesses. Similarly, there was a tendency to hold back if the person arrested by the constables was well known to the prosecutor or in a higher station of life. A glance at the surviving police registers in Pembrokeshire and Merioneth for a later period confirms the impression: up to 20 per cent of the people who were apprehended were 'discharged with no proceedings'. The most fortunate suspects were those who were young, respectable and local inhabitants. Even in 1883, S.H. Jones-Parry stated in his 'Crime in Wales' article that

> occasionally in petty cases, where the loss or injury sustained is trifling and concealment not likely to be discovered, [there is] a reluctance to prosecute. The cause of this reluctance is variously set down to ties of relationship; ... the only deterrent that is even hinted at in other than the most trifling cases is the fear of loss of time and money in prosecuting, and the feeling of dread at being placed at the mercy of lawyers.[22]

The most revealing document is that left by P.C. Evans of Pennal in Merioneth to his successor in 1887. In this private letter there are lists of suspected offenders in the area, names of witnesses who refused to support prosecutions, the identities of people who had settled matters out of court, a note of hostile residents who would not work with the police on any account, and a register of cases where the chief constable had arbitrarily stopped proceedings.[23] From this and other evidence, it is clear that in many parts of Wales prosecution and policing relied heavily on the community to function properly.

It was the realisation of this obvious but unwelcome fact which so alarmed the more extreme critics of Welsh society. No one now, of course, can estimate the dark figures of unrecorded crime that the people of this country accepted or ignored. Anyone who has looked at the manorial and religious records of eighteenth-century Wales knows that there were not only many offences which did not reach the Crown officials, but also many crimes which were dealt with by families and communities. Bruce Chatwin's account of border-country life at the beginning of this century rings true: the families of upland Wales fought battles of honour, cheaply and effectively, with their dogs, the brummock, and the blazing torch.[24] Only when matters got out of hand, or when 'outsiders' became involved, did such people resort to the Crown courts.

Some of the statistics of certain offences in nineteenth-century Wales bore no relationship to the incidence of the crime. It was said, in the Commission on the Constabulary force in 1839, that even murder and manslaughter were regarded lightly in parts of Wales.[25] This seems unlikely, though the number of babies' bodies found in pits, rabbit holes and boxes in a county such as Pembrokeshire highlights a little known but disturbing trend. Similarly, as the Welsh Land Commission noted in 1896, many cases of sheep-stealing and game and fishing offences went unrecorded. Thus, protested one Merioneth correspondent in 1856; 'in the neighbourhood of Corris and Minffordd great numbers of sheep are driven off the farms and sold in the different markets in the south', whilst the police records and calendars were 'indicative of the paucity of crime'.[26] Other offences which were widely regarded as under-reported in Wales were property disputes, family violence and sexual assaults.

One reason for this was the determination of some communities to deal with such matters in their own way. Public ridicule was the traditional method of punishment, and the Welsh newspapers supply the following list: throwing offenders into water, cutting a person's hair, placing earth down chimneys, breaking gates, placing people on ladders or poles, and burning effigies.[27] Wherever Edwin Chadwick, James Kay-Shuttleworth and Sir Edmund Head wished to illustrate the necessity for an improved police force in

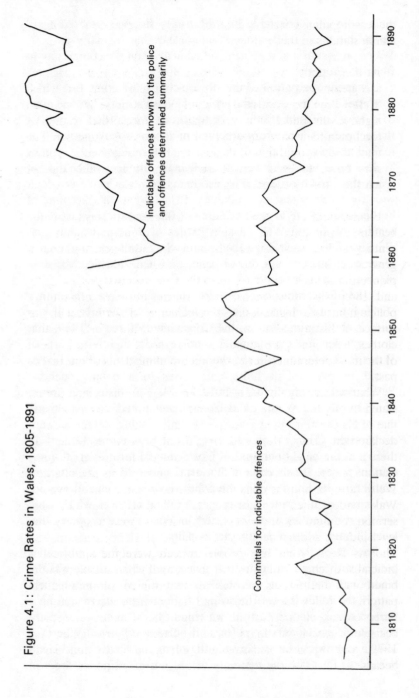

Figure 4.1: Crime Rates in Wales, 1805-1891

Indictable offences known to the police and offences determined summarily

Committals for indictable offences

the less-populated areas of Britain, they chose inevitably the latest manifestations of the Welsh *ceffyl pren*.

At the present time the magistrates of Cardigan and its vicinity are greatly embarrassed by the increasing practice, called the 'Ceffyl Pren' or wooden horse; a figure of a horse is carried at night in the midst of a mob with their faces blackened, and torches in their hands, to the door of any person whose conduct may have exposed him to the censure of his neighbours, or who may have rendered himself unpopular, by informing against another, and by contributing to enforce the law.[28]

Examples of *ceffyl pren*, especially against adulterers and wife-beaters, can be found in industrial Wales until the mid-nineteenth century, and in the south-west the custom was still practised over a generation later.[29] We know from Professor David Williams' pioneering studies that rural and industrial protest between 1815 and 1845 was often an extension of this form of community policing, but later instances of Rebeccaism have hardly broken the surface of history. Mobs with black faces, cattle skins, women's clothes, horns and pans, humiliated the people's enemies in some of the most determined yet poorly-recorded incidents of our recent past.

What we already know about Welsh crime in this period can be stated briefly.[30] The rate of indictable committals followed closely that of England, rising to a peak in the early 1850s. 'Never, surely', declared the gloomy Rev. John Griffiths of Aberdare in 1850, 'was there a nation in the state this is now', and the formation of Associations for the Prosecution of Felons, the complaints of embattled Welsh farmers, and the demands for the new police in the towns of Wales underpinned his message.[31] Yet for 50 years after Griffiths' sermon the number of serious court cases dropped to a very low level indeed, adding weight to the claims of Henry Richard and Thomas Rees. What few people noticed were the statistics of indictable offences known to the police, and, when these are combined with the figures of offences determined summarily, the pattern in Wales during the second half of the century was of a fairly consistent *increase* in recorded illegal activities. Partly because of new legislation such as the Summary Jurisdiction Act 1879, and the new licensing and education laws, and partly because of the establishment of more police and courts, the level of known crime was higher in the 1890s than in previous decades.

On the character of criminals the police and gaol records indicate that between one-fifth and a third of them were female, and about a third of the inmates of Welsh prisons in the second half of the century were in their twenties, though the age pattern rose significantly in the last decades. Deidre Beddoe has shown that the criminality and immorality of Welsh women was sometimes greatly exaggerated; but in Cardiff, Swansea and Merthyr Tydfil the ratio of female to male offenders in the mid-century was well above the national average, especially in cases of larceny and disorderly conduct.[32] The literacy and occupational statistics of prisoners are notoriously unreliable in Wales, but they suggest that those committed to penal institutions were from the least educated sections of society and tended to be unemployed or engaged as general labourers, mechanics, dealers, charwomen and domestic servants. About 60 per cent of them were of Welsh origin, and an increasing proportion were known to have had previous convictions. In the largest towns of the Principality there was a well-defined group of 'bad characters', but over much of the country the idea of a criminal class is not supported by the evidence.

The composition of recorded crime in Wales is somewhat different from that in England. Between a third and two-thirds of arrests in the nineteenth century were for drunkenness, assaults, stealing, vagrancy offences and malicious destruction. For much of the period when national statistics are available, it seems that the Welsh were more likely to be apprehended for drunken behaviour and violent or malicious attacks on people and property, and less inclined than the English to be committed for larceny and vagrancy crimes. If Taffy was a convicted thief or beggar he probably lived in the largest towns of Wales where as many as a quarter of known offences were of this type. Larceny offences were by far the largest category of crimes dealt with by the higher courts, but the proportion of people charged with various forms of stealing mirrors the declining rate of indictable committals generally in the second half of the century. Most other property offences, too — notably cases of malicious damage, and crimes against the Game and Fisheries Acts — were less common after the early 1880s. Committals for assault and drunkenness held up fairly well, however, and an increasing proportion of people found themselves in the dock for ignoring legislation to promote education, highway control and public hygiene. The typical Welsh offender at the end of the century was an aggressive working-class male, with too much beer in his stomach and too few of his children at school.

The character of criminal acts which did and did not lead to court appearances tells us much about Welsh society. Violence was more common than some contemporaries and historians have suggested. Murder and manslaughter were comparatively rare in the Principality, and executions for such crimes were almost unknown in some counties after the third decade of the nineteenth century. Yet violent attacks on people were a feature of rural life, of places experiencing the traumas of rapid urbanisation, and of seaport towns. It comes as no surprise, therefore, to find that Carmarthen was widely regarded in the first half of the century as one of the most violent towns in Europe. Its first policemen had to run the gauntlet of drunken farmers, half-clothed beggars, mobs from the slum quarters, affluent miners, brawling sailors, fishermen, navvies and prostitutes, and horse-riding young men with rifles in their hands.[33] Merthyr Tydfil had a similar reputation, as did Cardiff, Aberdare and Mountain Ash some years later. 'Under the heading of Assaults and Inflicting Bodily Harm, Cardiff has no parallel in Wales or England', ran one report in 1860, but this tends to minimise the high proportion of violent offences in many other parts of the country.[34] The occurrence books and newspaper reports make it plain that so much of this never reached the courts. It was the custom in certain rural districts to release men taken into custody when the victims of their attacks were said to be out of danger. As in the case of mass battles between Pembrokeshire villages in the early nineteenth century, it was thought wise and cheaper not to interfere. Violent recreations continued to be enjoyed in the Principality long after reformers had pronounced them extinct.

The most typical forms of violence were family conflicts, sexual assaults, clashes between neighbours, drunken brawls and attacks on constables, bailiffs and other officials. In nonconformist Wales there were subtle pressures to play down the real incidence of the first two categories, and the combined court figures of about 200 cases annually can be regarded with justified scepticism. In some areas policemen and magistrates almost always refused to accept the unsupported words of a beaten wife, and the cases which were heard in court revealed histories of horrendous assaults. The wives of James Reynolds of Haverfordwest and Albert Poole of Cardiff were brutally battered throughout their marriages, and 10 shillings, 1 month and 3 months gaol were the sentences meted out to their husbands. Mrs Reynolds, like so many others, was denied a legal separation order, for the Welsh authorities were more concerned with the costs of divided families.[35] When David Davies' wife was found covered in blood in Towyn in 1885, a constable was sent 'to keep watch a long time in case he would assault his wife again', but the chief constable firmly ordered that no proceedings should be taken.[36]

The number of instances of sexual assault which resulted in a trial reached a peak of only 65 in 1891, and at least half of these were from the county of Glamorgan. A considerable number occurred in the great iron town of Merthyr Tydfil, and have been described elsewhere by the present writer.[37] In defence of Wales, it was argued that sexual crimes were rare in the countryside, the 'land of pure morals' (Hen Wlad y Menyg Gwynion), but a closer survey shows that many incidents were covered up or never reached the final stages of the legal process. In the occurrence and charge books of the Merioneth police, for example, rape, indecent assaults and exposure, and bestiality make up a significant share of known offences. Yet, as these assaults were often committed by farmers' sons and servants, and by teachers, shopkeepers and ministers, many were hidden from the public gaze. Where respectable people were involved there was a strong tendency to reduce the charge to one of common assault only, and try the offender at petty sessions. In general, the victim of rape could not expect to win a case if she had no witnesses, or if she could not show physical marks of resistance on her body.[38]

Many of the reported acts of violence were associated with drink, and occurred at or near a beershop or public house. Such disorderly conduct was traditionally linked with outsiders — the Irish navvies, vagrants and seamen. Sailors in Cardiff and Swansea usually carried knives, and were often accused of serious wounding, armed robbery and rape.[39] Yet, as reformers bleakly admitted in the 1860s, the degree of native drunken behaviour was considerable, and the police diaries show that weekends, market and fair days were busy periods for those who had to maintain order. In both town and country, too, the bailiff, Poor Law officer, agent and police constable were constant targets of violent attacks. At least 500 people were committed each year for assaulting policemen, and in parts of rural Wales in the mid-century some of the mob violence against these new public order officials took on the character of community revolts.[40]

The pattern of property crimes bore no relation to the above, although there were some correlations with the state of the economy and food prices. In urban Wales stealing was the second most popular crime, with about a quarter of recorded offences and two-thirds of court cases in this category. Clothing, food, fancy goods, coal, wood, metals and other materials were the main targets. Much of this was stolen by women and young people, and its total value can be estimated at less than £30,000 per year.[41] This compared favourably with the losses sustained by the recorded embezzlement, fraud and forgery of accountants, clerks, commercial travellers and agents, but white-collar crime only captured public attention late in the century.

Petty theft usually took place in three environments.[42] First, there were thefts from shops, stalls and houses, especially where the owners were careless about securing their property; secondly, there were thefts from the person in the main streets, in brothels and in public houses; and thirdly, there was stealing from employers, by female domestic servants, dockworkers, canal boatmen and the like. In the industrial towns of Wales this type of crime was very prevalent, and the reasons for this are fairly complex. Coal was, of course, comparatively easy to steal, and hundreds of women and children were accused of taking it as free fuel. In fact, most of the stolen goods in the nineteenth century were kept by the offenders, though a very small number of gangs disposed of their loot via pawnbrokers, ironmongers, and keepers of brothels, beerhouses and lodging houses. As these receivers were often of non-Welsh extraction, this strengthened the popular claim that crime in the Principality was organised by outsiders.

The nature of stealing in the countryside was naturally different. The theft of clothing and, to a lesser extent, of money and jewellery, was fairly common, but so, too, was that of corn, eggs, cheese, butter, potatoes and turnips. In general, it was people other than employees who took these goods. The same was true of the stealing of farm animals. I have shown elsewhere that sheep, horses and cattle vanished in large numbers in the eighteenth century, and this continued to be the case probably until the 1860s.[43] Apart from a few notorious characters like John Jones of Bala, and a remarkably small number of vagrants, such rural theft was carried out by the resident population, and often by one's neighbours.

Perhaps the most characteristic and controversial offences of the type were those against the Game and Fisheries Acts. Opposition to these laws formed a significant part of the debate on the criminality and passivity of the Welsh, and some astonishing statements were made about the infrequency of court cases.[44] In fact, 1,000 persons every year appeared before the Welsh courts on such charges, and this represented only a small proportion of known incidents. Ground game and fish disappeared in large quantities and a wide section of peasant and semi-industrialised society participated in the crime. In general, the poaching of game tended to be carried out by individuals, but in some districts gangs operated throughout the century. At times the daring and violence of these people reached the ears of the Home Secretary, and authorities even considered setting up special police districts to control the poachers.[45] 'You are of course aware', wrote Thomas Mostyn to his chief constable on 31 December 1859,

> that Gangs of Poachers are, and have for some years been in the habit of making depredations in the coverts at Gloddaeth, where I reside, as well as in the woods of the Gentlemen who own the surrounding property; they not only shoot the Game, but they make great havoc in knocking down the walls and breaking the fences and gates. ... My keepers having become an object of hatred to these fellows, the ruffians are now in the habit of prowling about my premises in order to catch them and shoot them, and otherwise maltreat them.[46]

Along the largest rivers of Wales poaching frequently took on the character of a small rural war, with scores of people dressed up as Rebecca, and carrying swords and spears. In Caernarvonshire, Radnorshire and Montgomeryshire there was a strong element of community protest in the crime, as people battled over old common land rights, and as new game and fishery associations sought to impose restrictions and introduce outsiders to the sport.[47] Later in the century the crime of poaching was also drawn into the Welsh debate on the Land Question, and the publicity given to certain offences, and to the punishment of offenders on estates such as Rhiwlas and Powis in Mid-Wales can be fully understood only in this context. 'The workmen of this country', pronounced the *Cambrian News* in June 1881, 'do not recognize the divine rights of a game preserving class.'

Malicious damage was, as Thomas Mostyn noted, a related crime. Although not unknown in the towns of Wales, trespass and damage to property was especially common in the countryside. It comprised a considerable proportion of recorded offences, and involved the destruction of houses, walls, fences, gates, hedges, woodland, crops, machinery and animals. Such activity was the outcome of juvenile pranks and personal feuds, and was also a product of long-standing battles over common rights, encroachments and sheep walks. There was much anger in the nineteenth century as the Crown, great landowners and certain freeholders sought to establish their legal rights over the hillsides of Wales. Sometimes, as in the post-war years, and again in the 1860s, 1870s and 1880s, news of the troubles reached the press, as houses and fences were pulled down, sheepdogs killed, and bailiffs attacked. In Mid-Wales, on the Powis estate, the conflict was especially bitter, as some of my relations recall.[48] People whose grandfathers had built *tai-unnos* returned from market to find their families and furniture in the road, and new occupants in their cottages. As in the many instances of maiming and killing animals in rural Wales, the motive often given behind malicious destruction was 'for revenge'. Indeed, in some of the most serious outbreaks, which included the smashing of miles of fences and walls in Caernarvonshire between 1859 and 1869, there was a sense of lost rights. 'There is an opinion among the lower orders', wrote Sir Richard Bulkeley of the latter case, 'that they had a right to the commons as long as they were unenclosed.[49]

Perhaps the most feared act of vandalism was arson. The court records of this crime are comparatively rare, except in the mid-1840s and mid-1860s, confirming the common claim that the Welsh did not resort to incendiarism. In fact, these statistics are a poor indication of the extent of arson and even, for example, in the years 1843-44, there were many fires in the Welsh countryside which historians have so far ignored.[50] The police occurrence books and newspapers are a useful source for this crime, though, of course, we know that much arson went unreported. From these it appears that shooting moors and plantations were set on fire, as were enclosure fences, hayricks and farm outbuildings, and, more rarely, houses. Often the blame for this incendiarism fell on the tenant, labourer or ex-employee of the property-owner, and it was customary to take these people, and vagrants near the scene, into custody 'on suspicion'. Motives for the crime were many: from the angry response of tramps who were denied poor relief, to the bitterness of domestic and farm servants who were about to lose their jobs. As the later stages of the Rebecca riots indicate, in the days before the belated arrival of trade unionism in Wales arson was a useful form of protest and intimidation.

Some types of crime were widely regarded as acts of protest. D.C. Davies, writing in 1883, argued that 'although a law-abiding people generally, the Welsh, when fully aroused by a sense of wrong, are very apt to take the law into their own hands,' and he cited the Rebecca riots and the more recent Denbighshire election disturbances, and the clashes between colliers at Mold and Ruabon, to prove his point.[51] There were obviously more illegal forms of protest than the low court statistics suggest, although the evidence has yet to be comprehensively studied. The Rev. John Griffiths of Aberdare claimed, for instance, that the industrial working class was 'never [free] from discontent' and class feeling.[52] The Scotch Cattle movement on the South Wales coalfield was still active during the disputes of the 1850s, and although it is now fashionable to talk of the paternalism and passivity of industrial Britain in the mid-Victorian era, violence never ceased to be a part of the collective bargaining process. As Emlyn Rogers illustrated many years ago, physical intimidation was a way of life amongst mining families in Denbighshire and Flintshire at this time. In South Wales, too, there were several attempts by thousands of workmen to remove Irish and English families from the valleys in the period, and election riots continued until the 1880s.[53] We should also remember that the miners of the area joined probably the most serious insurrectionary movements of nineteenth-century Britain. It was small wonder that Lord Melbourne told Queen Victoria that such Welshmen had to be regarded with great suspicion.

In the countryside there was more tension and illegal protest than is generally recognised. The Master and Servant Act was used regularly to control and punish employees, and the direct action in the first half of the century required compromises, the introduction of soldiers, and the establishment of early police forces. Even later there are many incidents in the press, police occurrence books and Home Office papers which are not easy to categorise. In the mid-1860s and 1880s, when anti-landlordism was at its height, mobs occasionally roamed the countryside, and threatening letters, poisoned animals, arson and attacks on keepers and agents betrayed underlying friction. Occasionally in nineteenth-century Wales such tension broke through into the great community rebellion of Rebecca, the generations of enclosure riots centred on the Vaenol estate in North Wales, the enormous poaching raids in Radnorshire from the mid-century until the 1930s, and the extensive tithe riots of the 1880s and 1890s with their trumpet and bonfire accompaniment. We can make too much of all of these, but the historian has to be wary of labelling rural, and even upland, Wales as 'extraordinarily' or 'relatively peaceful'.[54]

The above analysis has shown why it was possible to hold two almost contradictory views of Welsh life and progress. In the early years of Victoria's reign Wales appeared to pose a significant threat to the integrity and peace of Great Britain, and even in later years a small number of people were unduly conscious of the upward trend in the recorded level of petty crime and the excesses of the nation's 'rebellious spirit'. Only when the memory of Chartism and Rebecca had receded, and the number of cases at the higher courts dropped away sharply, did the optimistic version of Welsh identity emerge triumphant. Judges and some police chiefs now suggested that the Welsh were the most law-abiding people in Europe, and attributed this to their interest in religion and education.[55] About the same time Henry Richard and his friends were rewriting Welsh history along similar lines, jettisoning even the Newport rising as something alien to the nation's spirit. It was a view of Wales which was to be used much at the turn of the century when, during tithe riots or quarrymen's strikes, the nonconformist media bitterly denounced the need for imported policemen and soldiers.

On one thing, however, the defenders and critics of Wales were agreed. Even Thomas Phillips, Lewis Edwards, Hugh Owen and Henry Richard admitted — at least in private — that the 'personal habits' of the *gwerin* needed improving, and that heavy drinking was a 'besetting sin'.[56] In Cardiff the campaign of reform, aimed at controlling prostitution, vagrancy, juvenile delinquency and drunkenness, began in earnest in 1859, but everywhere the arrival of nonconformists and Liberals on Watch Committees, and later on joint standing committees, was followed by similar civilising programmes. After 1873 almost one in three committals in the Principality was for a breach of the licensing laws, and the Welsh Sunday Closing Act 1881 signalled the triumph of one reforming lobby. The intense pressure for a sober Sunday was, of course, just one aspect of a wider cultural battle, as noted by Hugh Evans in his rural *Cwm Eithin*. Drunken revellers, unmarried mothers and hungry criminal families of the countryside were frequently denounced from the nonconformist pulpit at the turn of the century. 'The Welsh rural areas are still the location of "Hen Wlad y Menyg Gwynion",' said the Rev. Thomas Jones in 1900, 'only the southern industrial valleys have been corrupted through the influence of English people and their vicious habits.'[57] In heavily populated Wales control and reform were even more essential, and the intensity of some campaigns is recalled by old folk still living in the poorer parts of Swansea and Cardiff. Inhabitants of Greenhill or Canton, who were born at the turn of the century, still remember the levels of surveillance: the 30-minute police patrols, the school board men, the temperance missionaries, the bans on Sunday trading and entertainment, and the periodic attacks on swearing in public, drinking clubs and juvenile games. The comparatively high statistics of recorded petty crime at the turn of the century are partly a reflection of this civilising and modernising policy, and a testimony to the fact that working people were often the victims of the myths which their 'betters' so lovingly cherished.

Notes

1. Robert Lingen, in Reports of the Commissioners of Inquiry into the State of Education in Wales (1847), Part I, p. 4.
2. Ibid., Part II, p. 294.
3. PRO, Home Office (H.O.), 73/55, Report of 14 November 1839.
4. H.O. 40/45, letter of 6 November 1839. To put this section in context, see G.A. Williams, *The Merthyr Rising* (London, 1978); and I. Wilks, *South Wales and the Rising of 1839*, (London, 1984).
5. T. Rees, *Miscellaneous Papers on Subjects Relating to Wales* (London, 1867), pp. 17, 15.
6. See, for instance, H. Richard, *Letters and Essays on Wales* (London, 1884 edn), pp. 57-60; H.A. Bruce (Lord Aberdare), *Letters and Addresses* (London 1917), pp. 241-2, 265-6.
7. Rees, *op. cit.*, p. 17.
8. The statistics of this, and many other aspects of Welsh crime, have been taken from the unpublished Social Research Council report, D.J.V. Jones and A. Bainbridge, 'Crime in Nineteenth-Century Wales' (1975). Unless otherwise stated, Monmouthshire has not been included in the figures of Welsh crime.
9. D.J.V. Jones, 'The Criminal Vagrant in Mid-Nineteenth-Century Wales', *Welsh History Review*, VIII (1977) 3; K. Birch, 'The Merioneth Police, 1856-1950', M.A. thesis, University of Wales, 1980.
10. See, for instance, Rees, *op. cit.*, p. 15; T. Phillips, *Wales: the Language, Social Condition, Moral Character, and Religious Opinions of the People* (London, 1849), pp. 52-3.
11. A point which D. Richter recently underlined: 'The Welsh Police, the Home Office, and the Welsh Tithe War of 1886-91', *Welsh History Review*, XII, 1

(1984), p. 75.

12. For this section, see Jones and Bainbridge, *op. cit.*, pp. 177, 394-403 and J. Willet, *First Report of the Cardiff Associate Institute for Improving and Enforcing the Laws for the Protection of Women* (Cardiff, 1860). Neil Evans of Coleg Harlech kindly sent me a copy of this report. The various sets of instructions to policemen and the chief constables' reports for Swansea are also illuminating. These have now been catalogued and can be seen in the Royal Institution at Swansea.

13. Bruce (Lord Aberdare), *op. cit.*, p. 266.

14. *The Welshman*, 13 July 1860.

15. Parliamentary tables of the Revenue, Population and Commerce of the United Kingdom, IV (London, 1834), p. 418 (state of the gaols), and the detailed gaol calendars for the same period in the Pembrokeshire Record Office, Haverfordwest.

16. Willet, *op. cit.*, pp. 4-5, 13.

17. Cited by S.H. Jones-Parry, 'Crime in Wales', *Red Dragon*, III (1883), p. 524.

18. On the careful nature of Grand Juries, and the comparative leniency towards serious offenders in the second half of the eighteenth century, see D.J.V. Jones, 'Life and Death in Eighteenth-Century Wales: a Note', *Welsh History Review*, X, 4 (1981).

19. A point made some years ago by Bainbridge, *op. cit.*, pp. 261-9, 282-5. The quotation is from the *Carmarthen Weekly Reporter*, 25 July 1902. See R. Davies, 'In a Broken Dream', *Llafur*, III, 4 (1983), p. 29.

20. Pembrokeshire Record Office, Legal and Police Records, General Order Book, 1857-80. Instruction of 3 July 1877. I am grateful to Winston Jones for this reference.

21. See, for example, Birch, *op. cit.*, Appendix VI.

22. This, he suggested, was true even of cases of arson; *op. cit.*, pp. 526-7.

23. Merioneth Record Office, Police Records, Instructions left by P.C. Evans, Pennal, to his successor (1887).

24. 'Little by little, the war with The Rock flourished into a ritual of raid and counter-raid: to call in the law was beneath the dignity of either belligerent.' *On the Black Hill* (1982); Picador edn 1983), p. 78.

25. Report on the Constabulary Force of England and Wales (1839), p. 42.

26. *Caernarvon and Denbigh Herald*, 16 February 1856. The information on child deaths, gleaned from the *Western Telegraph*, can be compared with that on Carmarthenshire. Davies, *op. cit.*, p. 33.

27. Based on a study of the *Carmarthen Journal*, *The Welshman* and the *Western Telegraph*, 1831-64.

28. Report on the Constabulary Force (1839), p. 44.

29. For just three examples from the mid-century in Pembrokeshire, see the *Carmarthen Journal*, 2 July 1852, *The Welshman*, 30 March 1849 and Pembrokeshire Record Office, Police Records, copy of a letter from the Superintendent of Police at Fishguard to the chief constable, 27 March 1858. The last source was discovered by Dr. D. Howell. See also the *Cambrian News*, 1 October 1869.

30. The following section is based on published statistics in the Parliamentary Papers for the period 1805-91.

31. *The Cambrian*, 8 March 1850.

32. D. Beddoe, *Welsh Convict Women* (1979), S. Williams, Barry. On the proportion of females arrested for petty crimes in a place like Merthyr, the reports of the chief constable to the quarter sessions are a particularly useful source. These are located in the Record Office at Cardiff.

33. See P. Molloy, *A Shilling for Carmarthen* (Llandysul, 1980).

34. Willet, *op. cit.*, p. 7.

35. *Harverfordwest and Milford Haven Telegraph*, 14 June 1882.

36. Merioneth Record Office, Towyn Occurrence Book, 28 January 1885.

37. D.J.V. Jones, *Crime, Protest, Community and Police in Nineteenth-Century Britain* (London, 1982), p. 110.

38. See, for example, Merioneth Record Office, Penllyn Minute Book, 19 May 1869, and Towyn Occurrence Book, 6 April 1885, 9 August 1891. Cf. Davies, *op. cit.*, pp. 26-30.

39. See Bainbridge's work on Cardiff, *op. cit.*, section V.

40. For a few of the serious mob attacks on the police, see *Carmarthen Journal*, 25 July 1845; Molloy, *op. cit.*, pp. 27-123; and Jones and Bainbridge, *op. cit.*, p. 290. The chief constable's annual report for 1881 is also revealing about attacks on the police in Swansea: Records in the Royal Institution, Swansea.

41. The national estimate of losses is unfortunately no more than that. It is based on the small number of chief constables' reports which have survived, and which include such information. See ibid., reports, 1879-91.

42. The following analysis of property crime is based on the tables of indictable crimes known to the police and of cases determined summarily in the Parliamentary Papers, supplemented by reports from chief constables in the Welsh counties.

43. D.J.V. Jones, 'Life and Death in Eighteenth-Century Wales: a Note', *Welsh History Review*, X, 4 (1981), p. 539.

44. Report of the Royal Commission on Land in Wales and Monmouthshire (1896), pp. 509-10, cited by D. Howell, *Land and People in Nineteenth-Century Wales* (1977), p. 77. The number of game law cases in Carmarthenshire, for instance, is grossly underestimated. There were 1,032 cases at petty sessions in the county (excluding the county town) in the years 1875-91.

45. For one humorous episode in which extra policemen were drafted into a rural area, see Birch, *op. cit.*, pp. 80-1.

46. H.O. 45/6812.

47. I have described just one of these battles, in 'The Second Rebecca Riots', *Llafur*, II, 1 (1976).

48. I am currently doing research into this neglected subject. Hugh Evans, in *The Gorse Glen* (Cwm Eithin) (n.d.), p. 74, describes the bitterness of the conflict, and the Royal Commission on Land (1896), has much on the squatters' plight. On malicious destruction generally, there were about the same number of court cases as game law offences.

49. *Caernarvon and Denbigh Herald*, 6 July, 1867; J.O. Jones, 'The History of the Caernarvonshire Police Force 1856-1900', M.A. thesis, University of Wales, 1956, pp. 127-32. Animal maiming is, of course, a much-neglected subject. For a couple of Pembrokeshire cases, see the *Western Telegraph*, 27 January 1864, and the *Haverfordwest and Milford Haven Telegraph*, 1 March 1882.

50. See, for instance, *Caernarvon and Denbigh Herald*, 14 October-4 November 1843, and the *Monmouthshire Merlin*, for the spring of 1844.

51. He was very aware, however, that in some instances, the rioters had 'an admixture of Irish and Lancashire blood'! 'The Present Condition of the Welsh Nation', *Red Dragon*, IV (1883), p. 445.

52. *The Cambrian*, 8 March 1850.

53. The Scotch Cattle were in action in the winter of 1857-58; *Merthyr Guardian*, 26 December 1857. Although one can exaggerate their significance, the anti-Irish riots of 1849, 1850, 1857, 1866 and 1882, and the election disturbances of 1852, 1868 and 1874 in South Wales deserve to be studied. Cf. A. Burge, 'The Mold Riots of 1869', *Llafur*, III, 3 (1982).

54. Terms used in Howell, *op. cit.*, p. 156.

55. See, for example, *The Welshman*, 13 July 1860, and the *Carmarthen Journal*, 6 March 1863.

56. P. Morgan, 'From Long Knives to Blue Books', in K.O. Morgan and others, *Welsh Society and Nationhood* (Oxford, 1984), pp. 309-10; Rees, *op. cit.*, p. 21.

57. *South Wales Press*, 5 July 1900; Davies, *op. cit.*, p. 24.

BREAKING SILENCE: GWYN THOMAS AND THE 'PRE-HISTORY' OF WELSH WORKING CLASS FICTION

Dai Smith

In the summer of 1831 the times were excessively bad ....
Politics had little to do in the matter, though it was natural that
a suffering people should attribute their condition to many
causes, and think that 'Reform' would bring them better times.
As it was, Reform cries were occasionally heard, and, in the
sack of Coffin's house, women carrying away sides of bacon and
other things cried out, in Welsh, 'Here's Reform', thus misleading some to think it a political riot. (Charles Wilkins,
History of Merthyr Tydfil, 1867).

In 1867 — that year of ordered reform, the advent of Liberal
triumph, not least in Merthyr itself — earlier and 'misleading' ideas
connecting 'politics' to 'riot' must be seen to perish. For Merthyr's
Victorian chronicler, the town's nineteenth-century progress to
industrial order and civilisation cannot be held in doubt. The
moment of 1831 had to be fixed as an aberration. An historiography of Welsh political history was required both to establish the
relative insignificance of the summer of 1831 and to assert an
alternative, exclusive definition of politics.[1] Merthyr's working
class in this Whig concept of development could only play one role
in 1831: that of dumb, distressed and misled unfortunates. Despite
this early dismissal, the moment of 1831 in Merthyr — Gwyn A.
Williams' 'one year in the life of one Welsh town' — has echoed
and re-echoed through the history of Wales. The questions it
posed about politics and consciousness have continued to quiz
Welsh politics, divide Welsh historians, and overwhelm Welsh
novelists and poets.[2] From the historical wreckage of a lost history
the 'second' Welsh working class, refashioned in the late nineteenth century, was handed the produced memory that was sal-
vaged by amateur and academic historians in the interests of the
reformist politics of community service: an iconography of
emotional chaos and deplorable suffering topped up by the socially
acceptable innocence of a transparent martyr.[3]

The details restored by more recent scholarship have, at last, provided an alternative historiography of great power. Purely imaginative writing, bent under this accretion of detail and mes- merised by the suggestion of alternative paths the modern Welsh might have (will yet?) taken, has been crushed into unwonted — certainly unwelcome — subservience to mere facts. It is not the weight of history but of historiography which weighs on the minds of the Welsh imagination. The latter has atrophied in the harsh light of the historical scholarship which has been proceeding at such a pace since the 1960s. In particular, the history of a Welsh working class has taken on such epic proportions as its past actu- ality is restored that representation of its more complex, live reality, past and present, and necessarily available only in the con- juring-trick world of fiction, has been left to one side. This is a crisis especially for Welsh writing in the English language since it is this creature — so misleadingly and, conveniently for some, labelled 'Anglo–Welsh' — which finds itself caught rudderless in the sea-change affecting Wales in the 1980s. The automatic response had been to seek reassurance about an emerging future in the factual 'certainties' of history. As a traditional South Wales withers in the contemporary blast, so it is celebrated or keened over for its past. The historian who labours in that past surely did not intend its prior existence to swamp present initiatives, least of all creative ones. Society is not a family. Historical writing wants to liberate the imagination, not force it to make pious obeisance. The 'new' Welsh history has found its own voice through language and form as much as by virtue of dogged scholarship: any 'new' fictional representation of the Welsh working class needs to re- discover an independent boldness. A selective past, assembled for consumer use, shrinks from the confusion of the present. Its litera- ture, like its politics, avoids the hard questions, preferring the grand gesture of sympathy to the small detail of attachment. Con- temporary Welsh culture has so far silenced the impact of the one Welsh writer who did escape the cul-de-sac of the literal to pene- trate to the essential meaning of his industrial culture. Significantly enough his major work, too, centred on that early, and lasting moment of revolt, that weld of riot and rebellion, of social upheaval and political yearning, in Merthyr Tydfil in 1831.

The writer was Gwyn Thomas (1913-81); for if it can be said, as Gwyn Williams has phrased it, that in 'Merthyr Tydfil in 1831 the pre-history of the Welsh working class comes to an end', it can also be said that the pre-history of the literature concerned with that class came to an end with the publication in 1949 of Gwyn Thomas's novel about an insurrection in the 1830s *All Things Betray Thee*. The innovative structural intentions behind this work must be placed within the contemporary context of fictional representation of proletarian struggle. On the 1930s side of the divide was a formidable, if often clumsy, tradition of documentary naturalism; from the 1940s and with increasing power, whether the strain was 'right' or 'left' populism, the dominant form was the historical romance. The more circumspect, worthily honest genre, typified by the historical novel proper, scarcely surfaced in Wales. There were reasons, both specific to the novel form and to the Welsh working class, for the use made of these modes of writing and for their unsatisfactory outcome. In 1949 it was Gwyn Thomas's triumph — his 'remarkable creative achievement' in the words of Raymond Williams[4] — to break the fetters of history and of fiction, to break the silence entrapping lives once poised, by giving voice to their meaning even against the engulfing tides of a subsequent history. He had been perfecting the voice with these purposes in mind for over a decade.[5]

Gwyn Thomas's first published work dates from 1946. However, his themes and his distinctive voice stemmed from an obsessive interest in the unemployed of the South Wales valleys in the 1930s. It was their collective history he attempted to capture in the unpublished *Sorrow for Thy Sons*[6] and which he refined through a maturing comic vision in the 1940s. The rush of publications after the war was the release of this pent-up force. The prose was a heady mixture of the demotic and the hyperbolic. It was, strictly, unclassifiable. Reviewers, confronted with 'novels' that had no plots or social texture, reached for comparisons with Bunyan and Runyon. What was disturbing was the ambiguous manner in which an idiosyncratic style was being used to represent a drama normally confined by the honest simplicities of protest and struggle. He used a collective narrative voice which flitted through his black farces like a seared conscience. He was not interested in depicting the romance of individual destinies nor the epic of mass action. He was concerned with reflecting on the disjunction between the way his characters would have wished to live and the way they had actually lived in the interwar years. His intent was to lay bare the tragedy by revealing how conscious they were of their fate. There was no concession to traditional mimesis because no representational genre combined the force of lyric and philosophy.

He intervened directly in his books through an authorial tone
which does not allow the reader even a momentary sense of identification with the fate of the characters. By the end of the 1940s he
had completed his examination of all these unfulfilled left-over
lives which he saw as the ultimate agony of coalfield society in the
interwar years. He now turned, at the end of his first major
creative phase, to assess the more vital history that had dwindled
to this helpless rage. In order to do so he needed not only the
distancing effects of his mature style but also an issue which could,
in *its* reality and through *his* imagination, be made to stand for a
whole, and subsequent history. He chose, therefore, not the end of
a phase, the 1930s, but the 1830s, the identifiable beginning of all
that fascinated him about South Wales. He set the novel in 1835
and its action centres on a revolt of ironworkers in the new industrial town of Moonlea.

However, 1835 echoes 1935 as much as it does 1831. It was in
the early winter months of 1935 that Gwyn Thomas witnessed,
and as a university student participated in, the demonstrations
organised in South Wales against Part II of the National Government's Unemployment Bill.[7] This measure would have had the
effect of reducing still further the pittance the unemployed
received in dole. Its family-based means test provisions were
greatly resented. With great rapidity 'united front' committees
operating with the wider support of the South Wales Miners'
Federation began to organise a range of effective opinion across
traditional party and social divisions. The result was a series of
demonstrations on successive weekends in cold, blowing rain
through January and February. These marches were the largest
ever seen in South Wales. It was estimated that at one time over
300,000 people were involved in various, simultaneous demonstrations.

'Silent pain', wrote Aneurin Bevan, 'evokes no response.' This
articulation of pain *did* have a response. The government slapped a
'stand still' order on the regulations.[8] For the young Gwyn Thomas
this unprecedented physical occupation of the streets was a clear
sign that after the grim defeats of the 1920s the people of the coalfield still had the vital ability to protest. His 1937 novel used the
1935 demonstrations to pull his character, Hugh, a university
student, back to a belief in the power of collective being: 'Listening
to the speeches was of less importance than the mere, animal
intermingling of thousands of people gathered together in

one place for the same purpose.'

The novel, though, does not quite end there. Hugh leaves the valley. It is an exit both characteristic of the Welsh industrial novel in its actual removal of a main character, and quite distinct in its emphatic sense of a beginning. It is the valley's past as a more general catalyst for change which engages this Hugh. The history of South Wales has, more usually and more famously, entered into fiction as a compound of nostalgia and closure. *Only* the past possesses real meaning.

Another Huw leaves his valley, in Richard Llewellyn's saga *How Green Was My Valley* (1939), with a clutch of defiantly regressive questions on his lips:

> Are my friends all dead, then, and their voices a glory in my ears? ... Did my father die under the coal? But, God in heaven, he is down there now, dancing in the street with Davy's red jersey over his coat .... Is he dead?
>
> For if he is, then I am dead, and we are dead, and all of sense a mockery. How green was my valley, then, and the valley of them that have gone.[9]

And, quite startlingly similar in tone, though this time with heroic rather than nostalgic interest, Alexander Cordell rounds off *Rape of the Fair Country*, his equally famous 1959 novel, which spans 1826 to the 1839 Newport rising, with his first person narrator, Iestyn Mortymer, about to be caught for his part in the rising, asking:

> Is Idris Foreman gone, and Afel Hughes to his burned wife ...?
> Is Richard Bennet in the Great Palace, entering in his youth the portals of the dead when all his life he had fought for a heaven of the living? ... Is my father gone, he so great in strength? Is my country dead, this beloved land that has powdered the bones of other conquerors and trampled their pennants into dust? I see the mountains green again in the lazy heat of summer, and cold and black under the frozen moons of winter. Is the hay still flying from the barn down at Shant-y-Brain's? Is the canal still swimming through the alders from Brecon to Ponty?[10]

In 1939, using a family saga as romance, Richard Llewellyn closed down the expansiveness of an actual history by inflecting its rhythms with greed, stupidity and pettiness. In 1959 Alexander Cordell, employing the device of families as history, sought to restore an epic pattern by having his lusty individuals collide with events (as they would continue to do in succeeding books) from Merthyr and 1831, to Newport and 1839, and on to Penrhyn in 1900, Tonypandy in 1910 and Senghennyd in 1913. In 1949 Gwyn Thomas wrote a novel set in the 1830s with the 1930s in mind; the connecting passage of years would thereby not be dismissed (as in Llewellyn) because of the energies lost to South Wales society in the Depression. Nor did Thomas assume, as Cordell would do, that the convergence of actual public drama and fictional persona could be anything other than the incorporation of history, raw and unmediated, through the prior demands of romantic fiction. The power of the latter, so well done by Cordell, is dependent on the poetry of history which emerges from the detail.

Yet detail is not reality. The poetics of history emerges only when the detail is given a shape which reveals its meaning, rather than by being used to give colour to a purely fictional development whose basic device could be, and is, applied to almost any historical time. Gwyn Thomas tried to imagine a history for South Wales which would enable us to apprehend the shaping significance of a century. He strove to make clear how men and women assembled purely for the purposes of work made themselves into communities of purpose. His novel of 1949 is about an actual defeat which is an imagined victory because the moment, single and individualised, collectivises an experience. Or to use the dismissive yet deeply potent phrase of Charles Wilkins, it dares to discuss the implications of a 'political riot'.

'Can it be', asked Gwyn A. Williams in 1971,

> that it took the elemental passion of a traditionalist and archaic communal revolt to create that solidarity which made trade unionism possible? The difficulty lies in getting at the kind of evidence which would enable us to approach the problem. So much has been lost. ... Not that it will be easy to find. But if it could be found, and we could understand fully the relationship between the riots and the unions, we would surely take a giant step forward in social history .... If we solved that problem, I suppose we'd have solved the central problem of human history as such.[11]

Gwyn Thomas sensed, in the perspective of a history also ingrained in Gwyn A. Williams, that the connection between riot and rising, between revolt and unionism, between artisans and proletarians, between communal values and solidarity, between '1835' and 1935, was the key question, universal because specific, which was posed and answered in the history of South Wales. Revelation is another matter from representation. The historian's difficulty of evidences is, in a different but related sense, the novelist's problem of form. Gwyn Thomas's solution was to fuse his understanding with his characters' forming identities.

He wrote a novel about one year in the life of one town in the knowledge of what had subsequently unfolded. His narrative and his characters are, therefore, freighted with the burden of a history both subsequent to them and dependent *on* them. Their own altering individual lives are held in the focus of an early industrialisation that is the most dramatic social experience of modern humanity. Just as in the novels directly concerned with the 1930s he was anxious to illustrate, through language rather than action, consciousness of fate, so here, dealing with the 1830s, he narrates an action-packed story in which a heavily stylised language teases out the predestined discovery of consciousness for which South Wales reaches. At the end, after the revolt is defeated, the innkeeper, Jameson, explains to the harpist, Alan Leigh, the significance of what they have witnessed. The singer begins by doubting the song;

> 'no men should ever have so little chance as these. They bit at something that was unripe, bitter. They should have waited. They were in too much of a hurry. Has death some special call that lures these lads its way? They should have waited. They had too little cunning. Cunning is a slimy thing; it might have rusted away some of the fetters they've smashed their lives on.'
>
> 'We state the facts,' said Jameson. 'We state them now softly, now loudly. The next time it will be softly for our best voices will have ceased to speak. The silence and the softness will ripen. The lost blood will be made again. The chorus will shuffle out of its filthy aching corners and return. The world is full of voices, harpist, practising for the great anthem but hardly ever heard. We've been privileged. We've had our ears full of the singing. Silence will never be absolute for us again'.
>
> 'That's so,' I said, looking up at him, my head less heavy

now. 'That's so. The silence will never again be absolute. The
back of our dumbness will have been broken and it must have
been a granite sort of spine while it lasted. But the ears of John
Simon, that once could hear music in every voice, on every
wind, are stopped. Will that fact ever cease to make me sick, a
stranger to myself and the whole of life, in those moments when
it takes me by the thumbs and strings me up?'

'The fact will grow into you. Finally it will be all of you, your
new root.'[12]

The original title of the novel was *My Root on Earth*.[13] The idea
of community rootedness, of forced uprooting from the land, of
'slashed roots', of commitment and loyalty, recur over and over.
To the extent that this is all overshadowed by loss, defeat and
ambivalence, so the first published title, *All Things Betray Thee*,
does indeed describe the published novel.

Perhaps, though, the ambiguity Gwyn Thomas wanted in his
theme was best expressed in the title used in the 1949 American
edition: *Leaves in the Wind*.[14]

'We all have a choice,' said Connor ...

'I don't know,' said Jeremy Longridge. 'Men like John Simon
Adams and myself, we are not much more than leaves in the
wind, bits of painful feeling that gripe the guts of the masses.
From the cottages, the hovels, the drink shops and sweat mills,
anger rises and we are moved. No choice, Mr Connor, save perhaps the last-minute privilege of adjusting the key of the scream
we utter ....

We all have a choice. You and John Simon Adams could as
well have chosen a replete and sodden silence. ... But some of
us are cursed with the urge to be making assertions that are
either too big or too deep to fit into the box of current relations.
So we have to broaden the box or whittle down our assertions.'

'Have you a choice, harpist?' Jeremy asked me.

'I don't know. I've never seen life as you boys seem to see it,
a distinct, separate thing like a detachable shadow, to be
examined and kicked or kissed. It's just flown around me, not
hurting too much and I've never given a conscious damn. No,
I've never thought about this business of choosing. I wish I were
far away from here ... but hour after hour I stay here, like the
rabbit stays by the weasel. That puzzles me.'[15]

The puzzlement is unravelled in page after page of tennis-ball dia-
logue in which the harpist, winning game and set, never quite takes
the match. Finally, he has to be made to see that he *can* only win
within the rules of a game. Outside that framework his controlled
spontaneity of playing, his art, is shown to be child's play.
Longridge tells him:

> 'The whole instrument of your passion is being retuned. We all
> have a set of special pities which we work off in different ways.
> Harping is the simple way of doing it. But to look for and find
> the strings of significance that today hang loosely between men
> and which must be drawn tighter before any real sweetness of
> melody will be heard in living, that's the job, harpist. Do that
> and you will see the very face of the joy whose mere anus you
> have been fiddling with to date.'[16]

Jeremy Longridge is a leader of the rebellion; he represents the
call to arms, whereas the other leader, John Simon Adams, first
stresses the power of reason and of peaceful demonstration as persuasive enough even for those in authority. Both perish —
Longridge in a last, despairing fight with the military, Adams by
execution in prison. Earlier in their lives, we learn, they had
espoused opposite opinions. Their Janus-like leadership is of a part
with the mirror-images present throughout the book. Connor, the
radical lawyer whose father had been a 'great nephew of David
Hume', and had wished his son 'to become the philosophic
Napoleon of the day', has a professional rival in Jarvis, legal brain
for the landowner, Plimmon and the ironmaster, Penbury. Each in
turn is also reliant for a developed identity on others. Connor has
'everything except the hard tinder of real experience against which
my gift of logic could strike a spark and start to live.' Some lives,
however, will prove to be so encrusted with 'experience' that their
carapace of indifference, posing as hard-headed good sense, will
shield them against self-doubts. This is true of Radcliffe, partner in
and manager of the ironworks, who spots rising disquiet and, over
the dinner table, asserts that Penbury's guests can settle the discontent.

> 'You have a soldier, a minister, a lawyer. They symbolise the
> whole fabric of traditional guarantees against the folly of vin-
> dictive and presumptuous illiterates. If there is ever a hint of

disturbance, it will be in Moonlea and Captain Wilson, with a dozen troopers, few more, will put an end to it with a wave of his sword . . . .

Jarvis is the majesty of the law and you will never realise how fiendishly majestic the law can look when you are on the receiving end of it . . . . Then again, these folk are as responsive to Mr Bowen as women's flesh to bruises. At the touch of his words, when the full hue and cry of the passionate God-search is upon them, the stoniest spirits will crumble to a ruin that will make a lovely mould for our every molten suggestion and fiat. And if all else fails, set that fiddler and harpist to work their magic upon them.'[17]

Throughout the novel characters are forced to choose: to betray love for glittering power as does Helen, Penbury's daughter; to betray the rebel leaders for an illusory security as does the shopkeeper Lemuel Stevens; to struggle, perhaps to die, as do those around Adams and Longridge; to wish that a choice did not need to be made, as does the harpist. His dilemma is a tortured one, something that overwhelms his original, simple aim.

Alan Leigh travels to Moonlea to 'rescue' his friend John Simon Adams from the iron town for which Adams' father had left 'the North'. The harpist is a Romantic, a melancholic fatalist whose spirits are momentarily uplifted by nature, beauty, drink, love and music. He sees the moments as evanescent and then moves on:

'Around my harp, in all the villages of all the hills and valleys where I had stayed for a brief night or day, had crystallised whole layers of expressed longings and regret . . . [but] . . . there was that within me which set a fence around my pity and bade all other men and women let me be and pass.'[18]

Already, though, this is a past life for him since he comes to Moonlea bereft of the harp which a drunken drover has smashed. He sees this as a release: 'The harp's death left me free' (from 'ancient vagabondage and sorrowful bardry') since now he will settle down with his friend in an idyllic rural haven back in the North. The harpist's frustration will grow as he finds it impossible to uproot Adams from this industrial hell on earth, and inconceivable that anyone should willingly accept a 'slave' life as an 'iron-toiler'. The harpist's own unwillingness to be readily involved or overly attached to those for whom he has sympathy, but little more, is the fulcrum on which the novel depends for its balance. The harpist, as Orpheus, does represent a kind of fullness and human content which has been lost in Moonlea; the Promethean rebels, he will learn, understand that Orpheus's harp is splintered, and that only their efforts can restore, through struggle, an Orphic capacity to humanity.[19] Development cannot be an arrested state.

Gwyn Thomas rarely presents a collective history in general terms. He prefers to let that social impersonality work through the actions and words of his characters. In the novels set in near con- temporary Wales he can almost assume a familiarity with the public nature of his historical background. In this instance, though, he needs to recall the novelty of the break in human time brought about by industry. The broad contrasts are those between a pastoral and urban existence. Moonlea, with its hovels, beershops, acrid smoke, glowing ironworks and grasping truck shops is a Rhondda-in-embryo, the people's grim future. The 'field-folk' have been forced off the land by hunger and enclosure. The move- ment is abrupt and abstract.

> In my roamings I had seen the increase of wealth and power in the hands of the great landowners as the large estates broke their fences and drove out the small field-tillers. I had seen the empty cottages and quiet fields that had contributed their drop to the stream that was now flowing into the new noisy centres where cloth, iron, coal were creating new patterns of effort, reward, unease. The personal forces, the men of gold, the mighty, whose brains and hands directed these changes, I had kept well outside my private acre and as long as I could keep my moving undisciplined hide free from their manipulative frenzies I had cared nothing about them. Strong and fast they might be, I would always be too swift for them. I would never be found squirming in the life-traps they were creating in the new centres of power.[20]

Only in escape, then, does the harpist envisage being his own man. He has pity for the oppressed, contempt for those who glory in being oppressors. He will play his music for anyone, even submit to being respectably dressed by the ironmaster's daughter, but the lives of all who take industrial bondage seriously are, for him, lost lives. Coming to Moonlea without a harp means that he can acquire one to play *or* learn a new music. It is the first option which attracts him. He discovers, however, that the new world means he cannot play as before. The new patrons have allotted him a role which does not even allow him to stir up anguish in his listeners. He must purvey music to soothe or to lull.

Richard Penbury, second-generation ironmaster, calls him to play. He is offered a magnificent new harp. On this instrument the only tunes he may play are *muzak*. As a young man, Penbury had travelled in France and embraced the libertarian credo of Rousseau. Once home, the engrossing will of his father had bent him to the achievements of capitalism. In him the two great revolutionary impulses war. Insomnia allows him no rest. He is Faust the ardent architect of human attainment, and Faust the willing destroyer of the human scale of things in the interests of overarching visions. Penbury — whose 'whole existence ... was frighteningly opaque to me' — holds the harpist enthralled:

'I don't suppose you know much about the brain of man, harpist .... It would like to be calm but it is shaken grey and sick by savage angers, for it plays fantastically with the idea of worrying all stupid and tolerated hungers from their lice-holes and outlawing them from the earth. There will be days in its journey of crazy leaps and crawls when it will seem inscrutable and ruthless, festooned with stunted lives and quaking bellies, for it can work freely to its end only when a great heat of change and movement has been wrought, when the stuff of living and feeling can be made to run into another mould. That's how it was at the beginning, the very beginning ... with all things molten and awaiting shape. Then it sees the idiot grin of men and women willing the counter-coldness of obstinacy and death, clogging the stream of change and settlement for lifetimes on end. And this stupendous music of man's aim to make his unique genius the infallible sculptor of a controlled and kindlier universe sinks to a feeble moan while some feeble life-sickened loon makes an epic of pity about a few sores on the breast of Moonlea .... Not storm, nor pain nor death but the plain, filthy improvident helplessness of the world's unfit ... that's the enemy. Man's brain will devise new weapons of power and authority against nature with her puking jests of flinty soil and useless minds ... [and] ...

men like you will be a dwindling pack of pathetic and restless freaks.'[21]

The harpist, as artist, is trapped irrespective of his wishes. At the end it will only be Penbury intervention and Penbury money that will save him from Adams' fate. The harpist, shamed and fearful, is not able to embrace the martyrdom of his friend. He oscillates between the extremes of submission and rebellion since he sees both as alien to himself. He leaves Adams in prison, yet strives to rescue him. He almost urges on the armed revolt that will be crushed, but accepts his role as token of the mercy of the mighty in the knowledge that Adams must be the sacrificial victim as a counter. What tears at him is the divide between his growing awareness of his role and his limited ability to break the fetters that tie him down to an illusory freedom he actually shares with the despised Lemuel Stevens, the archetypal petty-bourgeois shop-keeper:

'To John Simon, you and I and Penbury are a squalid lot of intruders, and we are, too, you with your pennies and I with my constant and deafening chime of selfish moods. He isn't happy about us. He's part of a new disease of awareness that'll kill us off like flies on some distant day. You were born too small and I was born too loud to be able to do much about it. But tonight we are free to buzz and pollute to our heart's content. Where's my harp?'
'Two men are bringing it down from the mansion.'[22]

The novel is full of sound. The harpist's observation of the world of Moonlea proceeds almost entirely through conversation whose Socratic intent is frequently punctured by wisecracks. Gwyn Thomas uses his self-confessed 'clowns' and 'loons' to subvert by their comedy of word and deed a world they can scarcely influence otherwise. For the harpist, as for his 'dark philosophers' in the early novels, it is a mode adapted for survival. The joke is a measuring stick for reality. The quip is a side-step executed in the path of the juggernaut. None the less, it is the fury that really signifies. It is anger which makes the sound that the dumb *must* articulate. The harpist can tell Lemuel that he speaks in a way that 'isn't your idiom', and that his words are designed to 'make you giddy', but it is he who fails to understand the silent power being assembled in towns like Moonlea. Through John Simon Adams we hear of how the collective presence of an industrial proletariat will begin to shift.

> Here in Moonlea and places like it the people for the first time are not quite helpless. They are close together and in great numbers. Their collective hand is big enough to point at what is black and damnable in the present, at what is to be wished in the future. Back there in the fields they were in a solitude.[23]

The rebellion will inevitably be as complex as a society in flux. We meet characters who seek, and exact, individual revenge for injustice. Religion is seen as a 'practice ground' for change as much as a dose of opiate. Towns like Tudbury outside the industrialising centre are brush-stroked in to remind us of the proximity in space of different human times. Servants, jailers, soldiers, innkeepers, mothers and lovers all sing their comments on the central drama. It is a cast rich in the dialectic of opera. Their rhetoric is a social oratorio of discord and unison. This is the early industrial culture of places like South Wales brought to the pitch of events by the beat of its structure. The harpist is our opening eye. He is South Wales' unfolding history made cerebral through passion. And just as a more human society tries to break, prematurely, the mould in which it has been set, so a piece of writing, in Gwyn Thomas's heroic attempt strives, imperfectly, to reach a form (historical novel? fictive history? philosophical homily? political fable?) which will encompass that history whole. To do that is to restore conscious endeavour to men and women, to put politics into social history, ideas into the novel and interpretation of meaning into the depiction of happenings:

> 'Look Alan ...' [said John Simon Adams]. 'Today is always a muck of ails, shifts and tasks, a fearsome bit of time to stare at and tackle. A man always hates to make a hostile grab at the fabric of the existence he actually knows because he himself might turn out to be the first pulled thread. But yesterday's beliefs are nice, smooth drumsticks, and they are often brought to tap out reassurance against fears to which we have no answer at all. These people brought here from a dozen counties, have no common understanding, no common language. They are still frozen and made dumb by the strangeness of their different

yesterdays. Men are always shy to say clearly how the dream of freedom really strikes them.'

'So they talk of their souls and temples and sects and at the end of it all you will find a multitude of clear-eyed and clear-minded rebels to do war with the rule of wealth and squalor?'

'War?' He smiled and shook his head from side to side. 'Even to see, wonder and protest, that's a victory.'[24]

Between a quiescent past and a utopian future there is, for the harpist, only what may be taken in the present. The present, therefore, extends interminably. It is the individual ever-defiant in the ever-recurrent face of death. The rebellion for the harpist is an understandable outburst of anger. Victory for him would be a physical success — the burning of the mansion, the destruction of the ironworks, an end to hunger brought about by 'communal revolt'. The more elusive concept of 'solidarity', not umbilically connected to the short-lived satisfaction of 'winning', is one that eludes him. The old 'Jacobin' Abel, persecuted in his own youth for his politics, informs him, in advance of the rising, of the likely turn of events:

'There'll probably be another war and then there will be no muttering in Moonlea, no more talk of equality. There will be iron, there will be lives rotting into profitable slime in Penbury's cottages, there will be silence and a more confident whiteness in the columns that flank the master's hillside home.'

'And for you, who crouched in ditches, for John Simon who cracks his skull against the stone, no victory.'

'We don't aim to win.'

'What the hell are you out for then?'

'To break silence, that's all.'[25]

The question Gwyn Thomas posed in all his books was how this could be done in art ('When we find the things that really signify to say about such things, leaving no more to be said, great things will happen in the following silence'),[26] so that the reality of common experience could be understood in its collective as well as its singular shapes. He could not, writing out of *his* experiences of South Wales and grasp of its history, allow people to be merely individual or let crowds fragment into mobs or riots lose an informing direction. His work lay, deliberately, at a tangent to his subject-matter. He dramatised a 'history' at the same time as he commented on it. His nudging author's presence went even further than this: he speculated on the universality of his very local subject-matter. In this he was encouraged by the manner in which South Wales had indeed leapt from the parochial to the international within two or three forced generations, but the experimental prose form owed as much to the inadequacies of the traditional working-class novel. Within the bounds of the latter he had discovered that only certain things could be said. The subject was defined in advance by the form. Gwyn Thomas knew that the essence of his subject — the formation of a proletariat and its struggle to consciousness — was its fluidity. This had to be depicted in its working-out, not in any finished picture. The harpist is still exploring the contradictory tugs of his life at the novel's end although he has, at this stage, been taught and been fired by events. He has rejected the blandishments of the Penburys but his way forward now is not — cannot be — that of his friend, John Simon Adams. To be artisan is, maybe, to be more rebellious but less revolutionary than to be proletarian. The harpist is neither and both. Like his society he embarks on a journey whose end is clearer than its direction. Gwyn Thomas's novel is consciously removed by nomenclature and incident from any actual Wales in the 1830s in order to claim that historical territory's resonance for his fiction. The latter does not represent the history. It tries to make actuality signify its lasting reality in our understanding and in our subsequent activity. The actual would be reduced to mere transience if presented as a fixed heroic subject or a sentimental group portrait. The play of mind on matter is the irreducible care which art must represent.

When the novel appeared it was seen, and quickly dismissed, as a 'sport' at best, at worst an historical novel in which there was 'no sense of period, no feeling of an earlier age' (*Books Today*, June 1949).[27] Its trans-historical character was, it was felt, a decided oddity in a work set so squarely in the early nineteenth century. A more considered piece of criticism first came in 1950 when Howard Fast, American novelist and social-realist supporter of causes unfashionably left-wing in his contemporary America, singled out 'a young Welsh writer, Gwyn Thomas by name' who had already by 'writing experimentally and searchingly of the working-class ... managed to break loose from most of the iron-like taboos with which bourgeois culture encased his subject.' Now, in *Leaves in the Wind,* Fast thought he had surpassed himself by grappling with the combination of 'objective' reality and narrow 'subjectivity', through adding 'his own consciousness' to 'the consciousness of the Welsh workers' about whom he wrote: 'It is one thing to do this in an academic historical presentation — although it is sufficiently rare in the field of historiography — and it is quite another matter to do it well and artistically in literary terms.'[28]

It was precisely his success in bringing off this difficulty with such apparent ease that led to a subsequent neglect of his work within the field of working-class literature. Within Wales, a career as comic novelist, pundit and playwright saw him pigeon-holed to the detriment of any profound appreciation of his early, dynamic phase of creative writing. A generation from the 1960s who wished to comprehend the history of industrial Wales in terms of lucidity and utility resented not only his joking sensibility but also his free wheeling rejection of a Whiggish/labourist chronology. He sat as uneasily on the labour historiography of Wales as he did within the almost parallel canon of Anglo–Welsh literature. Gwyn Thomas was what those things were not — a revolutionary writer. This element in his work was intermittently recognised by a faithful band of admirers,[29] but it came as a shock to many when Raymond Williams stated a brief, but powerful case for him in the late 1970s and later in 1983:

> It is ironic that the best historical fiction about the Welsh working class has been written (though with its own kinds of fault and limitation) by a sympathetic outside observer, who could *read* as well as experience the history: Alexander Cordell .... The form does much, but with still significant and weakening connections to the historical romance. The way in which the form avoids some of the local difficulties as well as some of the hardest local recognitions can be seen in a comparison with the most important novel of this whole phase, Gwyn Thomas's *All Things Betray Thee* which significantly is centrally concerned with the problems of writing — speaking, singing — this complex experience: the clear objective reality as subjectively — but by a collective subject — experienced.'[30]

With *All Things Betray Thee* Gwyn Thomas put the British working-class novel onto a different plane. It is not enough to say that his own voice was strictly inimitable so that his 'tradition' was a dead-end. That voice was made by a culture. It was given weight by a history. Other voices do not have to be echoes in order to take on those characteristics. The dead-end was, rather, the dead hand of a provincial culture in which he, and his fiction, and his own people had had no part. It is the gravest calumny to depict him as either a one-off or as part of some marginal, anglicised Welshness. He was a major socialist writer emanating from a major socialist culture. He dared to be original. The academic history of the Welsh working class would, in its time, require an alternative historiography that would also need an appropriate style to capture its inevitable entanglement of 'subjectivity' and 'objectivity' within a 'collective experience'. To move beyond those awkward, necessary paraphrases, which at least distance such a history from the ice-skating narratives generally on offer, is to move into the close reading of a social texture which alone allows the significance of moments, years, events to be heard. Gwyn A. Williams has circled around Merthyr in 1831, 'drawn endlessly back to its flaring, noisy, exciting, distressing, "free" and reassuringly *peopled* Samaria',[31] because, whatever the meaning of that 'one year in the history of one Welsh town' may be, it is his meaning, too, as an individual, an historian and a citizen of South Wales. Gwyn Thomas, from the Rhondda a generation earlier, dedicated his great novel 'To the Valley and Its People', because he, too, could draw no distinction between audience and performer, history and the moment, root and growth. Both these socialist writers, historian and novelist, have broken silence about and for a culture which requires politics, in its art as well as its activity, for its social being to be made articulate. The words with which Gwyn Thomas ended his master work apply to more than the changed life of Alan Leigh, his harpist: 'I turned, walking away from Moonlea, yet eternally towards Moonlea, full of a strong, ripening, unanswerable bitterness, feeling in my fingers the promise of a new enormous music.'[32]

Notes

1. The whole issue can be seen as revolving around the words 'riots' and 'rising'. Gwyn A. Williams pointed out in his essay 'The Merthyr of Dic Penderyn', in Glanmor Williams (ed.), *Merthyr Politics: The Making of a Working-class*

Tradition (Cardiff, 1966) that only G.D.H. Cole had spotted the importance of what he, correctly, and in 1941, first called 'the Merthyr Rising' in *Chartist Portraits* (London, 1941). The dominant academic interpretation, applied also to the Newport Chartist insurrection of 1839, was that of David Williams, who saw matters in the more trivialising dimensions of Wilkins and a subsequent British liberal historiography. Since Gwyn A. Williams began reinterpreting the event in 'The Merthyr Riots: Settling The Account' *National Library of Wales Journal*, xi (1959) the term rising, has moved increasingly to the fore until with his *The Merthyr Rising* (London, 1978) it has become the leading partner in this semantic tango.

2. Poets were drawn instinctively to the martyred symbol of Dic Penderyn in the 1950s and 1960s: J.S. Williams, Harri Webb, John Tripp; in the 1970s it is social ambience and rebellion that was stressed in poetry: Mike Jenkins, Robert Minhinnick. This seems to reflect, as do the novels of Rhydwen Williams, *The Angry Vineyard* (1975) and Alexander Cordell, *The Fire People* (1972), recognition of historical complexity, though not perhaps of contemporary ambiguity.

3. This was brilliantly dissected by Gwyn A. Williams in 'Dic Penderyn', *Llafur*, Vol. 2, No. 3 (1978).

4. Raymond Williams, *The Welsh Industrial Novel* (Cardiff, 1978) p. 18.

5. The best general account is Ian Michael, *Gwyn Thomas* (Cardiff, 1977) in the *Writers of Wales* series.

6. This novel is first quoted and discussed in Dai Smith, *Wales: Wales?* (London, 1984), pp. 140-51.

7. See Gwyn Thomas, *A Welsh Eye* (London, 1964) p. 18, and idem., *A Few Selected* (London, 1968).

8. For an account of this, see Hywel Francis and David Smith, *The Fed: A History of South Wales Miners in the 20th century* (London, 1980), ch. 8, *passim.*

9. Richard Llewellyn, *How Green Was My Valley* (1972 edn). pp. 376-7. And see David Smith, 'Myth and Meaning in the Literature of the South Wales Coalfield in the 1930s', *Anglo-Welsh Review*, Spring 1976.

10. Alexander Cordell, *Rape of the Fair Country* (London, 1959), p. 301.

11. Gwyn A. Williams, 'Merthyr 1831: Lord Melbourne and the Trade Unions', *Llafur*, Vol. I, No. I (1972).

12. Gwyn Thomas, *All Things Betray Thee* (London, 1949), p. 312. This has never been reprinted.

13. See Michael, *op. cit.*, p. 19.

14. The American edition, *Leaves in the Wind* appeared under the imprint of Little, Brown in 1949. It was edited in such a way as to remove some Thomasian digression and so differs in small but striking ways from the English imprint by Michael Joseph. *Leaves in the Wind* was republished in 1968 by Monthly Review Press (New York) with a short, admiring introduction by Maxwell Geismar.

15. *All Things Betray Thee*, p. 205.

16. Ibid., p. 206.

17. Ibid., p. 91.

18. Ibid., p. 7.

19. For a dazzling elaboration of this theme as quintessentially applicable to Marx, see Marshall Berman, *All That is Solid Melts into Air* (London, 1983), p. 127, and *passim* for an account of 'The Experience of Modernity' (its sub-title) which fits South Wales like a glove.

20. *All Things Betray Thee*, p. 11.

21. Ibid., pp. 58-9.

22. Ibid., p. 104.

23. Ibid., p. 31.

24. Ibid., pp. 39-40.
25. Ibid., pp. 145-6.
26. Ibid., p. 310.
27. Michael, *op. cit.*, pp. 19-20.
28. Howard Fast, *Literature and Reality* (New York, 1950), pp. 67, 69.
29. See Glyn Jones, *The Dragon Has Two Tongues* (London, 1968); Eric Hobsbawm, *Primitive Rebels* (Manchester, 1959).
30. Raymond Williams, *Writing in Society* (London, 1983), p. 237.
31. Gwyn A. Williams, *The Merthyr Rising*, p. 52.
32. *All Things Betray Thee*, p. 318.

6 RURAL REBELS IN SOUTHERN ENGLAND IN THE 1830s

Roger Wells

Years ago, Eric Hobsbawm and George Rudé emphasised historians' 'shocking ... total ignorance of the forms of agrarian discontent between the rising of 1830 and the emergence of agricultural trade unionism in the 1870s.'[1] The complaint has been recently reiterated,[2] but excepting studies of arson[3] our ignorance largely obtains, despite the fact that agrarian communities were integral not foreign, to Edward Thompson's thesis in *The Making of the English Working Class.* Thompson asserted that the populist democratic experiences in the shadow of the French Revolution survived the Pittite repression, and that during the remaining 'war years there were Thomas Hardys in every town and many villages *throughout* England ... biding their time ... waiting for the movement to revive.' 'By 1832', Thompson continued, 'and on into Chartist times there is a Radical nucleus *in every county, in the smallest market towns and even in the rural villages.*'[4] His critics insisted that Thompson concentrated too heavily on artisans and workers in the domestic industries, thereby eschewing consideration of a representative cross-section of the proletariat, and compounded this by geographical selectivity, through focusing on metropolitan, Midlands and Northern theatres of plebeian agitation. If Thompson's thesis is correct, expressions of both class-consciousness and popular radicalism ought to be found in the principally rural and agricultural South; logically, they should materialise during the 1830s, perhaps the most traumatic decade in the English countryside in modern times.

Recurrent crises characterised that decade. The Captain Swing explosion of 1830 engulfed the South. The protracted Reform Bill crisis of 1830-32, with its revolutionary under- and overtones, penetrated the most serene rural communities. The case of the Tolpuddle Martyrs reveals a rural ramification of the intense trade union campaigns of the early 1830s. The Poor Law Amendment Act 1834, aimed primarily to sanitise the pauperised agricultural workforce, swept away the essential prop of rural plebeian society, the Elizabethan statutory social security system. Finally, echoes of the Chartist movement sounded through the countryside in 1838- 39.

Strangely, these events have never been studied in tandem in a regional context. Swing is customarily seen as the last labourers' revolt, located in an historical panorama extending backwards to 1381, or — to cite Thompson's curious self-contradictory conception — Swing represented 'the first and the last time (till the 1870s) when the labourers of the South and East, began to feel themselves to be, and to act as a class with common objectives.'[5] Any impact of the Reform Bill crisis on the rural workforce is ignored.[6] Tolpuddle 'killed ... agricultural unionism ... for close on forty years', according to the Martyrs' latest historian.[7] As an ideological issue it was highjacked by non-agrarian trade unionists and non-rural radicals, and used as a *cause célèbre* to advance labour organisations, and as an exemplar of Whig treachery to politicise the masses. Indeed, it 'is known only because of its urban repercussions'.[8] Labour historians have concentrated on Poor Law reform as the *leit-motif* of Northern popular protest, central to the genesis of Chartism, also traditionally perceived as the preserve of the urban and industrial masses. In the countryside, the 'Poor Man's Robbery Bill' is believed to have reinforced what is projected as the 'Cohesion of Rural Society',[9] and the opposition from those on the receiving-end in the South, as too weak to constitute more than a transient struggle.[10] These challenges to aristocratic hegemony in its last undiluted bastion galvanised the governing class's successful determination to use the state's repressive machinery to preserve that bastion intact.[11]

Swing, rural trade unionism and the anti-Poor Law protests — all represent noted confrontations between the state and agrarian proletarians. Historians commonly forget that interactions between the state and society are vital components in the historic process of class formation. If, for example, Ned Ludd drew political lessons from the textile unions' failure to wrest labour-protecting statutes from Parliament, why not the Swing rebels from their experience of power; the Home Office determined on the Special Commissions, deliberate creations *in terrorem*, and then endorsed judicial decisions to exile hundreds and hang a selected score. That same government, its authority bolstered by Reform, was responsible for the transparent manipulation of the law to transport the Tolpuddle victims. The Whig ministry was the author of the most

savage class legislation in the new Poor Law, which also irrevocably implicated the Tories. If radicalism had penetrated the
countryside by 1830, it should have partially conditioned these
confrontations, which in turn ought to have accelerated both
politicisation and class-consciousness.

I

A re-examination of Southern labour history necessitates a re-
evaluation of the alleged remoteness and isolation of agrarian
communities. This common contemporary view[12] has been
uncritically repeated by modern historians. 'Rural England
remained very isolated,' opines Tolpuddle's historian — an odd
conclusion considering her identification of the role of emissaries
from the ranks of those involved in that notoriously rustic organisation, the Grand National Consolidated Trade Union, in the
Dorset Farmworkers' Union.[13] Hobsbawm and Rudé are covert
subscribers to a subtle version of the isolationist interpretation. If
farm labourers had 'links with the world ... of wider national
ideology and politics', these turned on 'non-labourers' resident in
the villages; the parish, these authors claim, remained the
labourers' 'inescapable cage'. The corollary of this virtual seclusion
is to write off the labourers' ideological resources as the 'usual
luggage of the pre-political poor'.[14]

The real role of 'Southern market and county towns, ... generally passed over by social historians', comprises one key theme.[15]
Political radicalism established a foothold in scores during the
1790s. The original 'very shy' handful of radicals at Maidstone in
1792 survived legal repression and Reevite intimidation; by 1796
'party ran so high' that the town was 'a divided place', with opposing sides entrenched in partisan inns. Evidential fragments of the
presence of organised radicalism thereafter are scarce, but they
include payments through the London Corresponding Society to
the state prisoners' relief fund in 1801, and some groups emerged
with a notorious tradition, including the 'patriotic shoemakers of
Maidstone', so castigated for their active support of Swing protesters in 1830.[16] Many towns, including Chichester, Lewes,
Brighton and Horsham in Sussex alone, had roughly parallel
histories. The Earl of Egremont, the octogenarian Lord Lieutenant, in 1830 noted the 'bad principles ... instilled ... for many

years, & during the last war' among the population of Horsham
and the surrounding parishes, and testified to his frustration at
being 'without means of prevention ... in that borough for these
last forty years.'[17] The burgeoning labour movement in these towns
encompassed more than devotees to democratic principles.
Brighton hosted a significant cooperative. In the ports, various sea-
farers, pilots, fishermen and sailors were capable of industrial
action, in addition to ship-repairers and builders. Maidstone was
also an important centre of the paperworkers' highly-advanced
trade union since the 1780s; trade unionism in the building trades,
and amongst shoemakers and tailors, was found in most towns.

This trade unionist presence had a multifold significance.
Tramping systems were one of the vehicles whereby certain unionists had strong regional and metropolitan links, which were
engaged on occasions, notably by builders, tailors and papermakers, to coordinate strikes between London and Southern provincial towns. Some unionised industries, again paper but also
timber, were located in predominantly agrarian communities.
Numerous other unionised trades, especially the millwrights,
served such industries, and other smaller manufacturing plants (for
example corn mills) in rural areas. Hundreds of journeymen went
on the tramp to the countryside in search of work. Not incon-
siderable enterprises are found in some villages, employing up to a
dozen craftsmen. Builders — some from London — are
encountered at work on big projects, especially country mansions,
and even more numerously in the spa and resort towns being
developed across the South. These workers took their political and
industrial principles with them. Moreover, in addition to these
links with a more militant working-class culture, agricultural
labourers were not so imprisoned as supposed. Many migrated, on
a semi-permanent basis, to nearby towns and further afield to seek
work, and here encountered the same ideologies; but they maintained contact with friends and family, as revealed, for example, in
the numbers of young agricultural workers who flocked to spend
Christmas in Brighton. Many of these migrants were, before 1834-
35, also in receipt of some poor relief from their home parishes.
Other relevant migrations, including seasonal ones to the hop-
fields, coastal and afforested areas, also brought agricultural
labourers under different influences. And to all this we must add
Andrew Charlesworth's key linkmen of the road, who as carters,
drovers and drivers constantly brought and took news and views

over their extensive itineraries.[18]

The relatively rich evidence of the early nineteenth-century labour movement in Southern towns, contrasts with the sparse details of its rural equivalent. The Queen Caroline affair unleashed scores of demonstrations in the countryside which exhibited radical tinges, and the perennial struggles over poor relief, especially after 1815, indicate many ingredients of class struggle.[19] It would be idiotic to surmise that the constant criticism of beer-shops in the 1830s as venues for the consumption of the unstamped, and seminaries for radicalism, represented a neat conjunction of a new taste for hyperbole and a change in the licensing laws. In fact, they represented a feature of rural societies which had already developed. The radical group which met to read Cobbett at tiny Sutton Scotney in Hampshire, is well known through the involvement of members in Swing outrages, though the fact that these men had subscribed to send a delegate to the king with a 'petition ... about the poor' on behalf of the 'sovereign people' is rarely stressed.[20] Parallel developments were also taking place in East Sussex. Shortly before the Swing rising it was reported from Rye that

the labourers in ... ten of the adjoining Parishes have ... formed themselves into Association, to promote local and general Reform; they have committees to direct them, and subscribe one penny per week each to raise a fund upon the same principle as the Catholic Rent ... and if universally adopted could not fail to ensure a safe and effectual change in the general management of public affairs.[21]

Artisans, some of whom were 'on the tramp', and others who formed a regular group at Battle, called a public meeting in September 1830 to petition for 'the freedom of the press' in general, and to protest at the current prosecution of Levi Cohen, the proprietor of the radical *Brighton Journal*, to which they collectively subscribed.[22]

II

A number of key facets of the notorious agricultural depression which subsumed Southern England for more than two decades after 1815 warrant emphasis. The full economic effects are commonly missed, and the politics are too often restricted to the interacting 'cash, corn and commerce' problem faced by Tory ministries in the 1820s. For the labourers, downward pressure on wages was relentless, reflecting the cancer of under- and unemployment, and symbolised by the contemporary coinage of the expression 'surplus hands'. Parish followed parish in devising employment schemes; public authorities intervened on an unprecedented scale, and if a high percentage of farmworkers were subjected to this intrusion, none were more so than young, unmarried men, thousands of whom ended up in parish employ subject to penny-pinching, dictatorial vestries.

The depression also struck rural artisans and tradesmen, notably shoemakers and retailers, whose economic problems turned on the increasingly impecunious condition of the labourers.[23] Others were hit because farmers economised by the delayed or non-repair of implements and buildings, and through the postponement of investment programmes. Payment for work which was done was delayed, and farmers combined to force craftsmen's prices down: 'I have made ... the mechanic charge lower,' stated a Wealden estate manager; and a Surrey farmer confirmed that he and the others 'reduced their prices to the blacksmith and the wheelwright and so on'.[24] A price war broke out between tradesmen in some districts, but undercutting did not suffice to prevent many artisans and tradesmen being forced to solicit poor relief. Some suffered the grave indignity of being put to work on the roads, as at Midhurst where alongside agricultural workers we encounter papermakers, bricklayers, sawyers and carpenters under the Surveyor of the Highways.[25] Moreover, fear of technology, actual and potential, was not limited to the heavy inroads on winter-time demand for farmworkers caused by the threshing machine. A crisis engulfed the paper industry with the rapid introduction of technology; in 1830 two millowners near High Wycombe threw 300 out of work when £2,000-worth of new machinery was installed. Larger and more sophisticated engineering concerns were created. The Waterloo Foundry in Hampshire made sacking and agricultural implements, and it was said that 'the foundry was ruining everyone — carpenters, and wrights, and weavers, and everybody'. The populist response from farmworkers, village and market town craftsmen was 'down with all Machinery'. Through this agrarian workers discovered an identity of interests with their industrial and metropolitan counterparts.[26]

No farmer completely escaped the depression, though the smaller men bore the full socio-economic brunt. Whatever the latters' marginality in terms of their contribution to aggregate production, they were numerically strong in several areas, notably the Weald, where a proportion combined agriculture with modest businesses — milling, shopkeeping, the craft industries.[27] Their economic viability was jeopardised; their claims that they could not find profitable work for their own families, let alone hired labour, ring true. Hundreds were 'reduced from a comparative competency to want and misery, many having to subsist on the charity of friends, and others reduced still lower', to poor relief. Some ratepayers became claimants.[28] In addition to curtailing capital projects, the larger farmers cut production costs by less intensive methods; the curtailment of hoeing to below the minimum, for example, accounts for plebeian complaints that farmers 'grew weeds'.[29] The entire farming community suffered, be they small men reduced to barter or their grander neighbours, whose profitless years were exposed by annual audits, and their pride eroded by country bankers' refusals to entertain loans. With labour and other costs pared to the bone, attempts were made to reduce, or merely contain, escalating poor relief expenditure; the inevitable struggles further ruptured rural social relationships.[30] This served to throw other major issues (rent, tithes, taxes) into sharper perspective. Farmers increasingly saw salvation only through political representations. Tithes and taxes came within the prerogative of *laissez-faire* governments, and parliamentary petitioning punctuated the 1820s. Some sectoral interests petitioned almost annually, and none more so than the hop-growers. 'Petitions', wrote a pamphleteer, were the 'most *direct evidence* of ... impoverishment'; over 60 were presented from Kent and Sussex alone in the spring of 1830.[31]

Essentially negative ministerial responses generated a 'general feeling of dissatisfaction against government ... amongst the farmers in the supposed inattention to or neglect of the petitions.'[32] Political temperatures in the countryside achieved an unparalleled intensity, and a Wealden JP remarked that 'the mischievous practice of parochial petitioning [was] ... too generally adopted for other purposes than the benefit of the Petitioners.' Farmers, and other rural inhabitants, not only took 'more interest in political questions', but concluded that major political change was vital;

farmers were no longer 'the automatic and unquestioning champions of the *status quo*'. Attempts to reconstitute the Kent Yeomanry foundered on the political hostility of the farmers whose rhetorical responses included, 'Why are not the salaries of public offices reduced? Why are not useless places set aside?' Farmers asserted that the depression's causes lay in 'corrupt representation' in Parliament. This alienation penetrated all sectors of rural societies; when farmers vociferously and publicly ascribed their inability to employ more labour to taxes, tithes and rents, plebeians were effectively encouraged to turn against 'the rich, the gentry'.[33] Rapid politicisation is variously revealed. Eastbourne labourers reasoned that 'the Government won't do anything for the poor man or they would have done it before.' The depth of rural political hostility to both government and the political system was reflected in the apparently universal circulation of posters, published by radical London printers, entitled 'Nice Pickings', which detailed the incomes of selected nobles and senior ecclesiastics, 'received from the Labour of the People'. They were flourished in Kent, for example, by Swing rioters at Benenden, and at a farmers' assembly at Tonbridge. At the latter, Lord Brecknock's feeble response that 'several' incomes were 'grossly exaggerated' failed to avert a collective refusal to serve as special constables: 'the Government had turned a deaf ear to the just and reasonable complaints of the people', who 'could not cheerfully cooperate with ... Government'.[34]

III

In this broader social, economic *and political* context, many superficially strange aspects of Swing become more comprehensible. Once the revolt assumed quasi-insurrectionary proportions, the resultant mobilisations cut across occupational and indeed class divides, and represented more than the relatively narrow socio-economic grievances of the farm labourers. Farmers, both overtly and secretively, gave Swing much more support than that exposed by the handful of greatly publicised indictments against them. When Mr Justice Alderson told Farmer Target that his encouragement of rioters left him with 'blood on his hands', the courtroom erupted with 'loud applause and clapping'. Farmers certainly sidestepped their employees' anger, and redirected it on to parsons and landlords in opportunist attempts to wrench tithe and rent reductions. Farmers in some locations, including Barcombe, seized the initiative, and conspiracies hatched in their parlours resulted in the mobilisation of their proletarian neighbours.[35] The prosecution of such men was almost impossible.[36]

Swing was partly characterised by the wholesale destruction of threshing machines. But, just as the experience, fear and hatred of technology extended beyond farmworkers, Swing's campaigns targeted technologies beyond mechanised threshing. The resultant social juxtapositions are revealed, for example, by the sawyer and bricklayer, who together with artisans, left Chichester to join farmworkers in dismantling threshing machines at Oving and Bosham.[37] The Waterloo Foundry was sacked by agricultural and town labourers, aided by urban and country craftsmen.[38] Itinerant papermakers 'on the tramp through Kent & Sussex, ... sworn foes to machinery of all kinds', would have been supported by farm labourers like Francis Slade, who 'had been down to the Paper Mill & saw children chopping rags in danger of chopping hands ... this should not be.'[39]

Many rural artisans and petty tradesmen shared the labourers' hostility to Poor Law officers, and this helps to explain the spectacular and symbolic ceremonial cartings of such figures from scores of parishes. But Swing revealed a range of issues behind the militancy of these groups. Resisting price cuts and restoring past levels was one. The men of Kintbury specified wage rates for both agricultural labourers and 'tradesmen'. The struggle over the latters' income was also apparent in Hampshire, where the beer shop attached to William Reeves' blacksmithy had 'written in chalk upon the window ... a notice, that if he dared put a shoe on a horse for less than 8d his shop and house should be pulled down.'[40] 'Brickmaker' John Gaiter joined Swing 'to rescue ourselves', as he could not 'call myself quite a master. I haven't money enough to carry on my trade'; Swing might just have proved to be the rescue-vehicle for Gaiter, and other participants like the virtually bankrupt 'jobber in pigs and cheese', James Mould of Hatch.[41] However, vested interests did not propel all members of these classes to support Swing. Many had village properties which they let — often extortionately — to labourers, who also tried to use Swing to win rent reductions.[42] Wheelwright Moses Barlow refused to join labourers 'striking for Wages ... a Tradesman like me has no business with any such concern ... I should be thought worse of in the place working for all the Farmers.'[43]

Nevertheless, such men exercised a powerful sociological influence on Swing mobilisations. William Blackstone, a 33-year-old illiterate roadworker, provides a superb insight into this mechanism when a group informed him that 'they were going to break all the threshing machines ... by order of the Government'. Challenged by an incredulous judge, Blackstone explained, 'My lord, I am no scholar .... There were several respectable tradesmen, carpenters, and others in that mob, and when they told me so I could not but believe them.'[44]

The popular, political element to Swing has been seriously underrated by most historians, including Hobsbawm and Rudé, though their identification of the significance of village artisans in this respect is acceptable. The Chairman of the Hampshire sessions reported that 'Taylors, Shoemakers etc. ... have been found ... in the Mobs many miles from their homes ... always very eloquent, they are universally politicians.' Richard Price of Ashford, Kent, shoemaker, was typical. Active in at least three disturbances (at Stockbury, 27 October; East Malling and Yalding, 3 and 11 November), he informed the gentry that

he came to enlighten the people; they had been long enough in darkness ... the poor had got a large burden on their shoulders, and they wanted to throw it off ... he had joined the poor men ... for the purpose of obtaining an advance of wages, the tithes must be lowered in order that the poor might live by their labour ... it is your dandy house, your dandy habits, and your sinecure places that have brought the country to this state.[45]

The impact of the 'Nice Pickings' posters was perhaps behind Stephen Eaves' speech made at Goudhurst, 'about the large sums which some people got out of the taxes', and the attempts in East Sussex to force tax collectors to repay the cash they had amassed to the farmers.[46] Statements that only wage increases would enable farmworkers to 'live by their Labour', found in handwritten agreements which farmers were compelled to sign, may also derive directly from such radical literature, but some of the reported speeches of Swing leaders reveal their thorough politicisation. If others were less advanced, their self-perceptions were politically inspired. James Poulter, journeyman baker and Swing leader at Wadhurst, opined, 'that to release the country, the throat of the

Duke of Wellington must be cut'; and a Berkshire counterpart carrying a red and black flag would 'be damned if I don't wish it was a revolution'. A Kent activist anticipated a sort of rolling revolution: 'We will destroy the constables and threshing machines this year, next year we will have a turn with the parsons, and the third we will make war upon the statesmen.'[47]

These manifestations of radicalism, and other opportunist attempts to politicise the Swing crisis, cannot be solely ascribed to Cobbett's celebrated, if truncated, lecture tour in Kent and Sussex in October 1830, supported by the distribution of radical literature from London. The latter also came from Southern sources, including posters printed in Brighton by Cohen, and distributed to Sussex and Surrey villages by bill-posters employed by Horsham radicals.[48] At Maidstone, Cobbett's lecture was preceded by a working-class reform meeting, and followed by another 'popular meeting' on Penenden Heath, placarded with bills demanding 'Reform in the Commons ... vote by ballot in 2 years'. The papermakers struck for the day to attend, while Swing raged in the region. A 'conceited, mischievous Village Schoolmaster' convened a reform meeting in nearby Chichester, and at Horsham the 'influential agitating Party' was behind a mass refusal to enroll as special constables; instead they 'called a Meeting ... to take into consideration their grievances & to petition for Radical Reform.' Other towns, including Lewes and Canterbury, followed suit.[49]

London radicals were surprised by Swing, but soon took an opportunist view. The Home Office, partly in response to claims that Swing was orchestrated by metropolitan democrats, ordered reports from an experienced and temperate spy deep in the counsels of activists centered on the famed Rotunda. A 'long' and private conversation between Richard Carlile and others at the end of November concentrated on

the Fires and doings in the country. Their opinion (and that is all they have to do with it) are that they are going on very well and they hope they will continue until they rouse the people in London to join them in a general resistance to Government as nothing will do any good by a Revolution, and the sooner the better.

Subsequent intelligence was consistent: prolonged disturbances, tension and rural instability would weaken provincial authorities' capacity to rule, and might eventually trigger greater protests across the nation. Metropolitan radicals anticipated that this would facilitate politicisation, intensify hostility to the government, and stampede the Whigs into a more extreme reform programme.[50]

Much of the politics of Swing are obscure. In Kent, the shoemaker Price said that 'the burnings were necessary to bring people to their senses'. Many would have agreed with Kent's Lord Lieutenant — though with only a sliver of the evidence he amassed — that arson, after the suppression of overt mobilisations, 'arises from a System of Terror recommended & executed by those who wish Revolution in England.'[51] Such perceptions are not entirely fanciful. At Carlisle, a major centre of the working-class democratic movement, a lengthy industrial dispute in textiles was followed by an arson campaign against local farmers. The spy who penetrated the militant group responsible reported that these weavers avoided 'the Union Room' when finalising plans and arranging a supply of incendiary devices.[52] At Brighton at least two attempts were made to loot the barracks to arm the masses while Swing raged in the region.[53] Charles Inskip of Battle resigned from the Metropolitan Police rather than suppress 'some disturbance respecting the King's visit to the City', and returned home; here he went 'round to the neighbouring Village Beer Shops lecturing the Paupers after Cobbett's fashion' on democratic politics and revolution. His audiences were not all strangers to the subject, as six weeks earlier Battle petitioners for press freedom had registered that 'the glorious actions' comprising the French revolution of 1830 'are to be traced to the boldness and energy of humble ... operatives'.[54] James Thomas Cooper, Swing leader at Fordingbridge, Hampshire, had been employed locally for a mere six weeks. He did nothing to contradict his own followers' claims that he was Henry Hunt, but told them 'they had come 20 miles above London, and were going as far down the country as was any machinery to destroy it'. Cooper blandly told an interrogating magistrate that 'he had constantly attended the Rotunda' when in London.[55] Another regular attender at the Rotunda, the shoemaker Clark, also made a visit to a Swing epicentre, Tonbridge in Kent, about the same time.[56] None of this proves the existence, let alone the participation, of a centrally-directed, militant or physical force fraternity. It does suggest that political motivation — some of it adopting quasi-terrorist strategy — manifested itself during Swing. And this selection of evidence lends support to

Charlesworth's conclusions, based on comparative spatial analyses of Swing and earlier rural revolts, that the development of radical nuclei in many villages underlay the Swing explosion.[57]

Four other major points demand a brief mention. First, Grey's government could not afford to expose the politics of Swing. Grey needed the *committed and active* support of the new king to fulfil the Whigs' determination to effect parliamentary reform. William IV, mindful of historic and current continental events, was paranoid about the *sans-culottes*. His support for the Whigs would have been unobtainable if he had decided that political motivation, some of it revolutionary, underpinned Swing.[58] Damage control dictated the limitation of the government's retaliation to two principal political targets: Cobbett and Carlile, for riot incitement. A Bow Street detective, sent by Peel at the request of the Bench to investigate a 'conspiracy' among Horsham radicals to effect 'revolutionary objects, & for the excitement of the Riots', was withdrawn by Melbourne, much to the chagrin of Sir Charles Burrell MP. Burrell's protests were brushed aside by the new Home Secretary who also endorsed Burrell's final demand for professional help with the interrogation of an activist thought to be wavering under pressure, 'Nil'.[59]

Secondly, another major contemporary interpretation was also in the making through utilitarian opponents of the Poor Law. Nassau Senior immediately ascribed Swing to maladministration of the social security system in his *Three Lectures on the State of Wages ... [and] the Causes and Remedies of the Present Disturbances*, rushed out before the end of 1830. The Whig's commitment to radical Poor Law reform could only be advanced by this interpretative stratagem, which was soon complemented by the 1834 Report, with its rigged evidence showing that Swing's 'violence ... seems to have arisen from an idea that all the privations arose from the cupidity or fraud' of Poor Law officials.[60]

Thirdly, much of our evidence of Swing emanates from the Special Commissions which tried hundreds of participants. Historians have eschewed consideration of the distortions generated by the legal process. Many magistrates confronted the initial task of establishing cases against scores of prisoners. Obdurate and fearful witnesses created severe obstacles, not least because Swing regions remained tense. But even litigiously-minded witnesses, and those activists who turned King's evidence, were more likely to identify those whom they knew as neighbours, employees and workmates. This facilitated the escape of many strangers active in Swing crowds, or their prosecution only 'on the fact of their having been with the mob'. As 'A selection for prosecution' was 'made of those most guilty', a forum was also created for the exercise of judicial prejudice. Many magistrates selected artisans whom they believed had no justification for their participation in a revolt ostensibly by labourers over wages, a strategy endorsed by the Crown's legal officers and the courts. This produced an unrepresentative proportion of defendants from the ranks of non-labourers.[61] Artisans were more likely to be politically-motivated, but this potential source of distortion was neutralised by legal procedures. Prosecutions turned on overt acts of riotous assembly, assault, machine-breaking and 'robbery', the judicial euphemism covering Swing's exactions of subsistence and pecuniary contributions from the victims. Political motivation was an unlikely defence, but if it was marshalled by the prosecution, jurymen's sympathies would have been roused by the plausible counter-claim that defendants were the 'dupes of designing men'. A judge at Reading categorically stated that 'it is not my province in this place to inquire' into shadowy evidence of attempts 'to bring about a revolution'. Defence lawyers were repeatedly rebuked for trying 'to elicit something ... favourable to the prisoners' through questions pertaining to dreadful, rural socio-economic conditions; 'strict adherence to the rules of evidence was paramount'. 'What has that got to do with it,' boomed Mr Justice Alderson at Winchester. Told that the defence wanted 'to show the cause', Alderson riposted, 'We do not come here to inquire into grievances. We come here to decide law.'[62]

Finally, the survival of transparently incomplete political intelligence reports among the Home Office papers suggests that the Whigs preserved the secretive and systematic gathering of such material by that department since the 1790s. Much was furtively filed, destroyed or left in the hands of the London police, in accordance with a policy developed in the age of the French Revolution of observation, as opposed to blanket prosecution of radicals. Posterity may thereby have been deprived of Swing's politics. One of the Metropolitan Police's early commanders, Colonel Rowan referred to 'a little book called a remembrancer containing all my State Secrets of Police Espionage etc. etc. the knowledge of which by the world at large would of course ruin me.'[63]

IV

Swing proved to be the final factor in generating the massive accretion of support for parliamentary reform in the countryside. Governments under the current constitution had failed to confront the key issues (and Swing dramatically signalled that failure) so the existing political system rapidly became the favourite scapegoat. One of Wellington's correspondents attended the Kent sessions in December 1830 where 'he did not find, even among the most decided Tories, one man in twenty who will subscribe to' the Duke's anti-Reform stance:

> A conviction has gone abroad that Reform in some shape or other must be granted, and the only question seems to be the extent to which that Reform shall be carried. Whether this proceeds from intimidation or a mistaken belief in the wisdom of the measure, it is not worth while to enquire.

'It is difficult to find a person who is not an advocate for some degree of Reform,' chorused the county press.[64]

Swing was central to the Reform Bill crisis; every stage was played out in the countryside, thereby accelerating popular politicisation. Establishment political warriors injected respectability, and almost rivalled Cobbett at Reform rallies. Lord William Lennox warned against ignoring 'the innumerable petitions of the people complaining of grievances', which he contrived to juxtapose with the 'burnings of barns and ricks', while lambasting the 'enormous pressure of the poor rates'; he finally enounced 'sinecurists' who 'consume in sloth what the industrious poor have so hardly earned'. As the crisis deepened in March 1831, rural communities vied with the towns to petition for Reform. Southern farmers, notably in Swing theatres like Ringmer and Bosham, came to the fore; many who 'seldom mixed in politics' made powerful, public statements. Farmer Godlee appreciated that 'the contest had but just commenced', and 'strongly advised the people not to relax'. The Ringmer petition insisted that only Reform could 'restore that confidence between Government and the Governed, so essential to the best interests of society.' The parliamentary dissolution in May was celebrated by a 'general illumination' in the tiniest villages, and the withdrawal at the general election of the sitting Tory MP, Sir Edward Knatchbull, 'was hailed ... as a most

glorious triumph and celebrated ... in every town and village' in
Kent. Nobody escaped these ballyhoos: 'houses decorated with
flags, laurels and evergreens, and bands ... parading the streets',
playing the current favourite 'Turn the Rogues out'.[65] The Lords'
rejection of the Bill produced a fresh crop of petitions, including
one with the uncharacteristic 'unanimous concurrence' of Battle
residents that the Lords' speedy compliance was 'absolutely necessary to the Peace and Prosperity of the British Empire'. Nor did
the countryside escape the severe tensions accompanying the final
six months of the crisis. Genuine fears were entertained that the
example of 'what transpired at Bristol and other places' would be
echoed in rural locations, including Bognor. The presence of noted
opponents galvanised nervous apprehensions; the return of the
Bishop of Winchester to his palace at Farnham provoked a 'spirit
of Mischief', in the end theatrically played out with his Lordship's
displacement of Guy Fawkes as the effigy burnt throughout
Hampshire on 5 November.[66] A seller of the unstamped at
Avington, Hampshire, Swing centre and seat of the Duke of
Buckingham and Chandos, told estate workers that 'Avington
House & Store Houses would be levelled with the ground, because
the Duke voted against the Reform Bill.' Many retrospectively
believed that 'the political excitement ... ever since the Reform
Bill was first talked of' inspired 'a great deal of evil ... disorder
and immoral state ... among the agricultural population'. From
one Sussex village it was reported that labourers employed by the
parish

> are all politicians. In one field 30 or 40 are set to work breaking
> stones; and in the midst of them on a heap of flints at meal
> times, one of the most learned of their number, may be seen
> reading aloud the *Morning Herald*, and expounding the clauses
> of the Reform Bill, in which they take great interest, to his
> fellow workmen.

The Act's final emergence was universally celebrated across the
South, and the radical presence in scores of villages denoted by the
flying of tricolours.[67] More ominously, at plebeian levels, the Act
was interpreted as a panacea for all grievances. As one long-
serving sessions chairman put it: 'the lower orders have great
expectations absurd tho' it be, of increase of wages & lowering of
prices from the Reform Bill.'[68]

Did the triumph of reform dissolve anti-government hostility which was increased by the harsh suppression of Swing? First, as was poignantly observed in Hampshire, the Special Commissions punished 'at least one member of many families'. The government arranged the legal offensive against Swing, and its belated display of leniency in the commutation of some transportation sentences was attributed to a tardy recognition that machine-breaking was not, in fact, illegal — a common misconception with Swing rioters.[69] The commutations were instantly hailed as a popular victory. In Kent, 'the Peasantry openly stated' that 'Government' had been forced to retreat. The ambiguities were exploited by 'seditious spirits' in the countryside to discredit government.[70] Secondly, this mirrored metropolitan developments, where Bronterre O'Brien immediately marshalled the Special Commissions as evidence that the Whigs were 'secret enemies of the People', prepared to 'hang ... people instead of granting them relief though they are starving'. Mercy petitions flowed from the Rotunda, and though some factions predicted failure, others argued that they must be seen to fail to enhance politicisation.[71] Provincial radicals in the South also petitioned and made political capital. A Shaftesbury petition, drafted 'by individuals who are at all times anxious to oppose "the powers that be"', attributed Swing's

> popular exitement ... [to] extreme and long-continued public sufferings, produced by erroneous legislation — by the virtual subversion of public rights — and by the annihilation of all genuine popular weight and influence in the Commons.[72]

Judicial severity *vis-à-vis* Swing thereafter became a constant radical theme,[73] implicating the Crown's ministers and judges. Justice Alderson's eulogy on technology, printed on posters and flooded across Hampshire by county grandees, was ridiculed, as 'every villager ... knows ... that the threshing machine is a curse.'[74] Finally, Swing revealed the scale of agrarian deprivation, and therefore the huge potential of rural support for the popular democratic movement: moreover, Reform had no effect on the agricultural depression.[75]

Reform also failed to terminate popular rural radicalism in its pre-Swing footholds like Brede and Sutton Scotney.[76] Rural radicalism was strengthened by the formation of Political Unions (a product of the Reform crisis) in numerous Southern towns from Chard to Chatham.[77] The Yeovil Union's primary purpose was

> To circulate political knowledge by means of pamphlets, and other publications amongst all classes of society, for the benefit of the Manufacturing and Agricultural Population, that they might know their rights and privileges as men and their duties as subjects.[78]

The ensuing movement extended out into the countryside. Brighton activists responded to an approach from 'some of the Paupers' of 'very remote agricultural' Horsted Keynes in November 1832, with a delegation to launch a branch at a public meeting. Advance propaganda announced that 'Union is Strength and Knowledge is Power':

> all persons who feel the bitter pains of having their pockets picked by the holy and emasculated tribe of Priests, Sinecurists, Pensioners, and a long and dismal list of their supporters, who have for some years past been living riotously and faring sumptuously every day, on the hard-earned pittance of the Working Classes, will attend ... and judge for themselves.[79]

Their Horsham counterparts created branches at Billingshurst and West Chiltington. At the latter, weekly meetings convened under the auspices of a radical publican 'at whose House a violent Riot was hatch'd in Novr. 1830.' By February 1833 'nearly a dozen agricultural Political Unions' functioned in 'the vicinity of Horsham' alone.[80] These bodies were partly responsible for the marked upsurge in the distribution of Cobbettite and unstamped literature across the South. Many beer shops took extremist publications, and held regular public readings.[81] Their activities rarely made the headlines, but selective dealing to force petty shopkeepers into the movement occurred in Sussex villages, and 'a few agricultural labourers at Eastbourne' launched collections 'in pence' for radical causes. The Mayfield branch held a public 'REFORM' meeting in May 1833. By these means Southerners in town and country were drawn into national movements. Brighton sent delegates to the infant National Union of the Working Classes in October 1832. The unions' facilitated lecture tours by Hetherington and other campaigners in the 'War of the

Unstamped', and also repeated petitioning over national issues like the notorious Irish Coercion Bill.[82] The evidence, notably that relating to Horsham, Lewes and Brighton, also reveals the tensions between middle- and working-class radicals after 1832, so central to the emergence of purely working-class organisations and the genesis of Chartism.[83] However, in certain rural locations, especially those numerically dominated by petty agriculturalists, the farmer–labourer alliances revealed by Swing persisted; in the Burwash 'union of the working classes', 200 'farmers and their men join hand in hand' to advance the cause of democratic ideology which 'they well know will be an equal benefit to both'. Well might the Rev. Borlee ruminate over 'the great Injury ... inflicted on the Minds of the Agricultural Labourers'.[84]

Moreover, Swing's achievements, the victory over the threshing-machine, and the less secure triumphs in prising out increased wages and Poor Law provisions, required continuous reinforcement. Incendiarism became the dominant weapon against niggardly overseers and backsliding farmers. Covert action was natural after Swing, especially where the yeomanry was re-established (the 'only good result' from the revolt).[85] Collective action was never totally suppressed. 1831 witnessed a recrudescence of machine-breaking in Kent and broader resistance to the employment of itinerant labour; Poor Law disputes produced a crop of minor mobilisations, as at Beddingham where parish employees 'struck *en masse*' for more liberal payments.[86] Trade unionist principles made some progress among the rural poor. 'Many Parishes' in the battle liaised through delegations in 1831, and convenors summoned an '*annual meeting*' near Rye in November 1831.[87] At this time, much of the spadework for agrarian unionism — of which the famed Tolpuddle case is but a part — was achieved. The formation of the Grand National Consolidated Trade Union extended to the villages, 'upwards of 150 agricultural labourers', for example, collecting rule-books at Brighton in one week in April 1834. A shiver of fear ran through the ranks of agrarian capitalists, as strikes against wage cuts flickered in the autumn. Unionist mentalities conditioned the objections to Assistant Poor Law Commissioner Hawley's attempt to promote migration to the North. 'Strictly mechanical' work was inappropriate for farmworkers, and the entire programme was a mere 'inducement ... only held out to them for the purpose of breaking up the "Unions"', by flooding the industrial labour market.[88] A parallel rise in rural politicisation was detected by many magistrates concerned that 'the poison of some popular periodical publications was instill'd into' the agrarian proletariat, promoting 'An increase of information amongst the Peasantry'. Beershop conversations towards the end of 1834 were dominated by the soon to be implemented Poor Law Amendment Act. In West Sussex 'some fellows with Placards in their hats' were encountered 'hawking about at a cheap rate the New Poor Bill'. Market perceptions of early nineteenth-century pedlars speak more tellingly of the embryonically political rural poor than do historians' notions of isolation, backwardness and ideological underdevelopment.[89]

The New Poor Law proved unique, because it brought the 'concrete significance of national policies right to the doorsteps of the working poor'.[90] Southern popular reactions were neither muted nor ephemeral.[91] The rolling implementation of the Act provoked scores of riots, led in places by politically-motivated men as at Horsham by 'the Union of the Working Classes'.[92] Staggered effectuation of the Act prevented a recurrence of Swing's intensity because the issue was never universal at any moment, and further mitigations resulted from the lack of workhouse accommodation sufficient to implement the measure fully. This complemented the Poor Law Commission's policy of gradual consummation, effected in places by utilitarian enthusiasts who enforced the Act's provisions before they became law in a calculated endeavour to soften up Poor Law claimants. Nor did legal retribution against protesters parallel Swing; although over 60 people were prosecuted in Kent and Sussex in 1835 alone, sentences did not exceed two years imprisonment.

The Act stimulated a magnificent response from rural trade unionists with the formation of the 'United Brothers'. The Union aimed to recruit and amass a fighting fund during the spring and summer of 1835, prior to a strike in the critical harvest and hopping seasons if interim negotiations with employers failed to achieve substantial wage increases. Talks, initially through the Whig MP H.B. Curteis, collapsed; Curteis emerged not as an independent arbitrator, but the leader of a lock-out which broke the Union's back in its key south−eastern strongholds by midsummer. This prevented its extension, if not echoes, across the South.[93] The riots and the lock-out were superseded by a massive outbreak of incendiarism, animal maiming, other forms of 'malicious damage', and an unprecedented crime wave. The main victims, even of sheep rustlers, were those involved with the Act, especially the new Poor Law Guardians. The full spectrum of protest led an Irish visitor in the winter of 1835-36 to say that the Weald 'was in quite as bad a state as his neighbourhood in Ireland'.[94]

These covert protests endured. Guardian John Dick of Leominster, Sussex was just one arson victim following his Board's insensitivity to the plight of unemployed young farmworkers in 1841. The intensification of the crime wave represented labourers' 'determination ... to do anything' to evade the clutches of the 'Robbery Bill'. 'Criminals thieve to live, not live to thieve,' exclaimed a radical journalist; and his opinion was endorsed even by the Act's supporters, among them the Earl of Chichester who chaired the East Sussex sessions.[95] New criminal patterns were detected, including winter-time sheep-stealing 'sessions'; 'Pilfering is on the increase'; 'strict honesty is among the lower classes ... very uncommon', but 'not one case in a hundred is discovered', and detected employees were monotonously 'let off' by employers fearful 'of throwing the whole family into the workhouse', thereby inflating the rates and exposing prosecutors to the risk of secret vengeance.[96]

These multifarious protests must not be permitted to obscure the marked politicisation directly attributable to the Act and contiguous developments. One can almost feel the emergence of a politicised plebeian nucleus at Ringmer, stemming from the indictment of four men for forcing the new relieving officer to pay cash instead of flour. 'I expect it is no use what I have to say,' exclaimed John Trigwell from the dock in response to the evidence given against him by village worthies. Trigwell's family, in common with most, had no ovens and depended on the baker. The Bench was unimpressed and 'refused to suffer an offence of this kind to pass off' unpunished.[97] On occasion, JPs' own political prejudices got the better of them — Captain Richardson, for example, lectured protesting labourers in court on the iniquities of Whiggism, Melbourne and Lord John Russell.[98] The shortcomings of the Whigs were emphasised in the powerful political component of the United Brothers' crusade, which also proved that farmworkers were not isolated. Financial support came from metropolitan and urban-based Southern trade unionists,[99] and from political societies. Farm labourers meeting at Heathfield were told that 'We are not left to our own resources we have a solicitation to join a

Consolidated Union 25 thousand strong.'[100] Speakers from 'the London, Manchester and Birmingham Unions' addressed rallies, to which 'all Brothers of the different Unions' and 'ALL AGRI-CULTURAL LABOURERS' were specifically invited, 'as the Liberties of their Wives, Children and themselves are at stake.'[101]

The United Brothers' emphasis on the social, economic and political rights of labour mirrored the key objectives of campaigns for wages by urban and industrial workers, so central to the early nineteenth-century genesis of the British labour movement. John Goodard, who composed propaganda, aimed 'to promote' farm-workers'

> best interests, in establishing the rights of industry, securing the blessings of prosperity, and ... of affording them the means of promoting general knowledge, good habits, social friendship, peace, harmony, and brotherly love amongst them ... that they may give mutual protection, consolation, and assistance to each other, in the time of oppression or need.

At present, the right to work was obliterated by self-interested employers. John Storr of Eastbourne contradicted opponents' claims that unionists 'prefer a small sum in idleness to a larger one in wages'; union members

> admitted that the man who would not work for his family deserved solitary confinement till he would work but ... they did not feel it right to be forced into union Prison houses only because Tenants chose to grow crops of weeds instead of corn ... they wish to earn their bread before they eat it & by so doing become benefactors of their country.

Goodard, who made veiled references to incendiarism in print, was even fiercer on the hustings; at Heathfield he asserted that 'Your labour is exacted by Oppression by the ... Farmers' who were 'Petty Tyrants' and 'your immediate oppressors': 'No, No, No', chorused 'the Crowd' to his rhetorical 'Englishmen will you submit to Petty Tyrants?'[102]

However, the petty tyrants of the Southern countryside were not the sole targets. Goodard continued,

> We have got Reform have your expectations been realised. ...

[The] first reformd parliament passed the poor law Bill places &
punishment assign'd you directly you become poor and you are
punished [like] a common felon who would have thought the
first reformd parliament would have passd this despotic
Measure.

The worker, Goodard insisted,

gave birth to and still alone supports this world of commerce,
that which enables the statesman to roll in his gilded chariot that
which supports the dignity of the high churchmen and invests
him with that power with which he plays such fantastic tricks, in
short, all that exalts, embellishes, and renders life delightful, are
all the blessings and enjoyments proceeding from the sweat and
pain of industry and labour.

The attack on the Anglican clergy derived from more than
religious dissent and hostility to tithes, to reflect their contribution
to anti-union pamphleteering.[103] If, in its retreat, the union was
reduced to simple pleas for the re-establishment of old Poor Law
benefits, the refusal of local branches of the state to 'hold communications with persons who are assembled illegally and for the
evident purpose of ... intimidation' in the eyes of the Battle Board
of Guardians, operated further to indict the 'aristocratic tyrants'
who dominated the machinery of government.[104] They were
responsible for the Robbery Bill; the state expressly authorised
army detachments, posses of coastguards and special constables to
shadow union rallies, and despatched Bow Street Runners —
'police spies' — to intimidate leaders and members alike. The
system was denounced at rally after rally, and in poster upon
poster.[105] The emergence of Curteis as the employers' champion
earned him, the Whig Party and the reformed House of Commons
universal execration from the rural proletariat. Within weeks of the
union's collapse, Curteis was crowing about his role at political
meetings and agricultural shows across Sussex. The transparency
of his position did not pass unnoticed. His parliamentary career
hovered on a weak constituency base; he desperately needed
farmers' votes, and opposing labour was a sure way. The farmers,
in stark contrast to their workers, now had the vote, and Curteis
acted in farmers' interests because he represented capital not
labour. Curteis was the local epitome of Whig treachery, more des-

pised than the king of the Sussex grandees, and Cobbett's principal
target over the Amendment Act, the Duke of Richmond.[106]

V

The demise of the United Brothers increased agrarian terrorism,
but the *political* struggle against the Robbery Bill went on. Key
features, especially diet, discipline and separation of families in the
workhouse, were vigorously resisted. Ultimately the Act's implementation depended on the criminal courts. The prosecution of
protesting workhouse inmates gave a platform to a courageous
crusading few to expose the repressive realities of the new system.
Two such Sussex men were Henry Stapeley and James Dunster.
Stapeley was repeatedly in court in the first two years of the Act;
although Dunster appeared only twice, he was in close contact with
Brighton radicals, and Stapeley was keenly aware of the politics of
his protests. Theirs, and scores of less celebrated local cases, were
all grist to the mill of the radical *Brighton Patriot,* founded in 1835
as 'a Political Journal, established with the view of communicating
great political truths and principles ... to fight for the *cause of the
people.*'

The *Patriot* immediately won Cobbett's praise in the last weeks
of his life and, until it collapsed in 1839, waged unremitting war
against the Poor Law Amendment Act. This, like all issues, was
firmly placed in a political context. The 'interests' of the 'people'
— 'tradesmen, farmers, mechanics, artisans, labourers' — were
'distinct' from those of the tyrannical aristocracy whose monopoly
of political power could be demolished only through manhood
suffrage. In addition to full reportage of Stapeley and others' cases,
the *Patriot* also provided a forum for literate opponents, notably
Charles Brooker, dissenting lay preacher of Alfriston, described by
Assistant Poor Law Commissioner Tufnell as a 'sort of minor
Stephens in the Eastbourne Union'.[107]

The parliamentary inquiries into the new Act in 1837-38
proved that no major revisions would be supported by Whigs or
Tories. The investigations provoked a further round of petitions
against the Act, principally from the towns. Early in 1838 Brooker
tried to channel this opposition into a repeal association. But rural
hostility to the Act among the propertied had been reduced to a
rump of 'small farmers ... a few small shopkeepers ... and a few

well-intentioned & benevolent but unreasoning people', in Tufnell's estimation. The real opposition was principally proletarian. This enabled the High Sheriff of Sussex flatly to refuse Brooker's request to launch his new association at a formal county meeting. Instead, it was launched at Alfriston, Brooker advocating mass meetings in the early summer evenings so that 'the labouring classes would attend'. The plebeian appeal also dictated penny monthly subscriptions. The *Patriot* would provide regional publicity.[108]

The dilution of the original broad social opposition to the Act in the Southern countryside, warrants a brief analysis. First, the Act decimated relief costs; secondly, it disciplined the rural workforce; their notorious insubordination evaporated with the recognition that securing steady work, albeit with an unprecedented subservience to capital, was the surest mode of avoiding the workhouse. Farmers, notably the larger, almost unanimously reported a new deference, and some even calculated the value of enhanced *per capita* productivity. John Ellman opined that 'we have made friends of our best labourers and put the others at defiance, and that is as the thing should be.'[109] His comment reveals that the Act was responsible for a fundamental new division between workers, about which more later. Thirdly, a punitive mechanism, whereby the obdurate could be disciplined by the selective issue of workhouse orders, was provided. Fourthly, and almost paradoxically, the Act achieved acceptance because it was widely evaded. Surreptitious outdoor relief to able-bodied males is well known, but evasion in the South hinged on road maintenance. The highway rate, said an Assistant Commissioner, furious at his own impotence, was by 1836 'an indirect poor Rate'. Parishes put the unemployed to road-work. The survival of this source of autonomy enhanced the disciplinary powers of parish officials, who could expose recalcitrant workers to the full horrors of 'less eligibility' by a refusal to refer them to the way-warden.[110] Finally, this form of increased control was complemented by a rapid intensification of paternalism — with a new utilitarian face — wholly in tune with the 1830s. The creation of scores of agricultural societies, under aristocratic and gentry patronage, provided considerable numbers of valuable prizes for plebeians whose life-styles extolled Victorian values. Moral restraint, thrift, cleanliness, industriousness and deference, as represented by delayed marriage,[111] savings bank deposits, spotless cottages, verdant vegetable

gardens, church attendance and extended service for one
employer, brought their rewards in cash, clothing, fuel, seed potatoes, suckling pigs and allotments, ceremoniously handed down at
annual meetings. Many of the benefits paid as a right under the old
Poor Law were now bountifully bestowed by the affluent as
rewards under the new. Prizes promoted social cohesion, 'cult-
ivated a friendly feeling between the gentry, the farmers, and the
labourers'.[112] Paternalism's close link with the operation of the
Poor Law was neatly revealed by the Ticehurst Union Agricultural
Society, patronised by local grandees, who were joined on the
management committee by all magistrates, clergymen, church-
wardens and the entire Board of Guardians.[113]

The rapid acceleration of divisions between the rural poor,
detectable before 1834-35, was intentional.[114] Handbills supporting the Act announced the aim of making the '*Honest Industrious
Labourer ... much better off* than the idle or the Drunkard'. The
latter would be penalised, the former rewarded with independence.[115] This propaganda succeeded, especially where reinforced by the carefully contrived junketings of utilitarian paternalism.[116] Competition for prizes steadily increased, with farmworkers
out-bidding each other for the best reports from clergymen and
other village worthies. Winners despised those neighbours they
knew resorted to beershops, poaching and crime, though pragmatism commonly tempered their conduct: 'The better class of
labourers ... the steady working men ... will not give you any
information or opinion for fear of incurring the displeasure of the
others.'[117] Southern magistrates were soon designating another
manifestation as 'cottage robbery' or 'plunder', namely theft from
the poor by the poor, especially 'from the industrious poor who
were compelled to leave their houses unprotected' while at work.
The press of all political persuasions endorsed the view that the
poor 'not only plunder the more opulent but actually prey upon
each other.' Some of this larceny must be attributed to vagrants
and people on the tramp seeking employment, but the massive
proportions achieved in the later 1830s was principally due to the
Act. But there is also considerable evidence that the perennially
unemployed believed that the goods of their plebeian neighbours
in secure jobs were legitimate spoil.[118]

Brooker addressed his 1838 campaign to this divided proletarian order. His tactics centred on agricultural labourers proving
their tortuous experiences. Men mounted the hustings to detail the

ravages of under- and unemployment, indebtedness, dietary deprivation, begging by parents of emaciated children, and multifarious
struggles to avoid incarceration in the 'bastilles', details publicly
authenticated by other villagers. The campaign, despite Brooker's
argument that 'partisan ... politics' be excluded, unleashed some
decidedly political reasoning. The Burwash meeting ended with
cheers for 'Fielden and the seventeen who supported' his
Commons motion for repeal, and 'three groans for those who were
against the poor'. The resultant petition referred, logically in view
of recounted experience, to 'half-filled bellies and burning hearts',
but it also asserted

> the rights of labourers who cause the earth to produce all that it
> *does* produce ... to extend to something *more* than
> POTATOES AND RAGS ... they are deprived of those rights
> by immensely enormous taxation ... as takes from the pockets
> of your petitioners full one half of their pitiful earnings to be
> lavished upon thousands of idle and profligate hangers-on of
> the State.[119]

By 1838 Poor Law repealers — like Corn Law repealers — represented a threat to agrarian capital. The inevitable injection of radical politics further alienated agriculturalists who were at long last
beginning to benefit from improved prices and reduced costs. Not
surprisingly, 'every trick and intimidation', including threatened
dismissals, were used to stop farmworkers' participation. One
official even lobbied for London detectives to infiltrate a meeting
of 'the Labouring Class' at Brede.[120]

Developments in popular political circles in the more advanced
Southern towns in the mid-1830s were also portentous. The Lewes
Bundle of Sticks Club, originally a working- and middle-class
discussion group which mobilised behind Whig parliamentary
candidates, split over the performance of post-1832 Whig governments. The fissures were seen as 'the germ of a really independent
party', and by 1837 there was a canvass to 'shake off ... Whig
manacles' if ministries offered nothing 'but workhouse bastilles ...
police spies and armed soldiers'. The club split irrevocably when
the chairman refused to discuss the Charter in October 1838. A
faction opted to ditch the 'shallow-pated middle class' and 'unite
with our fellow men to effect our political regeneration'. Parallel
realignments can be detected in many other towns, notably in

1838, with the formation of 'Radical', 'Patriotic' and 'Working Men's Associations'. The *Patriot* also denounced bourgeois indifference to proletarian predicament under the Poor Law, which it correctly identified as 'the parent of Chartism'. Southern Chartists were not, in the event, deprived of all middle-class support, but these urban developments emphasise that the impetus for Chartism in the first 1838-39 phase was principally proletarian, and came through the towns.[121]

The *Patriot* devoted the entire front page to the Charter of its publication in June,[122] but Southern Chartism's potential was not particularly striking in terms of its existing organised base. Only one town — inevitably Brighton — sent delegates to the celebrated Westminster rally in September. Those delegates admitted that Southerners looked to the rest of the country for a lead, though they also stressed the alienation induced by the Poor Law. Westminster, the massive stirrings in industrial locations, and a visit from O'Connor, stimulated Brighton radicals. Many came from the Southern countryside, and knew the problems in the villages at first hand; they appreciated the potential represented by rural poverty and the Robbery Bill.[123] In December, Brighton Chartists formed a 'visiting committee' to take the cause to the villages in general, and address the 'agricultural labourers' in particular. Identical thrusts were made into rural hinterlands by Chartists from other towns, including Lewes and Chichester, and farmworkers also poured into town after town to attend Chartist rallies. The initial response of agrarian labour to the agitation was favourable.[124]

But that response also immediately revealed the nature and scale of the problem. Events at Patcham were typical. On 10 December scores of labourers assembled to hear the Brighton delegation who hired the 'large room' at the Black Lion; in the event, the '"gentlemen" of the village' pre-emptively packed the room, and although the farmworkers heard the speeches and voted for the Charter outside in the cold, subsequent meetings ended in confusion when booked venues were cancelled at the last minute. Meanwhile the farmers agreed to increase wages and to sack employees who openly persisted in their Chartism. One farmer withdrew customary Christmas gifts of mutton to men who had signed the Charter. Identical combinations of threatened dismissals and raised wages are found wherever Chartism appeared in the countryside. Wage increases were formally recommended by the prestigious East Sussex Agricultural Society, and the gentry of Kent and Sussex set the example, backed by the Anglican clergy, who tempered a further round of anti-democratic pamphleteering with vigorous philanthropy. Although 'visiting committee' speakers told farmworkers to take higher wages 'as a right', in Dorset the seasoned campaigner Henry Vincent reasoned that 'we cannot expect men to starve for us'.[125] Intimidation of those prepared to grant permission for Chartist meetings on private premises was not confined to vulnerable publicans. In Dorset, Vincent's hustings were surrounded by mounted farmers, and at Polegate the yeomanry were called out. Some magistrates sent informers ostentatiously to record the names of people composing Chartist audiences, or to denounce the speakers.[126] Brighton-based delegates were unable to hold public meetings in dozens of villages, and resorted to clandestine collections of signatures. Funding rural speaking tours posed problems; and inexperience also took a toll. The Canterbury Radical Association comprised 'mostly working men who do not possess the confidence or the ability to undertake addressing a public meeting.'[127] The press, with the exceptions of the *Kent Herald,* the *Maidstone Gazette* (soon in trouble with its advertisers) and the about-to-fold *Patriot,* was worse than merely hostile. The *Brighton Herald* specialised in disinformation,[128] the *Sussex Agricultural Express* lied about the numbers at Chartist meetings,[129] and the *Sussex Advertiser* refused to report speeches 'As we have no wish to disseminate the principles'. Instead, it comforted itself with claims of the royalism of the '"Clodpoles" of Sussex', and ridiculed plebeian political aspirations. Vincent insisted that Lovett in London should send Chartist accounts to the *Morning Advertiser* 'for if ... not ... the Dorset rascally accounts will be copied and the press will all echo the twaddle.'[130]

Initially, only Brighton in the South sent a delegate to the Chartist Convention, but John Good had served with the visiting committee, and appreciated that the agricultural labour force constituted an even larger depressed group than the handloom weavers. Other Chartist leaders, including Hetherington, Hartwell and Vincent, had their Southern contacts, and the Convention's mailbag soon contained appeals from isolated democrats demanding the services of experienced Chartist orators to take the movement to untouched locations.[131] Such experience determined the Convention to launch its missionary tours, and three significant thrusts were made in the South in the spring of 1839. O'Brien spoke in coastal towns from Brighton to the Isle of Wight, and was then replaced, first by Marsden, and then by Richardson and Dean. Only Marsden spoke in rural locations,[132] so while these tours maximised publicity, the real spadework in the villages was left to activists from the towns or indigenous stalwarts.[133] Although the 'national' Chartist press made exaggerated capital from the tours, their effect was not clear cut. Internal conflicts were generated by Marsden's refusal to denounce 'physical force'. Opponents claimed that the whole Southern movement was created by charismatic cheats, whose real object was to 'extract money ... for their own purposes'. A platform was also provided for real socioeconomic radicalism, notably O'Brien's. His heady denunciations of agrarian capitalism in general, and autocratic 'rural despots' in particular, sent a shiver of alarm through propertied agriculturalists; on his return to Brighton in August 1839 he devoted much of a three-hour harangue to land reform: Chartism meant land nationalisation.[134]

O'Brien's denunciations of the unprincipled exploitation of labour by the 'moneymongers' extended the revolutionary threat to all capital. There could be no doubt that Chartism was an integral part of early nineteenth-century class war. This stiffened the resolve of opponents in places like Dorking, a 'complete nest of Whigs and Tories', to sack workers who supported the movement and to drive it underground, as exemplified by the six trade unionists in 'one of the strongholds of Toryism', Richmond; if there was 'no chance' of any public meeting, dogged subterranean 'agitation among the public', and covert collections of signatures from 'a part of the working class' went ahead.[135] The repressive spirit even penetrated Chartist strongholds like Brighton, where the bourgeoisie were 'dismissing servants of many years' faithful service and ejecting tenants'. Seymour, the senior justice, was concerned at local Chartist advocacy of arming, and fearful that any disturbance would be supported by hordes of railway navvies. He planned an impressive contingency plan, in which pride of place went to middle-class special constables, organised in divisions. Even at Horsham a Chartist meeting was physically routed by a mob led by the sons of local grandees, and it was admitted that the emergence of Shoreham as a Chartist stronghold was principally due to 'Newcastle Seamen' engaged in the coal trade. The 1839 spring campaigns certainly elicited rural support; a Brighton emissary to

Burwash found that 'democratic principles continue to be cherished', and the new impetus briefly encouraged the 'agricultural labourers and the working class generally' at Rottingdean to hold open as opposed to secret meetings. The Duke of Richmond feared for his Goodwood empire. But the chairman of the East Sussex sessions put his faith in 'intelligent police, watchful magistrates & a numerous resident Gentry'; in the countryside 'peace officers & respectable inhabitants ... on the look out' could contain any threat. Moreover, he insisted, unless the North actually rose, in the South 'Numbers alone are evidently against a revolutionary movement, or there would have been 10 times as many at the Chartist meetings.' From Eastbourne, Marsden reported that he had 'repeatedly rated the poor working men for their submissiveness to their superiors'. If he detected 'a feeling ... rankling in their breasts', he concluded that it still 'required to be aroused'. As Shoreham Chartists candidly acknowledged, after holding a rally for adjacent villages in the shadow of the new workhouse on Ham Common, 'from the state of the surrounding population, they can scarcely hope with success to the national holiday.'[136]

VI

If failure accompanied the first phase of Southern Chartism, it cannot be ascribed to rural isolation, or the absence of countryside agitations. The majority of villages were neither socially nor politically remote. Nor were farmworkers somehow sociologically or psychologically incapable of identifying with urban workers of their class as is occasionally claimed;[137] nor were socio-political 'cleavages' between town and country deepened by the railway, and the very slow decline in long distance road transport and the 'linkmen of the road', so central to Charlesworth's analysis of Swing.[138] The recurrent conjunctions of rural and urban proletarians in the agitations of the 1830s reveal identifications of common causes. They also exposed significant differences, none more potent than in the relative scale of population. The larger towns facilitated not just confrontations between labour and capital, but gave labour a recognised chance of success.[139] Chartism was a mass movement which turned on public mobilisations of the masses. This exposed the weakness of the movement's engines when it penetrated the countryside. The underlying menace was already blatant in the competition for work which undermined the solidarity of the agrarian proletariat. Divisions made it easier for capital to exploit labour, while cementing its own authority. This cementation took many forms. Many of the under-employed avoided the workhouse, not through crime, but by appealing to the charitable — notably the Anglican clergy; the price exacted was plebeian docility.[140] Paternalism in its refurbished, institutionalised utilitarian form, also generated class-collaboration. Indeed, paternalism in the 1830s was a mani-festation of aristocratic tyranny. Chartism could not successfully confront this naked power, for as one activist said of the agri-cultural labourers, it was 'useless to attempt to organise them openly', they were too vulnerable.[141] Religious dissent was more tolerable to the rural establishment. Chapel attendance was a rela-tively safe mode of expressing hostility to Anglican squire and parson, and some support for Dissent also came from agrarian capitalists whose major grievance was the tithe. Dissent may have irritated Anglican egos, but it was normally an opiate. The excep-tion, the isolated rising of Boughton and the Battle of Bossenden Wood, required a charismatic religious maniac in the person of the self-styled Sir William Courtenay, exploiting an exotic mixture of poverty, superstition and engineered enthusiasm. It was then interpreted as a utilitarian triumph by Assistant Poor Law Com-missioner Tufnell. Those killed and captured meant that 'The worst gang in the County has been ... thoroughly annihilated ... & I thus get rid at a blow of 40 of the worst characters in [Kent].'[142]

   Nevertheless, there were progressions in the 1830s which are obscured through concentration on the failures of Southern, agra-rian Chartism. 'Swing originated Chartism in Kent', opined *The Champion*, 'Captain Swing' was 'a predial Chartist'. The link was enhanced class-consciousness of which there were many expressions, even if pragmatism dictated a subservience which pro-hibited many from expressing themselves. Sarah Ayling was one who dared. Outraged at the reduction of her pension under the new Poor Law, she told the Duke of Richmond that Halnaker plebeians were 'Greatly disturbd abaught' the Act, 'and it is all yr Grace's doings .... People say you Oppress the Poore.' 'As soon as ... all the Scamps ... heard' that the major landowner at Northiam, Frewen Breed, 'was dead they got into the Church & rang the bells.' Another Sussex landowner reluctantly agreed that

the County Bench could not be strengthened with Anglican clergymen as they were 'so much hated'. It was suggested that 'farmers
and influential gentlemen's' deepening devotion to cricket could
heal class divides, if they played plebeian teams which would 'serve
to generate a kindly and generous feeling between master and men
which ... each party are ... a stranger to'.[143] At Burwash,
paternalist support for self-help schemes foundered as the

> labouring Men appear to be so decided in confining themselves
> to their own views, that it is much doubted whether any Plan of
> a Sick Club would succeed with them which did not originate
> from their own Class, even if patronised by the principal Gen-
> try.

Historians will never know how many beershops functioned in
the same way as Thomas Ranger's St Leonard's establishment; on
Sunday mornings, the landlord 'normally read' to a coterie of
labourers who 'cannot read themselves', and received sterling support from farmworker Bungay who 'is a scholar, and wishing to
enlighten his fellow creatures with what is going forward in the
political affairs of the world ... read the news to them.' Such
activity helps to explain the unprecedented numbers of agricultural
labourers detected by candidates at the hustings in 1837, why
workhouse masters received censor's powers over 'all Newspapers
... delivered ... for the Paupers', and why Charles Brooker, while
riding across the Sussex Downs to the inaugural meeting of the
'Polegate Universal Suffrage Association', was given 'a paper ...
signed by 58 of the male poor persons in the Hellingly Union
Workhouse requesting me ... to have their names placed in [the
Charter].' Moreover, there were certainly more semi-organised
Chartist groupings in the villages than exposed by the sources, but
occasionally revealed, for example, by the sly comment of an
insurer that there were 'several Chartists' resident at Titchfield in
May 1840 when Farmer Moreley's rick was fired. Numerous
Sussex villages petitioned against the death sentences imposed on
the leaders of the Newport rising. Southern Chartists took up
O'Brien's case for land nationalisation as early as 1840, and here
may lay one origin of the marked interest subsequently shown in
the region for the Chartist land plan. But this Chartist programme
on its own did not represent a threat to the propertied; nor was
support, of necessity, open and public.[144] Nevertheless, major

economic changes, including rural depopulation, finally endowed agrarian labour with the key strength that could come only through labour shortage. In the 1870s and 1880s agricultural trade unionism in the South did finally realise the aspirations revealed by earlier struggles, and hit back hard at last.[145]

Notes

1. E.J. Hobsbawm and G. Rudé, *Captain Swing* (1973 edn), p. 242.
2. A. Charlesworth (ed.), *An Atlas of Rural Protest in Britain 1548-1900*, (1983), p. 164.
3. A.J. Peacock, 'Village radicalism in East Anglia 1800-50' , in J.P.D. Dunbadin, *Rural Discontent in Nineteenth Century Britain* (1974); D.J.V. Jones, 'Thomas Campbell Foster and the Rural Labourer; Incendiarism in East Anglia in the 1840s', *Social History*, I (1976). J.E. Archer, 'The Wells–Charlesworth debate: A Personal Comment on Arson in Norfolk and Suffolk', *Journal of Peasant Studies*, 9, No. 4 (1982).
4. E.P. Thompson, *The Making of the English Working Class*, (1968 edn), pp. 201, 806; emphasis added.
5. E.P. Thompson, 'Rural riots', *New Society*, 13 February 1969.
6. Instead, neo-Namierite perspectives generate laughable assertions; rural 'labourers had little or no effective contact with urban radicalism', yet the Swing 'uprisings were sparked off by the news which the local radicals brought of the revolutions on the continent' in 1830. M. Brock, *The Great Reform Act* (1973), pp. 123-4.
7. J. Marlow, *The Tolpuddle Martyrs* (1971), p. 271.
8. Hobsbawm and Rudé, *op. cit.*, p. 242.
9. A. Brundage, 'The English Poor Law of 1834 and the Cohesion of Agricultural Society', *Agricultural History*, 48 (1974).
10. A. Brundage, *The Making of the New Poor Law 1832-39* (1978), Ch. V. N.C. Edsall, *The Anti-Poor Law Movement 1834-44* (Manchester, 1971), Ch. II. M.E. Rose, 'The Anti-Poor Law Agitation', in J.T. Ward (ed.), *Popular Movements c. 1830-1850* (1970), pp. 78-82.
11. Marlow, *op. cit.*, pp. 34-5, 50-1.
12. 'The agricultural labourer is the last to receive information, and he is consequently the most degraded,' thundered *The Gorgon*, 26 December 1818. They were 'always behind, not having intercourse with the rest of society,' said the *Poor Man's Guardian*, 26 July 1834.
13. Marlow, *op. cit.*, p. 30.
14. Hobsbawm and Rudé, *op. cit.*, pp. 41-3.
15. R.D. Storch, '"Please to Remember the Fifth of November": Conflict, Solidarity, and Public order in Southern England, 1815-1900', in R.D. Storch (ed.), *Popular Culture and Custom in Nineteenth-Century England* (1982), p. 71. This paragraph is based on impressions gained from an extensive miscellany of sources; only those specifically cited are included in notes 16-18.
16. Reeves Association documents, B[ritish] M[useum], Add[itional] Mss. 16920, ff. 25-6; 16921, ff. 71-2; 16922, ff. 20-1; J.G. Jones, *Sketch of a Political Tour through Rochester, Chatham, Maidstone, Gravesend* (1796), pp. 79-85; *The Times*, 16 June 1800; Joseph Bacon's seized address book (1801), P[ublic] R[ecord] O[ffice], Privy Council, 1/3526; *Maidstone Gazette*, 16 November 1830.

17. The Earl of Egremont to Peel, 19, 21 and 26 November 1830, PRO. H[ome] O[ffice], 52/10, ff. 625-30.

18. D.C. Coleman, *The British Paper Industry 1495-1860* (Oxford, 1958), pp. 264-73; J. Rule, *The Experience of Labour in Eighteenth-Century Industry* (1981), pp. 182-3, 210; A. Aspinall (ed.), *The Early English Trade Unions* (1949), pp. 36-8, 211; A. Charlesworth, *Social Protest in a Rural Society: The Spatial Diffusion of the Captain Swing Disturbances of 1830-1831*, Historical Geography Research Series, 1 (Norwich, 1979), *passim*; B[ritish] P[arliamentary] P[apers], H[ouse] of C[ommons], S[elect] C[ommittee] Rep[ort], 'Poor Law Amendment Act' (1837), vol. XVII, Q[uestion] 16183; *The Times*, 28 December 1830; *Sussex Weekly Advertiser*, 15 January 1821; *Sussex Advertiser*, 28 December 1840; *Poor Man's Guardian*, 14 November 1835; G. Rudé, *Protest and Punishment* (Oxford, 1978), p. 117.

19. C. Calhoun, *The Question of Class Struggle: Social Foundations of Popular Radicalism during the Industrial Revolution* (Oxford, 1982), pp. 108-11; R.A.E. Wells, 'Social Conflict and Protest in the English Countryside in the Early Nineteenth Century: A Rejoinder', *Journal of Peasant Studies*, 8, No. 4 (1981), pp. 516-24.

20. The 17s. collected in pence was actually used to send a man to Brighton, where pavilion officials were 'obliged ... to call in ... the police to get rid of ... his importunities'; *The Times*, 25 December 1830, 3 January 1831; Hobsbawm and Rudé, *op. cit.*, pp. 88-9, 185-6; Charlesworth, *loc. cit.*, pp. 34-5.

21. *Kent Herald*, 18 November 1830. Activists at Brede, like their Hampshire counterparts, were caught up in Swing. For one member's account, see the confession of Joseph Bryant, 19 November 1830, PRO. HO. 52/10, ff. 422-3.

22. *Sussex Advertiser*, 13 and 20 September 1830.

23. Constable Winkworth, shoemaker of Sutton Scotney, wanted to prise wage increases from farmers, 'for otherwise he should not be able to get paid for the shoes which he had made' for the labourers, *The Times*, 25 December 1830.

24. The manager explained that 'if the wheelwright has little to do I have said, "you may make a waggon and if I can agree with you when it is made I will do so." I have offered him a price when he has made it, and if he has not taken that I have not purchased it.' The screw could not have been turned tighter on craftsmen, who, having financed construction, presumably had to sell at almost any dictated price. BPP., House of Commons, Select Committee, First Report 'Agricultural Distress', 79 (1836), vol. VIII, Qs. 903-6, 914, 3084: Second Report, 465 (1836), Q. 9450.

25. *The Times*, 25 December 1830; *Maidstone Gazette*, 16 November 1830; *Sussex Weekly Advertiser*, 25 January 1822; Midhurst vestry minutes (1816-30), W[est] S[ussex] C[ounty] R[ecord] O[ffice], para. 138/12/3.

26. Coleman, *op. cit.*, pp. 195-6; *The Times*, 22 December 1830, 3 January 1831; *Herts Mercury*, 20 Nov. 1830; C. Hulse, Fordingbridge, to Melbourne, 28 November 1830, PRO. HO. 52/7, ff. 248-9.

27. The significance of smaller farmers, including part-time agriculture by petty entrepreneurs and craftsmen, is subjected to an interesting re-evaluation by Mick Reed, 'The Peasantry of Nineteenth-century England; A Neglected Class', *History Workshop Journal*, 18 (1984). My thanks to Mick Reed of the University of Sussex for much informative material on south-eastern rural history; his forthcoming D.Phil. thesis should force a major reassessment of nineteenth-century agrarian capitalism.

28. Rye petition, cited Anon., *England in 1830 being a Letter to Earl Grey* (1831), pp. 91-2; *Sussex Weekly Advertiser*, 26 March 1826.

29. Sussex labourers 'say the farmer does not ditch it, nor grub it, nor trunk it, nor mend it enough, and that makes [demand for] labour scarcer'. 1834 *Poor Law Report*, Appendix A, pp. 14-15.

30. Wells, *loc. cit.*; Reed, *op. cit.*, pp. 61-3.

31. Annon., *op. cit.*, pp. 3-4, 38-51, 81-5.

32. Draft reply by George Courthope to the P[oor' L[aw] C[ommission] questionnaire (n.d.) [1832], E[ast] SCRO., SAS Co/C/230. Cf. speech by R.M. Austen at Tunbridge, *Maidstone Gazette*, 23 November 1830; and Tunbridge Wells JPs to the Home Office, 15 November 1830, PRO.

33. J. Cannon, 'New Lamps for Old: the End of Hanoverian England', in J. Cannon (ed.), *The Whig Ascendancy* (1981), pp. 113-14; Brock, *op. cit.*, p. 123; Tufnell to the PLC, 20 January 1837, PRO. M[inistry of] H[ealth], 32/69.

34. 1834 *Poor Law Report, loc. cit.*; *Maidstone Gazette*, 23 November 1830; T.T. Hodges, Benenden, to Melbourne, 11 November 1830: posters printed, Hetherington and Harrison, PRO. HO. 52/8, ff. 171-2, 320, 333-4.

35. *The Times*, 25 December 1830; J. Bryant's confession, 19 November 1830, PRO. HO. 52/10, ff. 422-3.

36. Four Herstmonceux farmers who were prosecuted owed their court appearances to a determined cleric, outraged that he had had to '*come among my flock* with a body of Dragoons . . . such was the panic'; Rev. G. Mathews to Melbourne, 3 February 1831, PRO. HO. 52/10, ff. 670-3; *The Times*, 24 December 1830.

37. At neighbouring South Bersted, where a farmworkers' 'strike' had already forced wage increases, no machine-breaking transpired; BPP, 'Poor Law Amendment Act', *loc. cit.*, Qs. 16921-43; J.B. Freeland, Chichester, to Richmond, 24 November, 9 December 1830, with many depositions; West Sussex Epiphany 1831, Quarter Sessions Roll, WSCRO. G[oodwood] Mss. 1477a; QR/W758.

38. *The Times*, 22 December 1830, 3 January 1831.

39. Papermills, which employed the wives and children of farm labourers, had an appalling safety record; Coleman, *op. cit.*, p. 311; H. Drummond, Abbey Park, Surrey, to Peel, 17 November 1830, PRO. HO. 52/10, ff. 199-200; Deposition of J. Prior, East Hangborne, Berkshire, November 1830, PRO. T[reasury S[olicitor], 11/849.

40. Kintbury evidence, cited by Hobsbawm and Rudé, *op. cit.*, p. 108, without appreciating the significance; *The Times*, 28 December 1830.

41. *The Times*, 1 and 3 January 1831.

42. A JP endorsed wage increases, but 'As to house rent he could say nothing; they must arrange with their landlords respecting that,' *Reading Mercury*, 3 January 1831. For the house rent issue in Sussex, see brief against Framfield rioters, PRO. TS. 11/1007/4051.

43. Barlow's deposition, November 1830, PRO. TS. 11/849.

44. *The Times*, 30 December 1830.

45. R. Pollen, Winchester, to Phillipps, 26 November 1830, PRO. HO. 52/7, ff. 25-7; Hobsbawm and Rudé, *op. cit.*, pp. 77-8; Treasury Solicitor Maule, to Phillipps, 5, 7 and 8 November 1830, PRO. HO. 40/27(2), ff. 58-63; *Maidstone Gazette*, 16 November 1830.

46. *Maidstone Gazette*, 4 January 1831; J.C. Sharpe, Northiam to Peel, and statement by T.L. Hodges, 9 and 11 November 1830; H.M. Collingwood, Battle, to the Home Office, n.d. [November 1830]; Bellingham, to Melbourne, with enclosure, 4 February 1831, PRO. HO. 52/8, f. 172; 52/10, ff. 386-7, 448-52, 458.

47. Cf. James Pearson, Swing activist at Aston Tirrold, Berkshire, who said, 'we mean to tackle you farmers first and then we mean to have at the Parsons & Bishops.' Deposition of W. Parson, November 1830, PRO. TS. 11/849; Sir G. Webster to Melbourne, 12 November 1830, HO. 52/10, ff. 397-8; *Brighton Chronicle*, 6 October 1830; *Sussex Advertiser*, 22 November 1830; J.L. and B. Hammond, *The Village Labourer* (1966 edn), p. 307.

48. Levi Cohen, publisher of the radical *Brighton Journal*, also ran off posters; one recipient, the grocer Steele of Horsham, paid a character to distribute them to every village beershop between Horsham and Dorking, and also designated at least one blacksmith who would pin up a copy at his smithy; T. Charlfont, to Melbourne, with enclosures, 28 November 1830, PRO. HO. 52/10, ff. 278-85.

49. Treasury Solicitor Maule, Maidstone, to Phillipps, 1 and 2 November 1830, PRO. HO. 40/27(2), ff. 54-7. Maidstone postmaster to Sir F. Freeling, 14 October; W. Burrell to Peel, 20 and 21 November; C.M. Burrell to Phillipps, 5 and 12 December 1830, PRO. HO. 52/8, f. 333; 52/10, ff. 550-1, 553-6, 565-6, 573-6; J.B. Freeland, Chichester, to Richmond, WSCRO. G.Mss. 1477a; *Sussex Advertiser*, 15 November, 6 December 1830; *Kent Herald*, 16 December 1830.

50. 'SS' reports, 27 and 29 November 9 and n.d. [December 1830], n.d. [January], 15 March 1831, PRO. HO. 64/11, ff. 130-2, 151-2, 165-6, 189-92, 231-2.

51. *Maidstone Gazette*, 4 January 1831; Camden to Peel, 12 November; J. Pearse, to Melbourne, 5 December 1830, PRO. HO. 52/6, ff. 14-5; 52/8, ff. 248-9.

52. See the large number of depositions, including statements by the informer, November–December 1830, PRO. HO. 52/6, ff. 491, 193-5, 499-503, 518-28, 534-42.

53. These attempts were taken seriously by the army: the CO demanded reinforcements, artillery was loaded on to a customs cutter, and a strict guard mounted on the remaining arsenal: Various correspondence, November 1830, HO. PRO. 52/10, ff. 307-10, 317-20.

54. Battle, clerk to the magistrates, to Melbourne, and postmaster to Freeling, 26 and 27 November 1830, PRO. HO. 52/10, ff. 431-2, 435-5; brief against Inskipp, PRO. TS. 11/1007/4051.

55. *Hampshire Telegraph*, 29 November 1830; J. Mills, Ringwood, to Melbourne, 26 November 1830, PRO. HO. 52/7, ff. 21-3; *The Times*, 21 December 1830.

56. 'SS' report, (n.d.) [early December 1830], PRO. HO. 64/11, ff. 130-1.

57. Charlesworth, *loc. cit.*, esp. pp. 45-61; A. Charlesworth, 'Radicalism, Political Crises and the Agricultural Labourers' Protests of 1830', in A. Charlesworth (ed.), *Rural Social Change and Conflicts since 1500* (Hull, 1982), *passim*; idem., 'A Comparative Study of the Spread of the Agricultural Disturbances of 1816, 1822 and 1830', *Liverpool Papers in Human Geography*, 9 (1982), esp. pp. 26-7.

58. Hammond and Hammond, *op. cit.*, pp. 313-14; cf. P. Dunkley, *The Crisis of the Old Poor Law in England, 1795-1834* (1982), p. 106.

59. Burrell to Phillipps, 5, 8, 10, 12 and 14 December 1830, PRO. HO. 52/10, ff. 565-6, 568, 571-7.

60. Dunkley, *op. cit.*, pp. 95-8, 106-7, 109-10; S.G. and E.O.A. Checkland (eds.), *The Poor Law Report of 1834* (1974), pp. 121, 123, 408, 410.

61. *The Times*, 21 December 1830, 10 January 1831; Collingwood to Phillipps; J. Walsh, Bracknell, to Melbourne, 18 and 28 November 1830, PRO. HO. 52/6, ff. 106-8; 52/8, ff. 91-2.

62. *The Times*, 28, 29 and 30 December 1830.

63. Rowan to Richmond, 20 September 1839, WSCRO. G. Mss. 1605. For political intelligence systems developed in the 1790s, see R. Wells, *Insurrection: the British Experience 1795-1803* (Gloucester, 1983), Ch. 2.

64. A. Aspinall (ed.), *Three Early Nineteenth Century Diaries* (1952), p. xxix, note 2; *Kent Herald*, 16 December 1830.

65. Letters to Richmond from, J.B. Freeland, 6 March, 17 April, D. Barclay, Mayfield (n.d.), A. Donovan, Framfield, 20 March, and W.C. Mabbott, 20 March

1831, WSCRO. G. Mss, 634; *Sussex Advertiser*, 14 March, 11 and 25 April, 16 May 1831.

66. Letters to Richmond from, W. Noakes, Battle, 28 September, R. Roper, Chichester, 2 and 12 October, H. Radwick, and Freeland, both 11 October 1831, WSCRO. G. Mss. 636; R. Clark, Bognor, to Phillipps, 9 November, and R. Stedman, Godalming, to Melbourne, 3 November 1831, PRO. HO. 52/15, ff. 371-4.

67. R. Wright, Itchen Abbey, to Melbourne, with enclosures, 29 May 1832, PRO. HO. 52/17, ff. 126a-127; *Brighton Gazette*, 31 May, 7 June 1832; BPP., H. of C. SC. 'State of Agriculture', 464 (1837), vol. V, Q. 4957.

68. C. Wood, London, 7 July, and cf. Montague Burgoyne, Tunbridge Wells, to Richmond, 17 October 1831, WSCRO. G. Mss. 635-6.

69. A point made, for example, by petitions for mercy for the three men finally sentenced to death in Berkshire; *Reading Mercury*, 10 January 1831.

70. Letters to Melbourne from, Rev. A.R.C. Dallas, 8 January, Deal JPs, 5 and 8 August, and J. Earle, Winchester, 11 October 1831, PRO. HO. 52/13, ff. 75-6, 81-2, 132-3.

71. 'SS' reports, 29 November 1830, and (n.d.) [January 1831], PRO. HO. 64/11, ff. 132-3, 189-92.

72. Rev. B. Donne, Shaftsbury, with printed petition, to Melbourne, 16 January 1831, PRO. HO. 52/12, ff. 5-7.

73. For example, Hunt's address to 'The People of England, Scotland and Ireland' in October 1831, copy, PRO. HO. 52/10.

74. *Hertford and Ware Patriot*, n.s. xxviii and xxix (1834); cf. *Poor Man's Guardian*, 24 September 1831.

75. *Radical Reformer*, 19 November 1831.

76. Webster, and Wright, to Melbourne, 28 March 1831, and 1 July 1832, PRO. HO. 52/13, f. 13; 52/17, f. 131.

77. Known branches include: Yeovil, Chichester, Horsham, Lewes, Brighton, Sevenoaks, Canterbury and Deal.

78. The Sevenoaks organisation would 'watch closely the proceedings of the Legislature and prepare and present Petitions ... wherever the Rights, Liberties and Interests of the Middle and Working classes are invaded, or whenever they can be restored or secured.' Sevenoaks union poster, 13 September; Yeovil secretary to J. Phillips, 1 February 1832, with enclosures, PRO. HO. 52/17, f. 211; 52/19, ff. 399-405.

79. *Brighton Gazette*, 22 and 29 November 1832; Horsted Keynes Political Union poster, 20 November; letters to Melbourne from, 13 East Sussex JPs, and Mabbott, 28 and 29 November, and Mabbott to Phillipps, 12 December 1832, PRO. HO. 52/20, ff. 12-3, 21-2, 24-5.

80. *Brighton Gazette*, 28 February 1833; Rev. Barlee to Melbourne, 5 May 1833, PRO. HO. 52/23, ff. 12-13.

81. Lord Carnarvon, to Melbourne, 5 February 1831, PRO. HO. 52/13, ff. 124-5. Ellenbrough diary, 2 November 1831; Aspinall *loc. cit.*, p. 154; *Brighton Gazette*, 18 April, 5 December 1833; *Kent Herald*, 11 April 1833; I. Thomas, Willingdon, to Chadwick, 20 September 1834, PRO. MH. 12/12854; *Brighton Patriot*, 22 September 1835; T. Hall, and J. Broadwood, to Richmond, 21 February 1831, and 30 July 1835, WSCRO. G. Mss. 669, 1575.

82. *Brighton Gazette*, 11 October 1832, 28 February, 21 March 1833; *Poor Man's Guardian*, 21 April 1832 and 19 October 1833; *Kent Herald*, 23 May 1833.

83. *Brighton Gazette*, 12 September 1833; *Brighton Patriot*, 16 February 1836, 5 September 1837, 7 August 1838.

84. M. Reed, 'Social Change and Social Conflict in Nineteenth-century England; A Comment', *Journal of Peasant Studies*, 12, No. 1 (1984), p. 116;

Barlee to Melbourne, *loc. cit.*

85. Heathcote to Sir J. Awdry, 16 August 1831; F. Awdry, *Sir W. Northcote Bart. A Country Gentleman of the Nineteenth Century* (1906), p. 46.

86. Rev. Poore, Sittingbourne, to Melbourne, 4, 5 and 8 August; T. Bradley, Sittingbourne, to Camden, 6 August; J.J. Moneypenny, Hadlow, Kent, to Melbourne, with enclosures, 5 February 1831, PRO. HO. 52/13, ff. 13-4, 70-3, 78, 87-8; *Brighton Gazette*, 19 May 1831; Freeland to Richmond, 14 and 29 July 1831, WSCRO. G. Mss. 635.

87. W. Deedes, Sandling, Kent, to Camden, 4 September; Webster, 28 March, Bellingham, 27 May, and Mayor Lamb, Rye, 9 October, 7 and 9 November 1831, to Melbourne, PRO. HO. 52/13, f. 31; 52/15, ff. 15, 22-3, 31-2, 39-40; BPP., H. of C. SC. Rep. 'Agricultural Distress', 612 (1833), vol v. Q.10977.

88. Hawley to the PLC., 17 December 1834, PRO. MH. 32/38; letters to Richmond from J. Woods, Chalgrove, Freeland, 5 and 6 November, Frankland Lewis, 7 November 1834, WSCRO. G. Mss. 1477; *Brighton Gazette*, 6 November 1834; *Poor Man's Guardian*, 15 November 1834; indictments and depositions against W. Bowling, November, and Naamah Denyer, December 1834, WSCRO. QR/W775.

89. Woods to Richmond, 28 October, 1834, WSCRO. G. Mss. 1477.

90. J. Bohstedt, *Riots and Community Politics in England and Wales 1790-1810* (1983), p. 220.

91. Edsall, *loc. cit.*; Brundage, *loc. cit.*; A. Digby, *Pauper Palaces* (1978), Ch. 12, But cf. J. Lowerson, 'The Aftermath of Swing: Anti-Poor Law Movements and Rural Trades Unions in the South-east of England', in A. Charlesworth (ed.), *Rural Social Change and Conflicts since 1500* (Hull, 1982); R. Wells, 'Popular Resistance to the New Poor Law in Southern England', in M. Chase (ed.), *The Victorian Poor Law* (University of Leeds, 1985), on the latter of which much of the following two paragraphs is based.

92. Letters to Russell from Poore, 8 and 9 May, and H. Stedman, 18 December 1835, PRO. HO. 52/26, ff. 144-144A, 152-3; 52/27, ff. 193-4; *Kentish Chronicle*, 26 May and 9 June 1835; *Brighton Patriot*, 29 December 1835.

93. Agricultural labourers in villages near Warminster 'struck for Wages' immediately the Amendment Act was implemented; J. Borr to the Home Office, 20 and 22 November 1835, PRO. HO. 64/5, ff. 66, 235; cf. Chairman, Hampshire Sessions, to Russell, 10 October 1835, PRO. HO. 52/26, ff. 80-1.

94. E. Cornford, Brighton, to Russell, 12 September 1835, and Rev. T. Monins, River Union, to the PLC., 12 December 1836, PRO. HO. 64/5, ff. 3-4; 64/6, ff. 7-8; C.H. Frewen of Northiam, to Richmond, 2 November 1836, WSCRO. G. Mss. 1870.

95. *Brighton Gazette*, 28 October 1841; *Brighton Patriot*, 23 February 1836, 7 February, 1 May, 13 November 1838.

96. *Sussex Advertiser*, 21 January 1839, 13 April 1840; *Brighton Patriot*, 20 February 1838; *The Champion*, 8 September 1839; Tufnell to the PLC., 14 July 1838, PRO. MH. 32/70. BPP. H. of C. Rep. 'Poor Law Amendment Act' (1837), vol. XVII, Qs. 2820, 5013, 5408.

97. *Sussex Advertiser*, 6 July 1835.

98. Ibid., 1 June 1835.

99. Including carpenters, stone-sawyers and polishers, bricklayers, plasterers, wood-sawyers, and from a 'Labourers' Lodge'.

100. *Poor Man's Guardian*, 22 August 1835; J. Goodard, Guestling, To S. Selmes, 29 April 1835, PRO. HO. 52/26, ff. 122-6. Secret report of Heathfield meeting by J.P. Durrant, sent to W. Day JP, 25 July 1835, WSCRO. G. Mss. 1575.

101. 'United Brothers of Industry' poster, 8 May 1835, PRO. HO. 52/26, f. 168.

102. J. Goodard, *An Answer to an Address from the Rev. C. James Curate of Playden to the Labouring Classes who have become, or are invited to become Members of the Friendly Society of Agricultural Labourers*, (Battle, n.d. [1835], copy in PRO. MH. 32/38; Durrant's report, *loc. cit.*; R. Raper, Chichester, and J. Storr, Eastbourne, to Richmond, 6 and 10 May 1835, WSCRO, G. Mss. 1575.

103. Ibid.

104. Bellingham to Russell, 25 July, enclosing copy, Battle Union minutes, 24 July 1835, PRO. HO. 52/27, ff. 212-213A. Ticehurst, 24 July, and Hawley, 29 July 1835, to the PLC., PRO. MH. 12/12747.

105. Bellingham to Melbourne, 17 May 1835, PRO. HO. 52/27, ff. 113-14; *Brighton Patriot*, 2 June, 21 July 1835. Hawley to Nicholls, 19 March, 9 May 1835, PRO. MH. 32/38.

106. 'So the farmers ... with Mr. Herbert Curteis at their head ... put us down,' exclaimed the Brede leadership in a letter to the *Poor Man's Guardian*, 22 August 1835; *Brighton Patriot*, 8 December 1835.

107. *Brighton Patriot*, 1835-39, *passim*; the citations derive from the 'Prospectus' in the first issue, 24 February 1835. For the campaigns of Dunster *et. al.*, see Wells, *loc. cit.*; Tufnell to Lefevre, 21 April 1839, PRO. MH. 32/70.

108. Tufnell to the PLC., 3 December 1838, PRO. MH. 32/70; *Brighton Patriot*, 13 and 20 March, 10 and 24 April, 8 and 22 May 1838.

109. Hawley to the PLC., 16 February 1836, PRO. MH. 32/38; BPP., H. of C. SC. 2nd Report, 'Agricultural Distress', 189 (1836), vol. VIII, Q.4529; cf. BPP., H. of L. SC. Report, 'State of Agriculture', 464 (1837), vol. V, Qs. 3498, 4266-7.

110. A Thanet farmer agreed that 'the highways have been the workhouse'; Hawley to Nicholls, 18 February 1836, PRO. MH. 32/38; BPP., H. of C. SC. Report, 'Poor Law Amendment Act' (1837), vol. XVII, Qs. 700-770, 1105-10, 1889,1899; BPP., H. of C. SC., 'Agricultural Distress', 3rd Report, 465 (1836), vol. VIII, Qs. 9522-3; BPP., H. of L. SC. Report, 'State of Agriculture', 464 (1837), vol. V, Qs. 1478, 1480-1; J.V. Mosley, 'Poor Law Administration in England and Wales: with Special Reference to the Problem of Able-bodied Pauperism', (unpublished Ph.D. thesis, University of London, 1975), *passim*.

111. Hurstpierpoint bachelors became eligible for premiums upon attaining the age of 27.

112. *Sussex Advertiser*, 28 December 1835, 10 June, 12 August, 23 September 1839; *Brighton Gazette*, 9 September 1841; *Brighton Patriot*, 15 September 1835; *Hampshire Telegraph*, 29 July 1833.

113. Ticehurst vestry book, note, 5 January 1837, ESCRO. para. 492/12/1/2; *Sussex Advertiser*, 19 October 1840.

114. R.A.E. Wells, 'Social Conflict and Protest in the English Countryside in the Early Nineteenth Century: A Rejoinder', *Journal of Peasant Studies*, 8, No. 4 (1981), pp. 525-6.

115. Bill, Glynde, 18 May 1835, WSCRO. G. Mss. 1574; cf. poster reprinted in the *Brighton Patriot*, 2 June 1835.

116. The grandees lauded the presence of 'so respectable a body of labouring men', and drank toasts to individual premium winners.

117. *Sussex Advertiser*, 21 November 1836, 10 June, 23 September 1839, 19 October 1840; *Brighton Gazette*, 9 September 1841; deposition of R. Gardiner, 13 December 1836, PRO. HO. 64/6, ff. 9-14.

118. *Sussex Advertiser*, 9 May 1836; *Brighton Patriot*, 19 September, 5 December 1837, 2 January, 2 October 1838.

119. *Brighton Patriot*, 13 March, 3 and 17 April 1838.

120. *Brighton Patriot*, 17 April, 4 December 1838; *Sussex Agricultural Express*, 1 December 1838; Ticehurst, Battle, to Chadwick, 26 November, with enclosed poster, and to the PLC., 4 December 1838, PRO. MH. 12/12747.

121. *Brighton Patriot*, 15 and 22 March, 22 November 1836, 5 September, 21 and 28 November, 12 December 1837, 7 and 13 February, 30 July, 7 August, 9, 23 and 30 October, 6 November 1838; *Sussex Advertiser*, 25 April, 9 August, 12 December 1836; Freeland to Richmond, 29 March, 3 November 1839, WSCRO. G. Mss. 1601.

122. *Brighton Patriot*, 12 June 1838. The sympathetic *Kent Herald* did not provide equal coverage until 21 March 1839, saying, by way of explanation, that few in the region appreciated the radicalism of the Chartists' political position.

123. Referring to the rural population, Brighton Chartists asserted that 'The discontent of the labouring classes ... is attributable to a deep-rooted sense of their own rights as men, forced on them by this almost intolerable condition of privation and wretchedness.'

124. *Brighton Patriot*, 25 September 1838, 8 January 1839; *Kent Herald*, 24 January 1839; *Maidstone Gazette*, 22 January 1839; Letters to Lovett from, J.C. Claris, Canterbury, n.d. [1839], R. Hawes, Canterbury, 21 February, and L. Snelling, Tonbridge, 28 February 1839 B[ritish] M[useum], Add. Mss. 34245A, ff. 12, 55-6, 78; B[irmingham] R[eference] L[ibrary] L[ovett] C[ollection], vol. II, ff. 241, 250; T.M. Kemnitz, 'Chartism in Brighton', (unpublished D.Phil. thesis, University of Sussex, 1969), esp. pp. 31, 150, 174.

125. *Brighton Patriot*, 11, 18 and 25 December 1838, 8 January 1839; *Sussex Agricultural Express*, 29 December 1838, 12 January 1839; *Kent Herald*, 13 December 1838; Vincent to Lovett, 16 and n.d. November 1838; and Vincent, *An Address to the Agricultural Labourers ...*, (London, n.d. [1838]), BRL. LC. vol. II, ff. 281, 285, 291.

126. Vincent to Lovett, *loc. cit.*; *Brighton Patriot*, 8 and 15 January, 14 May 1839; J. Blackman JP., Lewes, to Richmond, 26 April 1839, WSCRO. G. Mss. 1601.

127. *Brighton Patriot*, 8 January 1839; Hawes, and Snelling, to Lovett, *loc. cit.*

128. For example, claiming that a Chartist presence in Southern towns was confined to Brighton, for which it was blacked by the Chartists; *Brighton Patriot*, 4 June 1839.

129. Cf. *Sussex Agricultural Express*, 30 March, and the *Kent Herald*, 2 April and 4 July 1839.

130. *Sussex Advertiser*, 1 and 28 April 1839; Vincent to Lovett, 16 November 1838, *loc. cit.*

131. Letters to Lovett from anon., Kingston-upon-Thames, where the Charter had 'never yet been agitated', 13 March, W. Dale, Dorking, 21 March, E. Hallwood, Croydon, and six Richmond pipemakers, both 15 April, 1839, BM. Add. Mss. 34245A, ff. 13-4, 213, 289; *Brighton Patriot*, 19 and 26 February, 4 June 1839.

132. With the exception of O'Brien's speech at Cuckfield *en route* to Brighton, where he was met by the visiting committee. There may have been further delegations, like the badly-reported visit of Hartwell and Burns to Dorking, though the Wandsworth and Clapham Working Men's Association denounced the 'seeming apathy' in an address to the labourers of Surrey; *Brighton Patriot*, 26 March, 2 and 16 April 1839.

133. Convention sub-committee minute, 23 February 1839; James Moir and William Cardo, West Country delegation, to Lovett, 14 March 1839, BM. Add. Mss. 34245A, ff. 61-2, 128-9; *Kent Herald*, 24 January, 14 February 1839; *Brighton Patriot*, 9 April 1839.

134. 'The aristocracy monopolised the possession of the land, they ... consolidated the small into large farms ... they pulled down the cottages of the poor, and so drove them into the towns ... the land belonged to the nation; that meant all the people, but as it was impossible to divide the land equally among all,

the people should determine through their representatives, who should occupy it ... decide upon the various allotments ... the rent going to the nation, and the produce to the occupier.' *Brighton Patriot*, 26 February, 26 March, 2, 9, 16 and 30 April, 21 and 28 May, 4 June 1839; BRL. LC. vol. III, f. 14; *Hampshire Telegraph*, 1 April 1839; *The Champion*, 25 August 1839.

135. Letters to Lovett from, anon., Dale, and Richmond pipemakers, *loc. cit.*; *Brighton Patriot*, 9 April 1839.

136. *Brighton Patriot*, 26 February, 30 April, 7 May, 13 August 1839; *Sussex Advertiser*, 6 and 27 May 1839; *Sussex Agricultural Express*, 4 May 1839; J. Hindes, Shoreham, to John Frost, 27 April 1839, BM. Add. Mss. 34245A, ff. 318-19; Marsden's report on Southern tour, BRL. LC. vol. III, f. 14; letters to Richmond from, the Earl of Chichester, 5 and 27 April, 1 August, Freeland, 29 March, 22 May, 10, 11, 13 and 14 August, Seymour, 13 March, 18 July, 2 August, and estate-steward Rusbridger, 9 and 17 August 1839, WSCRO. G. Mss. 1600, 1601, 1606, 1863.

137. R.B. Pugh, 'Chartism in Somerset and Wiltshire', in A. Briggs (ed.), *Chartist Studies* (1959), p. 216.

138. Charlesworth's dedication to spatial analysis surely gets the better of his normally sensitive social perceptions when he claims that 'Chartism barely touched the countryside' due to a process of isolation caused by the railways in the 1830s and 1840s. A. Charlesworth, *Social Protest in a Rural Society: the Spatial Diffusion of the Captain Swing Disturbances of 1830-1831*, Historical Geography Research Series, 1 (Norwich, 1979), p. 46.

139. If the presence of master craftsmen and those farmers whom Reed persists in dubbing peasants for their dependence on family labour, means that it is an over-simplification to see these rural confrontations as straight fights between labour and capital, that was their overall complexion, whatever the permutations revealed by Swing, and never repeated on a parallel scale.

140. The Rev. Butler of South-east Hampshire returned unprecedented 'demand upon the clergy ... for alms', and a parishioner confirmed that he 'should have been nearly starved but for charity', BPP, H. of C., SC. Report, 'Poor Law Amendment Act' (1837), vol. XVII, Qs. 5106, 5120.

141. A.F.J. Brown, *Chartism in Essex and Suffolk* (Chelmsford, 1982), pp. 50-6, 64-5.

142. Tufnell to Lefevre, 3 June 1838, PRO. MH. 32/70; *Brighton Patriot*, 5 June 1838; G. Rudé, *Protest and Punishment* (Oxford, 1978), pp. 120-2, 212-13; P.G. Rogers, *Battle in Bossenden Wood. The Strange Story of Sir William Courtenay*, (1961).

143. *The Champion*, 20 October 1839; letters to Richmond from, Ayling, 23 May 1835, and C.H. Frewen, 21 November, 7 December 1836, WSCRO. G. Mss. 1573, 1870; *Brighton Patriot*, 5 June 1838.

144. *Brighton Patriot*, 2 May, 8 August 1837; clerk, Ticehurst Union, to the PLC., 15 July 1836, PRO. MH. 12/13138; Uckfield Union minute, 19 March 1842, ESCRO. G11/1a/2; D. Campigné, Gosport, to Normanby, 4 May 1840, PRO. HO. 64/10, f. 142; *Southern Star*, 26 January, 23 February 1840; A.M. Hadfield, *The Chartist Land Company* (Newton Abbott, 1970), pp. 22-4, 35-6; J. MacAskill, 'The Chartist Land Plan', in Briggs (ed.), *op. cit.*, pp. 316-17, 319, 321.

145. F. Carlton, 'The Kent and Sussex Labourers' Union 1872-95', in A. Charlesworth (ed.), *An Atlas of Rural Protest in Britain 1548-1900* (1983), pp. 173-7.

7 COMMUNICATION, COMMUNITY AND THE STATE

David Vincent

I

Throughout the nineteenth century, the accelerating pace of change raised the question of defining and measuring progress. In 1897, at the height of the celebration of Victoria's Diamond Jubilee, an additional criterion for evaluating the success of her reign was put forward by Henniker Heaton in *The Fortnightly Review*: 'If asked for a true index of the degree of civilisation attained in a given country, I should suggest the number of letters forwarded and received by its inhabitants.'[1] It was a large claim to make on behalf of so tangential an aspect of social behaviour, but there were valid reasons why postal flows might be used as a touchstone of national achievement.

In the first instance correspondence, unlike almost every other form of cultural activity, was susceptible to precise statistical calculation. Occasional sets of figures could be obtained on the state of the book trade and newspaper industry, but it was virtually impossible to gain a detailed perspective of the production and consumption of the multifarious forms of popular literature. The periodic attempts to measure the provision of schooling were fraught with technical difficulties, and the comparison of examination results under the Revised Code was undermined by frequent redefinition of the standards. The literacy tables derived from marriage registers, which first became available in 1839, offered the prospect of charting the progress of education, but even at the time it was recognised that it was dangerous to attach too much significance to a single signature inscribed on just one occasion in an individual's lifetime. By contrast, the flow of mail displayed not just the possession but the application of literacy. A letter had to be written, by or on behalf of the correspondent, and it had to be read, by or to the recipient. Prior to 1840, the scale of the Post Office's business was the subject of fierce controversy;[2] only its profits, which were running at around 70 per cent on turnover in the 1830s, could be stated with any accuracy.[3] Once the system had been reformed, however, it became possible to compute, year by year, the employment of the skills the elementary schools were seeking to inculcate.

The figures did indeed seem worthy of celebration. In the 60 years following the reduction of the price of a letter from an average of 6d to a flat rate of a 1d, the volume of correspondence increased 30-fold, from an estimated 76 million items in 1839 to 1,977 million in 1900. Per capita deliveries of letters in England and Wales grew from an official figure of four in 1839 to eight in 1840 and thence to 32 by 1871 and 60 by 1900.[4] Few other indices offered such convincing evidence of the progress of Victorian England. In Chapter 3 of his *History of England*, Macaulay reckoned that the flow of mail in 1848 was 70 times greater than it had been at the accession of James II.[5] Year by year the returns dramatised the widening gulf between the present and the past, and between Britain and her competitors. As early as 1862, Matthew Davenport Hill was able to draw a gratifying international comparison:

Indeed it is hardly too much to say that the amount of its correspondence will measure with some approach towards accuracy the height which a people has reached in true civilisation. As when, for instance, we find that the town of Manchester equals in its number of letters the empire of all the Russias, both in Europe and in Asia, we obtain a means of estimating the relative degrees of British and Russian civilisation.[6]

Subsequently, the tables compiled by the Universal Postal Union following its creation in 1875 confirmed that in the sphere of communication, the United Kingdom led the world.[7]

The sheer volume of letters was undoubtedly impressive, but there was a more fundamental reason for associating correspondence with civilisation. Heaton enlarged upon his theme by characterising the state of England prior to the introduction of the penny post:

It need not be hastily inferred that our grandfathers were barbarians. But certainly the masses were almost as much restricted to oral communication and local commerce as their ancestors were under the Stuarts, or as the Turks are under

Abdul Hamid. The country was, generally speaking, one dead
level of isolated communes, each absorbed in its own politics
and interests, and knowing no more of other communes at a
distance than one Russian village knows of another a hundred
miles away. The gentry and professional men in the rural districts, and the citizens of the great towns, maintained sufficient
intercommunication; but while the more elevated points were
thus tinged with light, darkness reigned below.[8]

Written communication was the engine as well as the index of
progress: its promotion was the responsibility of the state, whose
existence was justified by the level of integration of its citizens.

From the outset, the extension of the post to the masses represented an attack on the traditional perception of community. The
oral transmission of information depended upon and in turn
helped to define a sense of neighbourhood. A mutual knowledge
of people and place made conversation possible, and the continual
exchange of news, opinions and gossip created a shared identity.
The occasional letter might cross the boundary of the known
world, but the correspondence was likely to be between close relatives on matters of private family interest.[9] This association of
communication with locality was now challenged by the introduction of a flat rate pre-paid charge for letters which, it was
hoped, would eliminate the dimension of distance in contact
between individuals and thus overcome the barriers which stood in
the way of the emergence of a new sense of nationhood.

The machinery of large-scale posting demanded a new level of
impersonality. If costs were not to rise in proportion to volume, the
efficiency of sorting and delivery had to be transformed. This
entailed not only organisational improvements, but the introduction of the ready-gummed envelope which had to be properly
addressed. For the letter to reach its destination with a minimum
of delay, the correspondent had to distinguish with much greater
precision between the recipient and his or her family, between the
home and the street, and the street and the village or town. Previously the letter carrier worked on the basis of personal contact;
letters were so infrequent that each addressee had to be sought
out, and once found a charge had to be made, which often
involved prolonged explanation and negotiation.[10] Now every
inhabitant was to be described in such a way that he or she could
be located by a total stranger. Much trouble was caused to the Post

Office in the early years of the new system by writers unwilling or unable to differentiate between individual and community. On one sample day in July 1843, 3,557 letters were sorted bearing only a name and 'London'.[11] Three-quarters of the 2 million returned letters in 1861 were 'owing to the letters being addressed either insufficiently or incorrectly; more than 10,000 letters having been posted without any address at all'.[12] Not until the 1880s was the Postmaster General able to report a decline in the business of the Returned Letter Office: 'attributable probably in part to the increase of education, which causes letter writers to exercise more care and accuracy in addressing letters than was formerly the case'.[13]

The 'unrestricted circulation of letters' which Rowland Hill sought to achieve in 1840 was to replace the patchwork of private communities by a network of communicating individuals. The 'religious, moral and intellectual improvement of the people' would be attained by exposing to rational intercourse the prejudices and delusions which flourished unchecked in the enclosed oral culture. The bonds of society would be strengthened partly by the spread of common values, and partly by the reinforcement given to family ties by the habit of correspondence. In the debate prior to reform, which coincided with a deepening economic and political crisis, witness after witness drew attention to the importance of encouraging 'epistolatory intercourse' within the families of the labouring poor.[14] It was partly that the difficulty of maintaining control over long distances was inhibiting husbands and sons from travelling in search of new forms of employment, and partly that such mobility of labour as had taken place was undermining the structure of domestic affection and authority which increasingly was seen as fundamental to the stability of the social order. All this could be achieved in the name of abolishing a further tax on knowledge. Despite its shortcomings, the pre-reform Post Office constituted an immensely profitable state monopoly, which produced a net income in 1839 of £1.5 million, equivalent to 50 times the government grant to elementary education.[15] The spread of schooling could now be promoted not by imposition and expense, but by stimulating demand by providing new opportunities for using the skills of literacy. 'And to the poor', wrote Rowland Hill,

it will afford the means of communication with their distant friends and relatives, from which they are at present debarred. It will give increased energy to trade; it will remove innumerable temptations to fraud; and it will be an important step in general education: the more important perhaps, because it calls on Government for no factitious aid, for nothing in the shape of encouragement, still less of compulsion; but merely for the removal of an obstacle, created by the law, to that spontaneous education which happily is extending through the country, and which, even the opponents of a national system will agree, ought to be unobstructed in its progress.[16]

It was, indeed, the quintessential Liberal reform; social advance promoted by a reduction in taxation, progress attained by releasing the creative powers of free individuals.

II

Fourteen years before the accession of Queen Victoria the most salient use by the labouring poor of this form of communication was punishable by death.[17] For a century the anonymous threatening letter had been an integral element of collective protest, and although it had ceased to be a capital offence by the time of Captain Swing, it remained a widely employed illegal weapon in the sequence of intimidation and violence.[18] At the same time, letter-writing was an inescapable practice in the emergent campaign for parliamentary reform. It is no accident that the prototype organisations of the 1790s should have chosen to describe themselves as 'Corresponding Societies'. Written communication was central to their identity and function, as it was to be in every working-class political organisation from then onwards. Nothing brought into focus more sharply the changing relationship between protest and the sense of community amongst the uneducated than the contrasting function of correspondence in the differing forms of agitation during the final years of the unreformed Post Office.

In their separate ways both the threatening letters which accompanied every major Captain Swing outbreak and the correspondence which filled the columns of the *Poor Man's Guardian,* the standard bearer of the unstamped press during the Reform Bill crisis, were a reflection of the comparatively high levels of literacy which had been achieved in the absence of state intervention. By

the time the Whig government decided to make a token contribution to the work of the church societies, two-thirds of the adult
male population could sign their name in a marriage register.[19] In
every neighbourhood and every village were to be found those who
possessed at least a basic command over the skills of written communication.[20] 'Are the operative classes in general sufficiently educated to be able to write?', Richard Cobden was asked by the 1838
Select Committee on Postage. 'Not so much educated as one could
wish,' he replied, 'but still the operatives living so much together,
and generally having families, there is usually one in the family or
connection who can write.'[21] It was not uncommon for those
unable to read or to write to seek the assistance of relatives or
neighbours when the need arose — William Lovett, the secretary
of a succession of working-class organisations from 1828 through
to Chartism, gained his first experience as a correspondent composing letters for the inhabitants of Newlyn where he spent his
childhood.[22]

It might not matter who actually penned the sentences of a
domestic letter, but when the correspondence was to be used as a
medium of protest, the identity of the author was of critical
importance. Here the concealment of the writer by the use of a
pseudonym both united and separated the different forms of agitation. The anonymity of the threatening letter was a direct consequence of the strengths and weaknesses of its author's community.
On the one hand it exploited the uncertain local intelligence of the
magistrates and landowners by the use of the collective pronoun
and the inflation of the strength of the rioters: 'so pull down your
Thrashing Maschine or els Bread or Fire without delay', ran a
letter to a Whitney farmer in November 1830, 'For we are 5 thousand men and will not be stopt.'[23] On the other it reflected the vulnerability of the individual agitator to identification and harsh
punishment.

The more selective employment of anonymity in the *Poor
Man's Guardian*, which was receiving over 50 letters a week in
1831,[24] was by contrast a consequence of the vulnerability of a
much larger community to internal division rather than outside
repression. Letters which were concerned with ideology or policy
were almost invariably signed with a pseudonym, although the
paper insisted on knowing the name of the author: 'these are times
when all good men should be known to each other'.[25] 'A Poor
Man', 'A British Slave', 'Republican', concealed their individuality

partly to generalise opinions which might not be widely shared, and partly to avoid the danger of trivialising policy disagreements by reducing argument to the level of personality. The only exceptions were the frequent communications of agreed statements from fraternal organisations, which would bear the secretary's name. Where, however, a letter was seeking to broaden support for the movement by drawing attention to hardship or repression it would be signed, and often the address would also be given. This was partly because with the much broader constituency addressed by the *Poor Man's Guardian*, the suffering of an individual might go unnoticed, thus for instance letters were carried giving accounts of the victimisation of particular newspaper vendors, and partly because it was now recognised that in the battle to win recruits for the cause of parliamentary reform and the unstamped press within the working-class community, a general injustice was more tangible and more persuasive when presented as a private drama.

The most striking distinction between the separate forms of correspondence lay in their respective use of language. The syntax, punctuation and spelling of the threatening letter were more often derived from the cadences of the local dialect than from the increasingly rigid conventions of formal literature:[26] 'So now if you acts like jintelmen it shall be all fery well,' ran a letter left after a fire on the Isle of Wight in 1830:

> But if you dont you will Shurley go to Hell and as for this litel fire Don't be alarmed it will be a damd deal wors when we Burn down your barn. So no I hope that you will stand a poor felow frend or els in a Midel of a fier you shall Stand.[27]

There was some sense of a rough epistolatory style, the occasional trace of a literary influence, and in the early decades of the nineteenth century an indication of the spread of elementary education, but in essence the letters belonged to an oral rather than a written tradition. In this they may have reflected the general approach of the non-literate to the unfamiliar task of composition. Surviving domestic letters and manuscript autobiographies show a similar tendency to adapt the rules of grammar and spelling to the sounds and rhythms of the spoken word.[28] However, in the highly-charged atmosphere of intimidation, the form took on a particular meaning. The violence done to polite standards of writing reinforced the violence threatened to polite standards of behaviour. The letters combined the force of the generalised, impersonal statement with the shock of the face-to-face verbal assault. And above all the disparity between the style of the Swing letters and those of the magistrates who communicated with the Home Office vividly conveyed the gulf between the rioters' community and that of their intended victim.

Whereas there is a possibility that some of the Swing writers may have been exaggerating the contrast in modes of expression, their contemporaries in the parliamentary reform movement were doing everything to reduce it. The language of the correspondence in the *Poor Man's Guardian* belongs essentially to the world of print rather than the world of conversation. There is no change of tone or vocabulary as the columns move between articles and letters. In this the contributors were upholding a tradition of public communication established by the London Corresponding Society which from the beginning had adopted a formal declamatory style for all its writings, whether in the form of letters, addresses or pamphlets.[29] Its central purpose was twofold. First, it dramatised the distance between the respectable and non-respectable sections of the labouring poor. Both the political movements and the early trade unions, whose rule-books consistently abjured swearing, assumed that language reflected and reinforced behaviour. Secondly, it served to emphasise that reformers and unreformed belonged to a community of rights and that in demanding a change in the structure and exercise of authority the radicals were merely insisting on the correct application of established political conventions.

The sheer volume of properly construed and, for that matter, accurately printed prose which was published in the 1830s was a tribute partly to the capacity of the ill-educated to move with ease between differing modes of expression, and partly to the increasing role played by what Samuel Bamford called the 'expert writer'.[30] Every organisation had to have its secretary, responsible for making a formal record of meetings and membership, and conducting official correspondence. The leading representative of this class was William Lovett,[31] whose career illustrated that for the growing minority of self-educated workingmen, participation in the prose community of the educated classes presented no intellectual strain. His wide reading of polite literature and his practical experience of writing in his youth — he even courted his wife by

means of 'a kind of controversial correspondence'[32] — had prepared him for the tasks which lay ahead. The examples of his
labours in the *Lovett Collection* reveal a neat, rather schoolboyish
handwriting, which contrasts with the elaborate flourish of the
government secretaries and the hasty scrawl of professional writers
such as J.S. Mill.[33] He was none the less, able to reach each
audience on its own terms, compiling fluent, rhetorical denunciations for bodies such as the London Working Men's Association
and at the same time engaging in the rituals of official communication when arranging a meeting with a Minister's secretary.[34]

Another life-long scribe was Gravener Henson, who by the time
he was called before the 1838 Select Committee on Postage could
look back on 30 years' service on behalf of a series of representative bodies in the Nottingham hosiery industry.[35] His evidence provided a detailed conspectus of the actual and potential use of
correspondence within the working class. In the first place he con-
fimed the gulf between the private and public employment of this
form of communication. Whereas his participation in organised
agitation had invariably involved a heavy burden of correspondence, the high cost of postage, together with the system of
payment on delivery,[36] severely curtailed its use for domestic purposes:

> So far as regards the working classes, I consider that it prevents
> almost all correspondence between them; for my experience in
> writing letters for them has satisfied me that they never write
> unless it is almost upon life and death, unless they can send a
> letter free of postage.[37]

He also confirmed the government's fears that where the need to
communicate was sufficiently pressing, the local community had
long been accustomed to exploiting its own resources to establish
an alternative postal system, which although inadequate and
unreliable represented a serious loss of official revenue. Any workman known to be travelling in a certain direction was liable to be
entrusted with unstamped mail, and any parcel of goods to a
distant destination was likely to contain undeclared letters.[38]

More generally, Henson dwelt upon the sense of isolation which
the absence of an effective system of communication imposed
upon a particular locality. Husbands and sons who travelled away
in search of work, daughters who went into domestic service, virtu-

ally disappeared off the face of the earth until such time as they could be physically reunited with their families. The more organised and ambitious trades societies and political bodies became, the more conscious they were of the barriers which surrounded them. In terms of the exchange of information, a vast distance still separated adjacent centres of population: 'We frequently know no more of what is going on in Leicester, and Leicester knows no more of what is going on in Nottingham, than people residing in different states.'[39]

The introduction of cheap postage would strengthen the resources of the community: families would be able to organise their affairs more effectively; knowledge of employment opportunities, news of the affairs of distant relatives, would no longer depend so heavily on the undertaking of journeys; and where mobility was necessary, the dislocation of relationships would be reduced.[40] But above all, the availability of an affordable system of sending letters would enhance the power of the collective bodies of the working class. Whilst recent improvements in the technology of communications, ranging from the press to the railway, had been exploited by radicals and trade unionists, there was a strong sense that even greater benefit had accrued to the government and the political and economic organisations of the middle class who possessed the wealth and expertise to make more effective use of the new facilities. Henson, who was primarily a trade unionist, was particularly sensitive to the shifting balance in the sphere of labour relations. Employers were displaying an increasing tendency to meet wage demands by making claims about the state of the regional, national or international market which the union representatives were unable to counter:

> I know that, even between so short a distance as Nottingham and Derby, masters make statements that are not true; that they can have their work done at prices, or have more work put in, and that wages have thus been lowered 20 or 25 per cent., which would not have been the case had there been a regular open communication between the workmen in each place.[41]

III

In relation to the hopes that had been entertained, the implementation of the penny post was a sobering failure. The preliminary parliamentary return on 12 March 1840 revealed that instead of the expected five or sixfold increase, postal flows had merely doubled.[42] In the first complete year, gross revenue fell by almost a half, and with costs rising steeply, profits fell by nearly three-quarters, costing the Treasury £1.2 million in lost income.[43] The volume of post did not reach its original target until the mid-1850s, and it was not until the mid-1870s that profits finally regained their pre-1840 level.[44]

Rowland Hill and his supporters now found themselves on the defensive, and in the ensuing *post mortem* only the vaguest arguments could be made for an increase in correspondence amongst the labouring poor, whereas striking claims could be made for the exploitation of the new service by a wide variety of businesses and commercial interests.[45] It seemed difficult to resist the verdict of a hostile pamphlet published in 1844:

> Thus, where the poor man receives, say eight letters, from his sailor-son, or his daughter in service in the capital, or in some distant town, and thus gains a shilling in the year by cheap postage, let any one consider how much is gained and saved by this Penny Postage in such houses as Loyd, Jones and Co., Baring Brothers and Co., Morrison and Co. &c. Indeed, the point is too plain for argument, that Penny Postage is a boon to the rich instead of the poor, and is a sacrifice of national revenue to swell the coffers of a class which does not require it.[46]

Not for the last time, the middle class was taking the lion's share of a flat-rate benefit designed for the underprivileged.

The one undoubted advantage of the new system lay in the precision of the statistics which could now be calculated, and when in 1863 a table was compiled showing the change since 1854 in the rate of per capita deliveries in each postal district, the consequences of reform became abundantly clear.[47] The heaviest users of the service, with more than 30 deliveries a head a year, were either middle-class resorts such as Malvern, Leamington and Brighton,[48] or large commercial and trading centres such as London, Bristol and Liverpool, whilst the towns with the lightest flows were all in the northern industrial belt — Bury, Burnley and, bottom of the table in 1854, Oldham, with just three deliveries a year to each person and one receptacle for every 23,553 inhabitants wishing to make a reply.[49] A decade later, with the Post Office's network now complete, the pecking-order remained unchanged. The principal beneficiaries of the penny post were those with money to make or money to spend.

There were a number of reasons why the bulk of the labouring population were so slow to exploit the opportunity. First, there was the gap between nominal and functional literacy. In all inspected elementary schools, before and after the Revised Code, 'writing' meant copying, not composing. Not until 1870 did composition, which in practice meant setting out a simple letter, enter the curriculum, and even then it was only encountered at the 6th Standard, which a mere 2 per cent of pupils passed each year.[50] Throughout the nineteenth century the great majority of the 'literate' working class were never taught anything more than a basic manual dexterity with the pen.

Secondly, despite the rapid expansion in population which had taken place in the first half of the nineteenth century, the northern mill towns were still too compact to require much internal communication by letter.[51] Most information could still be exchanged through conversation. Not until the urban community reached the size of Birmingham or Liverpool did it begin to generate a substantial proportion of its own mail. By 1863, 47 per cent of London's 161 million letters came from within the capital and were delivered in the inner area no less than 12 times a day.[52] In spite of the large-scale migration into the towns, most working people continued to live close enough to their original families to remain in contact through an occasional visit. There is some evidence that the fashion first for Valentines[53] and then for Christmas cards[54] extended below the middle class, but it was only when the labouring population could at last afford to travel for pleasure that they turned on a large scale to corresponding for pleasure. The floodgates were opened in 1902, when the Post Office finally permitted a message to be written on the same side of a halfpenny card as the address, leaving the other side free for a photograph of the destination of the day trip.[55] When Henniker Heaton's isolated communes began to communicate with each other, it was by way of the seaside.

Finally, although the professional political communicators like Lovett and Gravener Henson welcomed the reform, in practice it made little difference to their mode of operation. There is no doubt that the reduction in the price of postage and, which in some ways was more important, the extension of pre-payment, removed what had been the cause of considerable inconvenience. Letters could now not only be sent but received with much greater ease. In the past newspapers and organisations had frequently been forced to adopt a policy of refusing all incoming mail unless the postage had already been paid.[56] In 1839 the first Chartist Convention found itself in the embarrassing position of having to send back large and desperately needed contributions to the national petition because it could not afford the bills of £3 and £4 which accompanied them.[57] However, there were limits to the use which could be made of the new facilities.

In spite of the national character of Chartism, its institutional form, as had been the case with every movement since the London Corresponding Society, was essentially local in character. In the 1790s, correspondence had been used only to connect largely autonomous organisations. The elaborate structure of classes ensured that the bulk of the political communication could take place on a face-to-face basis.[58] The LCS was held together by oral rather than written ties, and the same was true of the branches of the National Charter Association. Under the Seditious Meetings Act 1817, it was still illegal for societies, their members or officers to correspond with each other. Hence even greater emphasis was placed on the newspaper as an agent of integration.[59] Whereas in the outbreaks of rural unrest the letter was subordinated to physical intimidation, in the more sophisticated forms of radicalism correspondence always appeared as a branch of journalism. Most of Lovett's letter-writing was either to newspapers, about newspapers or, when directed to institutions and organisations, couched in a form which would lend itself to publication. In so far as working-class politics benefited from a revolution in communication in this period, it was through the independent and initially illegal radical press, rather than the government-sponsored expansion of the Post Office. It is only amongst the nascent bureaucracies of the early federated unions, such as the Operative Society of Masons, that it is possible to see correspondence as a central component of organisation.[60] Even so there was no dramatic expansion in the use of the mail. As late as 1881 a mere 0.6 per cent of the total expenditure of the branches and the Executive Committee of the OSM[61] was going on postage. It was only in the large-scale unions towards the end of the century that organisers became virtually full-time correspondents. In 1898 the miners' leader, Edward Rymer calculated that in his career he had composed 10,000 letters, reports and communications, and engaged in a correspondence which amounted to 35,000 letters, telegrams, postcards and circulars.[62]

By marked contrast, the reform was of immediate and substantial benefit to the great middle-class organisation of the time, the Anti-Corn Law League, which had taken an active role in the campaign for the penny post, and now reaped its rewards. The League's resources and expertise enabled it to pioneer the use of the mail for mass communication with the electorate.[63] In 1844 it sent out 300,000 letters together with over 2 million 'stamped and other publications'.[64] It was only proper that Richard Cobden should write to Rowland Hill to thank him for a reform which had been 'a terrible engine for upsetting monopoly and corruption: witness our League operations, the *spawn of your penny postage*'.[65]

IV

Although the slow response was disappointing, it was still possible to argue that once educational facilities improved and the working class became more accustomed to communicating across the boundaries of its communities, the original ambitions would be realised. The real threat to the association of communication with civilisation came not from the Postmaster General's annual returns, but from the state itself. Since at least the middle of the seventeenth century, governments had been interfering with the mail to gain information on criminal or seditious activity.[66] Over the years the Post Office had developed a considerable expertise in the art of opening and re-sealing a letter without the recipient's knowledge.[67] The turmoil of the Revolutionary wars and their aftermath had caused an extension of the practice, with warrants being issued by the Home Secretary either for opening the correspondence of named individuals, such as Horne Tooke, Despard, Thistlewood, Watson and Orator Hunt, or for detaining any suspicious correspondence passing through particular post offices.[68] There was another flurry of warrants during the Reform Bill crisis, and again in 1838 and 1839 as Chartism grew in strength.[69]

By this time, all leading working-class politicians assumed as a matter of course that any letter sent by post was liable to be read by or on behalf of the Home Office. When Robert Lowery arrived in Dundee on a lecture tour in the aftermath of the 1839 Convention, he was appalled to discover that a local Chartist had just received a letter from Dr John Taylor discussing the manufacture of explosives. He insisted that the individual concerned take immediate action to prevent further damage:

> It is too bad for such a fellow to send letters about at a time when we have every reason to suppose that the Post-Office is tampered with, thus putting men's liberties in jeopardy, and I advise you instantly to write to Frost and inform him of the letter you have received from Dr. John and the danger of such letters. I would save the midnight post at once, but mind be cautious in writing about it, put in no names, Frost will understand you without that.[70]

Lowery's suspicions were well founded; both his own and John Frost's mail had been under surveillance since early August, and a warrant for opening Taylor's correspondence was issued on 21 December.[71] As the Home Secretary deliberately chose individuals with the widest range of contacts in the movement,[72] letters to or from a very large number of Chartists were at risk. The sense of mistrust was intensified by the long-standing fear of government spies, and by the fact that usually the only sign that a letter had been opened was an unexplained delay in transit[72] which, given the inefficiency of the unreformed Post Office, was a common occurrence at the best of times.

It is not surprising, therefore, that working-class politicians preferred to keep to their own channels of communication rather than take up the offer of cheap postage. The government, on the other hand, faced with a resurgence of Chartism, was eager to exploit the opportunities presented by a possible increase of correspondence amongst its opponents, and in the first three complete years of the new system, a record number of warrants were issued.[74] Most of these were for individuals suspected of fomenting domestic discontent, but in March 1844 the surveillance was extended to the letters of Joseph Mazzini who was then staying in London. Like the Chartists, Mazzini was quick to suspect that he was a victim of espionage,[75] but unlike the working-class radicals, he had influential connections in the Liberal establishment. He encouraged

William Lovett and Henry Hetherington, themselves the subjects of earlier warrants, to write him a specimen letter,[76] and when it was delivered with a tampered seal, took the evidence to the MP Thomas Duncombe, who presented a petition on his behalf to the House of Commons. The ensuing public controversy painfully exposed the tensions in the relationships between the state and the growth of communication in society.

The Home Secretary, Sir James Graham, at first refused on the grounds of national security to discuss the matter at all, and when he was subsequently forced by mounting public clamour to yield to Duncombe's demand for a Select Committee, insisted that its proceedings be held in secret. His defence was conducted behind a smokescreen of precedent. In its report, the House of Commons Committee sought to deflect attention from the recent past by dwelling at inordinate length on the more distant history of the practice.[77] Governments of every hue, from the Commonwealth onwards, were shown to have engaged in the opening of letters of suspected conspirators and criminals. The Parliamentary Liberals stood accused of hypocrisy, but the government's most telling argument concerned the consequences of its predecessor's reform of the Post Office. The ease with which disaffected elements could now communicate in private with each other presented an unacceptable threat to the country's security. The reduction in the cost of postage, together with the spread of literacy, demanded more rather than less state surveillance. If the powers of the Home Office were removed,

> every criminal and conspirator against the public peace would be publicly assured that he should enjoy secure possession of the easiest, cheapest and most unobserved channel of communication, and that the Secretary of State could not under any circumstances interfere with his correspondence.[78]

In opposition Duncombe's campaign initially aroused great indignation in the national press, whose shock at the exposure of a practice so familiar to its victims was itself revealing. 'It is clear,' wrote *The Times*, 'that however uninterrupted and undisputed this tradition may be in the Home-Office, its discovery is a surprise to the nation.'[79] Within Parliament, eloquent support was given by Macaulay in the Commons and by Denman, the Lord Chief Justice, in the Lords. The protest took the form of an appeal not to an abstract notion of human rights, but to a national tradition of liberty. 'It was disgraceful to a free country' thundered Duncombe,

> that such a system should be tolerated — it might do in Russia, ay, or even in France, or it might do in the Austrian dominions, it might do in Sardinia; but it did not suit the free air of a free country.[80]

Particular exception was taken to the attempts to conceal the fact that a letter had been opened: 'Now, is such a state of things to be tolerated in a civilised country?', asked Denman. 'He would say, without the slightest hesitation, that it ought not.'[81] The *Westminster Review* saw the deception as a 'principle of administration ... subservient of all the moral obligations of society'.[82] While Graham sought to defend civilisation from the dangers of privacy, his critics placed the sanctity of private expression at the centre of a civilised state. The essence of the conflict was whether an individual extended or qualified his realm of privacy by engaging in written communication. Macaulay was in no doubt about the matter:

> I cannot conceive how we can make out that there ought to be any difference in principle in the way in which we should treat a letter in transit, and a letter after it has been delivered ... they are both alike my property; and the exposure of my secrets is the same, and attended with the same consequences, whether from the reading of a letter which is yet to be delivered, or from the reading of a letter which has been delivered.[83]

It was a principle which overrode any short-term considerations of national security:

> So I say in the case before us, the experience of many years shows us that the benefits arising from the strict observation of the security of private life, without the exercise of arbitrary power, much more than counterbalances all the advantages to be derived from a contrary system.[84]

In the event, the Home Office weathered the storm. *The Times* accepted the Select Committee's arguments that the powers were only exercised in a national emergency, and that by implication their use would now be confined to threats from below.[85] When Duncombe produced new claims that his own mail was being opened, Graham felt confident enough to refuse to confirm or deny the allegation.[86] The only administrative reform caused by the controversy was that the Home Office prudently ceased to keep a record of the warrants that were issued. Nothing was settled — least of all the flaws which had been exposed in the equation of a growth in communication with the progress of Victorian civilisation. The attempt to replace the pattern of 'isolated communes' with the network of communicating citizens threatened on the one side the security of the state, and on the other the security of the individual. The ambiguity of the reform of 1840 was nowhere better illustrated than by the fact that Richard Cobden, for whom the penny postage was 'a terrible engine for upsetting monopoly and corruption', had his own correspondence opened by the Home Secretary by order of a warrant issued on 19 August 1842.[87]

Notes

1. J. Henniker Heaton, 'Postal and Telegraphic Progress under Queen Victoria', *The Fortnightly Review*, CCCLXVI (June 1897), p. 839.

2. On the prolonged and confused debate over the size of the Post Office's business in the 1830s, see R. and G.B. Hill, *The Life of Sir Rowland Hill and the History of the Penny Postage* (London, 1880), pp. 298-9.

3. [J.W. Croker], 'Post Office Reform', *Quarterly Review*, LXIV (1839), p. 532; B.R. Mitchell and Phyllis Deane, *Abstract of British Historical Statistics* (Cambridge, 1971), pp. 393, 396.

4. *Twenty-seventh Report of the Postmaster General on the Post Office* (London, 1881), p. 11; *Forty-seventh Report* (London, 1901), p. 25.

5. T.B. Macaulay, *History of England* (London, 1866 edn), p. 303.

6. [M.D. Hill], 'The Post Office', *Fraser's Magazine*, LXVI (September 1862), p. 319. Hill was referring to a return for 1855, published in *Fourth Report of the Postmaster General* (London, 1858), p. 17.

7. In 1900 Great Britain had the largest flow of letters and postcards, although if all items of mail were taken into account, she was overtaken by the United States in the 1890s. *Union Postale Universelle, Statistique Générale du Service Postale, Année 1890* (Berne, 1892), p. 2; *Année 1900* (Berne, 1902), p. 2.

8. Heaton, *art. cit.*, p. 839.

9. *Second Report from the Select Committee on Postage* (1838), PP. 1837-38, XX Part II, pp. 143-209.

10. Howard Robinson, *The British Post Office* (Princeton, N.J., 1948), pp. 198, 204.

11. *Report from the Select Committee on Postage* (1843), PP. 1843, VIII, p. 282.

12. *Seventh Report of the Postmaster General on The Post Office* (London, 1862), p. 12; also pp. 126, 302.

13. *Thirty-fourth Report of the Postmaster General on the Post Office* (London, 1888), pp. 4-5.

14. *Second Report from the Select Committee on Postage* (1838), pp. 41, 79-80, 105, 136, 199, 200, 213, 215-16, 222-3, 258, 399.

15. Mitchell and Deane, *loc. cit.*; E.G. West, *Education and the Industrial Revolution* (London, 1975), p. 186.

16. Rowland Hill, *Post Office Reform; its Importance and Practicability* (London, 1837), p. 67.

17. E.P. Thompson, 'The Crime of Anonymity', in Douglas Hay *et al.* (eds.), *Albion's Fatal Tree* (Harmondsworth, 1977), p. 283. After 1823, letters threatening murder or arson could still attract a sentence of transportation for life.

18. E.J. Hobsbawm and George Rudé, *Captain Swing* (Harmondsworth, 1973), pp. 73, 88, 93, 94, 103, 104, 111, 113, 116, 132, 166, 171-5; A.J. Peacock, *Bread or Blood* (London, 1965), pp. 53, 61, 64-6.

19. R.S. Schofield, 'Dimensions of Illiteracy in England 1750-1850', in Harvey J. Graff (ed.), *Literacy and Social Development in the West* (Cambridge, 1981), p. 207.

20. For the distribution of literacy within communities, see David Vincent, *Literacy and Popular Culture in England 1750-1914* (forthcoming, 1986), Ch. 2.

21. *Second Report from the Select Committee on Postage* (1838), p. 49.

22. William Lovett, *Life and Struggles of William Lovett* (London, 1967 edn), p. 17. For other workingmen gaining experience in the use of literacy by writing letters for others, see Timothy Claxton, *Hints to Mechanics* (London, 1839), p. 10; Moses Horler, *The Early Recollections of Moses Horler* (Radstock, 1900), p. 8; John Younger, *Autobiography of John Younger, Shoemaker, St Boswells* (Kelso, 1881), p. 373.

23. Hobsbawm and Rudé, *op. cit.*, p. 105.

24. *Poor Man's Guardian*, 10 December 1831, p. 208.

25. Ibid., 12 May 1832, p. 391.

26. On the codification of grammar and spelling, see Dick Leith, *A Social History of English* (London, 1983), pp. 49-57.

27. Cited in Thompson, *art. cit.*, Appendix 1, p. 315.

28. See the letters of the Mycock family (Staffordshire Moorlands farmers and labourers) 1811-31 (private possession) and the MS autobiographies of Anthony Errington ('Particulars of my Life and Transactions'), James Bowd ('The Life of a Farm Worker', *The Countryman*, vol. LI, No. 2, 1955) and Joseph Mayett. See also David Vincent, *Bread, Knowledge and Freedom* (London, 1981), p. 7.

29. Cf. the addresses of the London Corresponding Society included by Thomas Hardy in his *Memoir of Thomas Hardy* (1832), reprinted in David Vincent (ed.), *Testaments of Radicalism* (London, 1977), pp. 45-55, and the addresses of the London Working Men's Association in Lovett, *op. cit.*, pp. 76-121.

30. Samuel Bamford, *Passages in the Life of a Radical* (London, 1893 edn), p. 12.

31. The role of William Lovett as secretary is discussed in David Lodge, 'William Lovett', in Patricia Hollis (ed.), *Pressure from Without* (London, 1974), pp. 110-11.

32. Lovett, *op. cit.*, p. 27. The correspondence was largely concerned with theological differences which threatened to keep the couple apart.

33. For Mill and Lovett's handwriting, see the exchange of correspondence in July 1842 concerning Mill's offer of books to the library of the newly-formed National Association of the United Kingdom, for Promoting the Political and Social Improvement of the People, in July 1842. *Lovett Collection* (Birmingham Central Library), vol. 4, 225.

34. See, for instance, the correspondence between Lovett and the secretary of the then Home Secretary, Lord John Russell, concerning the presentation of a petition from LWMA in September 1837, reproduced in Lovett, *op. cit.*, pp.

101-2; also the correspondence between Lovett and Peel in *Lovett Collection*, vol. 4, 216f.

35. For Henson's career, see Joseph O. Baylen and Norbert J. Gossman (eds.), *Biographical Dictionary of Modern British Radicals* (Hassocks, 1979), pp. 219-21.

36. 'They have generally complained to me,' stated Henson of his neighbours, 'that it was not the paying of the postage, but they were afraid of the answer coming when they had not sufficient money to release it.' *Second Report of the Select Committee on Postage* (1838), p. 215.

37. Ibid., p. 209.

38. Ibid., pp. 207, 210, 215.

39. Ibid., p. 221.

40. Ibid., pp. 208, 213, 215, 216.

41. Ibid., p. 215. See also pp. 209, 212.

42. Hill and Hill, *op. cit.*, vol. 1, p. 395.

43. Rowland Hill, 'Results of the New Postage Arrangements', *Quarterly Journal of the Statistical Society of London* (July 1841), p. 85.

44. Robinson, *op. cit.*, p. 323; Mitchell and Deane, *op. cit.*, pp. 393, 396.

45. *Report from the Select Committee on Postage* (1843), PP. 1843, VIII, pp. 13, 15, 267, 282.

46. *The Administration of the Post Office from the Introduction of Mr. Rowland Hill's Plan of Penny Postage up to the Present Time* (London, 1844), p. 196.

47. *Tenth Report of the Postmaster General on the Post Office* (London, 1864), pp. 6-11.

48. The resort figures have to be handled with some care, as the calculations relied on the preceding census which understated the seasonal populations and thus inflated the apparent per capita flow of mail. None the less, the findings are striking; in 1863, with similar census populations, Brighton had 4.6 million deliveries, Wigan 832,000.

49. These figures, as in most aggregate returns of the nineteenth century, were for incoming mail, but comparisons later in the century with a table for outgoing mail in 1891 suggests the volume of deliveries reflects the general level of correspondence.

50. *Report of the Committee of Council on Education 1872-3* (London, 1873), pp. 6-10; *Report of the Committee of Council on Education 1880-81* (London, 1881), p. 115.

51. As late as 1861, no provincial town except Newcastle had a municipal area in excess of 6,000 acres — about 9 square miles. David Cannadine, 'Victorian Cities: How Different?', *Social History*, No. 4 (January 1977), p. 462.

52. *Tenth Report of the Postmaster General*, p. 8.

53. 'The Post Office', *Fraser's Magazine*, Vol. XLI (February 1850), p. 227; *Twelth Report of the Postmaster General on the Post Office* (London, 1866), p. 15; *Seventeenth Report* (London, 1871), p. 20; W.H. Cremer, St Valentine's Day and Valentines (London, 1871), pp. 10-13; Frank Staff, *The Valentine and its Origins* (London, 1969), pp. 25-38; Ruth Webb Lee, *A History of Valentines* (London, 1953), pp. 109-35.

54. *Twenty-fourth Annual Report of the Postmaster General on the Post Office* (London, 1878), p. 10; *Twenty-fifth Report* (London, 1879), p. 10; *Thirty-sixth Report* (London, 1890), p. 2; George Buday, *The History of the Christmas Card* (London, 1964).

55. Cards bearing views became legal in 1894, and grew in popularity until the final reform of 1902 allowed both a picture and a brief message. Norman Alliston, 'Pictorial Post-Cards', *Chamber's Journal* (October 1899), pp. 745-8; Frank Staff, *The Picture Postcard and its Origins* (London, 1966); Robinson, *op. cit.*, p. 414.

56. The problems encountered by the *Poor Man's Guardian* are discussed in

the issue of 26 May 1832, p. 407.

57. *Lovett Collection*, vol. 2, pp. 331-2.

58. For the structure and proceedings of the LCS, see Francis Place, *The Autobiography of Francis Place*, ed. Mary Thale (Cambridge, 1972), p. 131; Hardy, *op. cit.*, pp. 44-5.

59. For the organisation of the NCA, see Eileen Yeo, 'Some Practices and Problems of Chartist Democracy', in James Epstein and Dorothy Thompson (eds.), *The Chartist Experience* (London, 1982), pp. 352, 360-2, 364-5. The offence was punishable by up to seven years' transportation.

60. Operative Society of Masons, *Fortnightly Returns*, 1834-40 (Modern Records Centre, University of Warwick).

61. Operative Society of Masons, *Biennial Auditor's Report*, 1880-81.

62. Edward Allen Rymer, *The Martyrdom of the Miner or a 60 Years' Struggle for Life Dedicated to the Mines of England, 1898* (Middlesborough, 1898), p. 32.

63. Norman McCord, *The Anti-Corn Law League 1838-1946* (London, 1958), pp. 163-87.

64. Henry Ashworth, *Recollections of Richard Cobden, M.P. and The Anti-Corn Law League* (2nd edn, London, 18XX), p. 185. In one election in London alone, 40,000 tracts were posted to electors. The *Administration of the Post Office*, pp. 59-60.

65. Hill and Hill, *op. cit.*, p. 478.

66. Howard Robinson, *Britain's Post Office* (Cambridge, 1953), pp. 25, 47, 55, 91-2.

67. William Lewins, *Her Majesty's Mails* (2nd edn, London, 1865), p. 223.

68. *Report from the Select Committee on the Post Office* (1844), PP. 1844, XIV, p. 13.

69. Ibid., p. 11.

70. Robert Lowery, *Robert Lowery, Radical and Chartist*, ed. Brian Harrison and Patricia Hollis (London, 1979), p. 155.

71. F.C. Mather, *Public Order in the Age of the Chartists* (London, 1959), p. 221.

72. As the 1844 Select Committee explained: 'the object in issuing [the warrants] has been, in many cases, to ascertain the views, not of the party receiving, but of the party sending the letter' (p. 14).

73. See the debate on the subject at the 1839 Convention, at which numerous delegates complained of unexplained delays. *Lovett Collection*, vol. 2, p. 331.

74. *1844 HC Select Committee*, p. 11.

75. His suspicions were aroused when he noticed that the original postmark had been over-printed with a later one in an attempt to conceal the delay in transit. Joseph Mazzini, *Life and Writings of Joseph Mazzini* (London, 1891), vol. III, pp. 186-7.

76. Lovett, *op. cit.*, pp. 247-8.

77. See in particular the 100-page Appendix to the Commons Select Committee. The House of Lords inquiry, which was conducted at the same time, confined itself to a generalised discussion of recent practice.

78. *1844 HC Select Committee*, p. 19.

79. *The Times*, 26 June 1844, p. 6.

80. *Hansard* (1844), 3rd series, vol. LXXV, col. 899.

81. Ibid., cols. 980-1.

82. *Westminster Review*, vol. LXXXII (September 1844), p. 225.

83. *Hansard*, vol. LXVII, col. 841.

84. Ibid., cols. 842-3.

85. *The Times*, 4 August 1844, p. 4.

86. *Hansard*, vol. LXVII, cols. 690-1. Debate on 18 February 1845.

87. Mather, *op. cit.*, p. 221.

8 ARTISAN ECONOMY, ARTISAN POLITICS, ARTISAN IDEOLOGY: THE ARTISAN CONTRIBUTION TO THE NINETEENTH-CENTURY EUROPEAN LABOUR MOVEMENT

John Breuilly

I. Introduction

One field in which Gwyn Williams has made a major and pioneering contribution — notably in his book *Artisans and Sansculottes* — is the comparative history of artisans. It was his work which first stimulated my interest in the subject and which led, ultimately, to this essay. My intention here is to pull together a number of arguments about the role of small workshops in industrial development, the part played by artisans in the political labour movement, and the sorts of ideas to which these artisans were attracted. My focus is on the period 1830 to 1870 and involves comparisons between England, Germany and, to a lesser extent, France.

By artisan I mean skilled craftsmen in sectors dominated by production in small workshops. The craftsman may be the owner of such a workshop or, more often, an employee. He will have served a formal apprenticeship, or at least have had to complete a term of training before being fully accepted into the trade. 'He' will be a man. By labour movement I mean a set of organisations and related ideas which bring people together in their general capacity as workers rather than being confined to specific occupations.

There are problems with these broad terms. What is a 'small' workshop? What is 'skilled'? What is 'training'? What about craftsmen who move between small workshops and larger enterprises? But this is only intended as a broad point of departure. In any case, some things like the size of the unit of production and its technology have to be seen in terms of a continuum and in relation to other types of production units, and not simply as a separate branch of the economy. So some of the problems raised by the use of these terms will be taken up in the course of the essay.

The choice of the period 1830 to 1870 has been made for a number of reasons. The major one has to do with the development of the labour movement. In the German case, which I know best, a labour movement only begins to develop in the form of journeymen's clubs and workers' educational associations from the 1830s. Clearly, in England, one can write of a labour movement prior to the 1830s but it develops on a new scale after the Reform Act 1832. In France it is during the July Monarchy that one sees the development of labour organisations which are interested in political activity, the labour question and socialism. The establishment of the German Second Empire between 1866 and 1871 involving the emergence of independent labour parties contesting elections to a national Parliament based on universal manhood suffrage signalled a sharp change in the character of the labour movement. The Reform Act 1867 and the adaptation of the Conservative and Liberal Parties to popular politics, the formation of the Trades Union Congress and new trade union legislation passed in 1871 and 1875 also marked a change — if not so sharp — for the character of the English labour movement. The Paris Commune, and its repression in 1871, and the formation of the Third Republic with a sovereign Parliament elected by universal manhood suffrage likewise ushered in a new period in the French labour movement.

One can also make out a case in economic terms for this choice of period. It is increasingly recognised that the industrialisation of the period before 1870 (if by this is meant primarily a shift of production to large enterprises with rational divisions of relatively unskilled labour using new types of machinery powered from inanimate sources) had had only a very limited impact by 1870, even in Britain.[1] The general development of much of what we associate with industrial society — separate working-class areas in industrial townships, the numerical and economic dominance of the manufacturing sector within the whole economy, especially that based on factory production — had hardly yet taken place. Whether it ever took place in these forms outside of the imaginations of those seeking to come to terms with large-scale and unprecedented changes is another matter;[2] but certainly the period up to 1870 — apart from specific branches of production — was not dominated by such a development. As a consequence certain aspects of labour politics and labour ideology, which are often seen as 'backward' in this period, need to be reinterpreted once the assumptions about industrialisation which often underpin such perceptions are challenged.

I shall begin by setting out the problems I wish to consider. Then I shall examine the typical economic changes to which artisans were subjected. Next I shall look at how such changes could push artisans into taking up ideas and forms of action which transcended occupational boundaries. Finally, I shall consider the nature of artisan politics. In a brief essay, it will only be possible to make some general points and to illustrate these with some examples with no pretension to a detailed or exhaustive treatment.

II. The Problem

I begin with three quotations:

> let all the useful and valuable members of every trade who wish to appear respectable, unite with each other, and be in friendship with all other trades, and you will render yourselves worthy members of society, at once respectable and respected. (John Gast, 1826)[3]

> *Article 1.* The Brotherhood of Workers is intended to create a strong organisation covering workers of all occupations, an organisation based on mutuality and brotherliness in which the rights and desires of the individual shall be reconciled with the whole, and work shall be linked to pleasure.
> *Article 18.* The local association shall meet at least once a week. Its tasks are: to investigate the needs and difficulties of workers both in specific occupations and generally, and to help in these matters; to advise and to guide workers on their working and economic conditions; to promote mutuality and brotherliness amongst workers through labour exchanges and the establishment and democratic management of voluntary funds for sickness, death, invalidity and other purposes; to spread knowledge and education amongst workers by means of instruction, libraries, model workshops, etc.; and thereby to realise the purposes laid down in Article 1. (From the Statutes of the Brotherhood of German Workers, (*Arbeiterverbrüderung*) 1850).[4]

> We wish to conquer our dignity as men and our rights as citizens ... we are determined to educate ourselves, constantly to seek moral improvement, to practise union and fraternity. We are

determined to force the bourgeois and the rich to respect us and to listen to our claims. (From 'Des ouvrier, à leurs camarades', 1842)[5]

John Gast was a shipwright and leading activist in the London labour and radical movement in the first decades of the century. He participated in trade union, educational, agitational, cooperative, and many other collective ventures. These ventures took the form of occupational action, intra-occupational cooperation between artisans, and supra-occupational action which sometimes extended beyond the world of artisans. In Prothero's study centring on John Gast we have a rich and detailed view of the artisan world of London.

The Brotherhood of German Workers was the most important labour organisation established in Germany before the 1860s. It drew its membership overwhelmingly from artisans. The 'other purposes' mentioned in the statutes quoted included, in practice, the establishment of a national newspaper and producer and consumer cooperatives.

The final quotation is taken from a petition of communist workers which had been drawn up by 20 men on 6 December 1841. It was published in the artisan journal *Populaire* at the end of January 1842. By this time it had attracted some 1,150 signatures in Paris alone, and about another 500 signatures from Lyons and other places.

Against this background one can make some general points about the passages quoted and the contexts in which they occurred. First, they refer to a common set of values concerning respectability, security, and solidarity. The interlocking of these three concerns underpins artisan actions and ideas throughout this period. Second, they indicate the very great variety of associational activity. In many cases — whether within, between or beyond specific occupations — these activities were not expressed through single-purpose associations. An institutional approach to labour history which separates trade unionism, benefit societies, educational associations, cooperatives and political organisations from one another can easily overlook this essential feature of the artisan labour movement. Third, a closer look at these associations, especially when one moves beyond specific occupations, suggests that it is certain artisan trades which dominate these associations — above all, tailors, shoemakers, cabinet-makers, and skilled building workers. This is admittedly rather clearer for Germany and France than for England.

These observations suggest a number of tasks. First, it would seem useful to identify, by means of a systematic description, the similarities and differences between these artisan organisations across national boundaries. One narrow front on which this can be carried out is in relation to the labour internationalism of the period as expressed in organisations such as the Fraternal Democrats and the International Working Men's Assocation (IWMA).[6] The common values of the members of these organisations point to a common set of experiences in each of their countries. Labour internationalism of the period is not intrinsically significant — it had a very limited membership and no power — but it is interesting as one point of entry into such cross-national comparisons.

The next step beyond some comparative description of artisan associations is an investigation into the reasons artisans acted together in these ways. The obvious way to begin would be to look at the economic difficulties faced by artisans of various trades. In general terms this is not too difficult to do and the plight of various crafts is, in some respects at least, well documented. But this could leave untouched any consideration of the general significance of these difficulties. It also would remain to be established how connections and understandings across occupational boundaries could develop.

The most common way of providing such a general framework has been through the employment of the contrasting concepts of 'pre-industrial' and 'industrial' society. It is commonly recognised that craftsmen played a prominent role in the labour movement in the early phase of industrialisation. Two basic reasons are given for this, one negative and one positive. The negative reason is that these craftsmen were resisting the threat which industrialisation posed to them. Industrialisation threatened their chances of independence by undermining the viability of small units of production, and it threatened their status as skilled workers through the introduction of machinery which could use less-skilled labour. The positive reason was that these craftsmen had certain resources — organisations, traditions, literacy, etc. — which enabled them to put up a spirited and collective resistance to industrialisation. One could treat these workers sympathetically. One could argue that this early phase of the labour movement had important positive influences upon the later phases — for example, with its attachment to socialist critiques of industrial capitalism, with its emphasis upon organisation and democracy. But the sympathy is frequently tinged with a sense of regret that the battle was doomed to failure, and the sense of any continuity qualified by the view that there had to take place eventually a fundamental shift towards a labour movement based upon industrial workers who accepted the fact of industrialisation, and operated on the basis of that acceptance.[7]

For a long time the only argument of importance against this view was one which removed any sense of major discontinuity. It was argued that the 'artisans' of the early nineteenth century were largely skilled workers protecting as best they could their sectional interests, and so too were the skilled workers of the later nineteenth century. Clearly there had been some shifts in the occupational structure, in the political context within which the struggle was conducted, and in the scale of organisation which could be constructed. But these were changes of degree rather than kind. More recent work on the continuity of craft trades and controls after 1870 carries with it similar implications.[8]

I do not find either of these views satisfactory. The first neglects important continuities and is based upon dubious assumptions about the nature of pre-industrial and industrial society. The second makes too much of continuity and neglects the point that the changes in context amount to a fundamental disruption of the world in which the artisan labour movement took shape. The problem is to find another, more satisfactory, framework within which to place a study of the artisan labour movement. The first step in dealing with this problem is to question the assumption of the centrality of factory production to the economic development of the period. This assumption underlies some of the most influential interpretations of the course of the·labour movement. For example, the argument that reformist and 'Lib–Lab' politics in Britain was based upon the development and dominance of an aristocracy of labour has involved distinguishing this stratum both from an earlier class of pre-industrial craftsmen and a later class of less-skilled industrial wage-earners. In the German case the absence of such a phase in the labour movement has been attributed to the more abrupt transition from a pre-industrial era to an industrial society dominated by a relatively unskilled and concentrated labour force. The lack of such a clear trend in the French case has been related to the slow, uncertain, even 'laggard' course of French industrial development and the continued importance, therefore, of pre-industrial figures in the labour movement. From this one can go on to make the well-worn contrasts between a 'mature' industrial society in Britain (with its correspondingly 'mature' and pragmatic labour movement); a new and vigorous industrial society in Germany (with its correspondingly militant and class-conscious labour movement) and a rather backward French economy (with its correspondingly backward labour movement attracted to such notions as anarcho-syndicalism).[9]

There has been no shortage of criticisms of this approach. The general economic perspective was already placed in question by Clapham, and much of what has recently been proclaimed as if new was given fairly full recognition in his work.[10] The present de-industrialisation of Britain, the growth of advanced branches of technology which do not need to be concentrated in factories, the development of twentieth-century versions of the 'putting-out' system controlled by multinational companies on a global scale, the absolute and relative decline of the industrial wage-labour force within the total labour force well before it had constituted the best part of that labour force — all this has perhaps compelled historians to question more closely the focus upon 'industrialism'.[11] In German labour history for the period up to 1870 there has been new work emphasising continuities between the labour movement before, during and after 1848. Work on the period after 1870 has shown how artisan concerns frequently underlie the 'modern' Marxist ideology of the German Socialist Party (SPD).[12] In France, economic historians have questioned the conventional wisdom of backwardness, and labour historians again have started to go below leaders and programmes to reveal the complex continuities of actions and ideas within the labour movement.[13] In England there is a rich body of work penetrating beneath leaders and programmes, though perhaps the tendency either to finish or begin around 1850 in much of this work has meant that the problem of continuity has not been as effectively tackled as it should be.[14]

However, I think this work could benefit by being brought together into a comparative perspective. To do this requires the establishment of an explicitly general framework. This is what I shall try to provide. First, I shall develop an argument which stresses the centrality of small workshop production and craft labour in the economic development of the period. That means that the response of the artisan labour movement to economic developments was of central importance and should not be seen as backward or increasingly peripheral. Second, I shall try to show how the participation of these artisan trades in the growth and development of the period led to a crisis which stimulated organisational and ideological innovation, especially at a supra-occupational level. However, these responses varied from one case to another. Comparative history, working from the basis of an explicit general framework, should bring out differences as well as similarities in the cases it considers.

III. Economy

I shall begin by rather crudely equating the economic sector in which artisans are of central importance with small workshops producing manufactured items. Any detailed investigation could not operate for long with so crude an equation, but it is a useful starting point.

We can begin with some rather interesting statistics assembled by Wolfram Fischer for Germany.[15] In the Federal Republic of Germany (excluding West Berlin and the Saarland) in 1962 there were 700,000 small workshops employing some 3.5 million people. This was about $12\frac{1}{2}$ times the number of industrial enterprises, and the numbers employed amounted to about half those in factory employment. The average number employed by a small workshop was just over five, and these units of production accounted for about 11 per cent of GNP. By all the criteria mentioned here, craft-shop production had increased in importance between 1936 and 1962.

It is interesting to look at developments over a much longer time span, though statistics furnish only the roughest indications of what was happening. Around 1816 official Prussian calculations suggest that those engaged in small workshop manufacturing accounted for about 4 per cent of the total population. By 1843 the figure had risen to about 4.3 per cent, and by 1858 to about 6 per cent. The figure for Germany as a whole in 1895 was about 4.5 per cent. Regional investigations do suggest that the labour force of this sector did decline quantitatively between 1875 and 1890. But they also suggest that the decline was sharpest in the less industrialised and industrialising areas, and that small workshops expanded both absolutely and relatively in areas of industrial development during this period.[16] Figures suggest that there was a general upward trend in the small workshop share of the labour force after 1895, at least for a decade or so. Very generally, over the whole period 1815-1962 the labour force in small workshops and its dependants may have increased from about 15 per cent of the total population to about 25 per cent.

One must emphasise that these are very crude figures. Their meaning changes over time with alterations in census definitions, practices and precision. They measure a very arbitrary thing: the numbers of manufacturing units and the numbers employed in those units above and below certain levels. All that they suggest is that the small workshop has a significant and expanding role to play in a period when industrial capitalism was establishing itself in Germany. Expansion of numbers of units, employees and share of the labour force does not, of course, signify prosperity. The figures tell us nothing about what sorts of goods and services are produced, the occupational character, technology and divisions of labour within workshops, the relationships between owners and employees, between these workshops and other economic units, the role of credit in the operation of these workshops, or the nature and extent of the market in which the goods or services are sold. There were significant changes in all these areas so that the nature of the 'artisan' sector and its relationship with other economic sectors is quite different by the end of the period from what it was at the beginning. Those who try to use these figures to argue that there was prosperity and steady continuity within the small workshop sector are going beyond what the figures can bear. Above all, during this period there was a general shift of economic activity from the primary to the secondary and tertiary sectors which meant that craft-shop production ceased to dominate the manufacturing sector and the urban-industrial economy. Nevertheless, the figures do suggest that there is something wrong with the assumption that industrialisation involved the destruction of small workshops. Figures on skilled workers in these workshops should also give pause to those who would argue that industrialisation means the decline in such occupations in the face of the rise of an unskilled and semi-skilled class of factory workers. One can argue about the definitions of occupations and the measurement of skill, but the figures do pose a problem for those who equate industrialisation with the growth of factories using sources of power and types of machinery and techniques which reduce the significance of skilled craftsmen.

This trend in the expansion of small workshops is clearly documented for Prussia and other German states for the period 1830-70. It is a trend which exists irrespective of whether laws encouraged the free practice of trades or recognised and favoured restrictions by corporations. It is also a trend which can be demonstrated elsewhere. As has been mentioned, Clapham made the point in relation to Britain many years ago.[17] More recently, Raphael Samuel has provided a mass of detail which breathes life into the dry statistics.[18] In a different way, the point has been made for France where the dominance of an artisanal economy has long been recognised. But now French economic historians have insisted that rates of growth in the French economy are not especially slower than in neighbouring economies, so one cannot equate an artisanal economy with a slow-growth economy.[19] Clearly, much of this economic growth was concentrated in domestic industry, often located in rural areas, and that sort of development raises a set of issues quite separate from the concerns of this essay. But the rapid economic and demographic growth of cities such as Paris and Lyons was marked by a rapid expansion of small workshops. This has led some historians to argue that these cities remained 'pre-industrial' centres, and that the labour movement characteristic of these cities was in large measure 'pre-industrial'.[20] But once the image of industrial development as meaning the dominance of factory and unskilled factory worker is questioned, so is such an understanding of those cities and those workers. The same sort of point can be made for even further afield. Olga Crisp, for example, has pointed to the expansion and significance of craft-shop and domestic manufacturing in the Russian economy of the late nineteenth and early twentieth centuries, though it does appear to be domestic, 'cottage' [*kustar*] production which is of especial importance. The focus in the Russian case upon the state and the forced development of large factory production in a few centres such as St Petersburg may have led to an unbalanced account of Russian economic development.[21]

We should not be surprised by any of this. The economies of nineteenth-century Europe had a plentiful supply of labour for manufacturing purposes. This available labour force was not very well organised and did not have high expectations about wage levels. Large sections of it could be trained beyond the level of unskilled work quite easily because there were high literacy rates and no great obstacles of 'acculturation'. The craft-workshop sector was the most important institution for the provision of such training (and thus for the supply of skilled workers to larger production units) and could be expanded quite rapidly simply through the setting-up of more small workshops and the recruitment of extra workers at the lower end of the age and wage scales.[22] What needs to be explained is rather why capital should be diverted into large, fixed investments in factory buildings and advanced machinery which could not be flexibly reduced or expanded in line with levels of demand and profit.

One can identify a number of specific reasons. In some cases there were technical imperatives, such as those involved in opening up deeper mines or using chemical processes. In some cases there was a very rapid increase in demand, perhaps due to the securing of certain export markets, which could only be met quickly by means of a shift to new technology and large units of production and where anticipated profits justified investments of this kind. In some cases there might have been very specific labour supply problems (due to the scarcity of particular types of skilled labour or perhaps the organisational strength of workers with those specific skills) which would make it advantageous to invest in machines or types of production organisations that would overcome those problems. But in many cases capital was more rationally invested in the reorganisation of marketing and credit arrangements or in intensifying the use of labour and elaborating the division of labour. None of these changes necessarily reduced the quantitative role of the small workshop. Indeed, in many sectors changes of this sort boosted the role of such workshops by making them more productive. A small increase in the average size of workshops in a specific area might indicate the introduction of more fixed and elaborate divisions of labour. It might be associated with the withdrawal of the employer from a production function to a more purely management function. It might involve the production of a larger number of standardised items for a few (maybe only one) customer rather than a very heterogeneous output for a large number of customers. It may, though only from about 1900, have meant the introduction of electrical machinery. All this could involve a transformation of the nature of such a workshop and a vast increase in its productivity. The statistics on the number of workshops and employees may, therefore, underestimate the trend in output of this sector.

There are also specific reasons why there should be an increase in the number of small workshops in one sector which could balance their decline in another sector. Factories demanded certain goods and services (components, servicing and maintenance, etc.) which might best be supplied by small workshops. The decline of certain production and service functions within the household could provide growth areas for certain types of small businesses.

One can see, therefore, that small workshop production was of continued, even expanding, importance in an industrialising economy and that there are good reasons for this being so. But this is all rather general. To connect to the concerns of this essay it is necessary to outline a number of ways in which small workshops and craft workers could develop within an industrialising economy. Then one can go on to see what problems this would pose for the types of workmen concerned and how this in turn can be related to certain political and ideological responses which found their way into the labour movement.

One can broadly distinguish between five types of craft production. First, there is the range of occupations actually created — or at least transformed and expanded — by industrial growth. The engineering trades are the best example of this type. Some of these trades continued to be practised within small workshops — supplying components to larger producers using or making complex machines, for example. Sometimes the work was carried out in units, often virtually autonomous workshops, within larger units of production. These shade over into the second type of craft production, that which retains earlier skills and occupational identity but much of which is shifted into larger-scale units of production. Printing is an example here. It is not surprising that these are the trades which are often selected as examples of a labour aristocracy. Some writers see in the continuity of skills, high earnings and occupational exclusiveness indications of a continuity between artisanal and skilled trade union concerns.[23] Others see in the change produced by increased dependency on large units of production and employer control a shift from the independent position of the artisan producer to the dependent position of the skilled wage-earner.[24]

A third type of occupation is one which was destroyed by domestic industry or factory production. Textile crafts are the best example of this kind of change. These are the types of trades which are taken to illustrate the radical discontinuity between the 'pre-industrial' or 'pre-capitalist' artisan and the industrial wage-earner under capitalism. The struggles, for example, of handloom weavers can be seen as typical of the doomed fight against the imperatives of economic development.

A fourth type of trade is one which hardly changes during the period. This may be due to the type of product. An expensive luxury item such as jewellery or something embodying a large amount of personal service such as barbering do not lend themselves to displacement by machines, diffusion into domestic production or concentration into factories. Another reason may be that the market is too restricted or static to merit investment in new forms of production. Until the rise of large retailing establishments, something which occurs largely after 1870, these points apply to a large part of the labour force preparing and selling food in towns. So skilled workers in the food trades, luxury trades and personal services exhibit continuity over this period.

It is upon a fifth type of occupation that I wish to concentrate, because I consider that it is this type which is central to the artisanal labour movement. These are trades which supply basic demands of the domestic population. This means that there is a large, stable market for their products. It is possible, unlike in those food trades dealing in perishable goods, to separate production and distribution. There is some scope for de-skilling, but through more complex divisions of labour rather than through the introduction of new machinery. Examples of these trades are shoe-making, tailoring, furniture-making, and the rather special case of building.

The separation of production and distribution means that the establishment of large-scale distribution units can take place without any corresponding concentration of production into large-scale units. The continued importance of skill means that the production unit still tends to be the small workshop (or the building site) rather than the household. The limited technical innovation means that start-up costs for a small firm are not very high. The diffuse, large and fairly fixed market for bulky, site-produced or inexpensive products is largely impenetrable to foreign competition. So one should not expect either a sharp contraction brought about by import-penetration or expansion and transformation brought about by export growth. However, shifts in centres of production within a region might take place. Unlike capital goods producers, such as engineering, one does not encounter sharp cycles of activity but rather seasonal fluctuations (e.g. due to bad weather, as in the building trades), erratic cycles related to food prices, and the level of real wages which determine the level of demand, and long-term growth due to an expanding and increasingly prosperous population. Generally, therefore, there will be an expansion in the output of this sector of the economy in each country, and that expansion will largely take the form of a multiplication of small units of production. This distinguishes this type of trade sharply from those created or destroyed by industrial growth. But it is also very different from the trades which remain largely unchanged. In this fifth type of trade there were significant changes in distribution, credit, divisions of labour and some technological areas.

Perhaps the most important area of change involves large-scale capitalist control over distribution. The expansion and concentration of demand in towns encouraged such a development, which could then be extended to a region, even perhaps in a limited way to a national economy. Clothing production was especially vulnerable to this sort of development. Tailoring in large cities such as Paris, London, Berlin, Vienna and Hamburg was increasingly concentrated into a type of putting-out industry dominated by women, though with a significant element of the higher quality market continuing to be supplied by skilled male workers.[25] Sweated production came early to the London shoemaking trade and some operations had already ceased to be located in workshops by 1830. Instead, domestic manufacture increased in importance, as in the Northampton area from about this time.[26] In some cases, such developments could lead to a centre of production being established which virtually supplied a national market. Certain types of Parisian tailoring seem to be moving in this direction by the 1830s.[27] Hat-making in England provides an especially vivid illustration of how far this concentration of production into an area could develop.[28] But the development of sweated production, which blurs the line between craft-shop and household production, was based upon the rise of a type of merchant who sold directly to the consumer, or who controlled the links between producer and retailer. Increasingly, such merchant figures intervened in the production process and this could lead to the reduction of nominally independent producers to a *de facto* wage-earner status. But that was the final point which was by no means reached in many of these occupations. Just as important was the pressure it placed upon the small workshop.[29]

Furniture production displays the same general pattern of development, but in a much more limited form, perhaps because the scope for a division of labour and technical innovation was more limited. In various towns there did grow up central warehouses through which cabinet-makers and other craftsmen could sell their products, and there was a noticeable amount of hawking of home-made articles. The building trade was distinctive because production shifted from site to site. There was very little in the way of production of standardised components for supply to the site. But large building contracts (for non-domestic purposes — railway stations, factories, town halls, etc. — as well as for blocks of housing) could promote the rise of larger operators, the 'general contractor'. The role of the small employer, perhaps, diminished more rapidly in this trade as a consequence but the continuity of skilled craft labour with considerable control over work on the site continued.[30]

Examples of this type of development could be multiplied indefinitely. What is important is that these trades were expanding and were of central importance in the economy. They were not forced into contraction or extinction, so their problems cannot be seen as a struggle for survival. They were not completely transformed or even created by economic development, so existing organisations and ideas could be used constructively to respond to their new problems. They were sufficiently numerous and of sufficient economic importance for their responses to have significance for the development of the labour movement as a whole. They have been neglected in economic history because they do not represent dramatic growth or decline, and there are no easy measures of the sort of changes which do occur in these trades. They have been accorded much more attention in labour movement history quite simply because they are at the centre of so much of the labour movement. But there is a danger that if the basic economic context is misunderstood, so too will be the role they play within the labour movement. The next step is to see how new collective responses could be generated within these trades.

IV. The Move Beyond Occupation

Much of the response to these new problems took place within occupational boundaries. The traditions of these craftworkers were occupational ones. The struggles over control of recruitment, the redefinitions of work tasks, and the work process — all this led to the development of new forms of occupational organisation. These forms were rather different from later craft unionism. Workers often owned their own tools, fixed levels of output at the same time as negotiating on the price of their work, and carried out many 'managerial' tasks concerned with the pacing of work and the sequence of operations. Owners often possessed influence by virtue of their status as skilled workers. There were widespread expectations about treatment at work which could be enforced if necessary. There were funds to cope with unemployment, sickness, injury and death. These often had the market function of reducing competition in the labour market.

These actions were carried out mostly at an occupational and local level. Attempts to dilute apprenticeship and expand recruitment met with an enforcement of apprenticeship regulations upon the employer; such a move might well receive the tacit support of other employers, so one should not see such actions simply in terms of a conflict between skilled workers and employers. Attempts to alter established work practices were resisted for a number of reasons. Most obvious was the defence of recognised skills and controls. But it might also be to preserve employment when changes would reduce the time taken to do the job.[31]

Some actions extended beyond the locality. Unemployment benefit, for example, was often paid to artisans who had come from another area. It was necessary, therefore, to have a system for equalising the income and expenditure of the different branches of an occupational benefit scheme. Linked to this was the support given to the tramping artisan (*wandernden Gesellen, compagnon*). Workers often maintained 'houses of call' (*Herbergen*) to which newly-arrived craftsmen reported. Often the workers running these hostels sought to control the procedures of hiring, and these issues were a constant source of conflict. The hostels could become the centre of occupational organisation and the place which sustained the rituals and ceremonies of the trade. From it could be built up a network of contacts between different towns. In this way a supra-local solidarity could be developed, though confined to the occupational level.[32]

This cannot be seen in terms of class conflict. Frequently the same functions were performed by organisations controlled by masters and by skilled workers, though the issue of control was a very real one. Disputes often cut across master–men lines. At times of general political crisis this could lead to forms of populist politics which had only indirect links to labour movement politics. The lack of class-consciousness and conflict in these trades had little to do with the size of the unit of production or the likelihood of skilled workers becoming masters.[33] Class attitudes appear no more marked on large building sites than in small workshops. In many trades it can be shown quite simply through the master–men ratios that most skilled workers would not become a master, and that this had been the case for generations. It is difficult, therefore, to believe that such an expectation figured very prominently in the minds of those men;[34] we need to look elsewhere for the changes which lead to supra-occupational collective action on some sort of a class basis.

One final point should be noted about these occupational organisations. They were very unspecialised. Benefit funds were not rigorously devoted to specific purposes, a fact which could lead to financial difficulties and provide grounds for government intervention. The use of funds to pay benefits had close connections to the ability to withdraw labour in a dispute. The house of call could act as a focal point for collective activity of all sorts, including a type of labour exchange under the control of craftsmen. Many of the early labour movement institutions which extended beyond the occupation also took on this unspecialised character. This lack of specialisation, along with the local and occupational basis of much collective activity, meant that much of that collective activity was expressed in informal terms. Legal prosecution also encouraged informality of organisation, or the carrying-out of one set of actions within the framework of a formal organisation ostensibly concerned with other matters. Overlapping interests, legal intervention and uncertain finances often meant that particular formal organisations were in any case short-lived. But one should not equate formal organisation with collective action.[35]

There were limits to what occupationally-bounded collective action could achieve in the face of growth, increased competition, a more elaborate division of labour and the penetration of merchant capital. One response was a more clear-cut type of trade union resistance at the occupational level. I shall not consider that response here. Rather, I shall look at the moves towards collective action at a supra-occupational level.

This could take a number of forms. Government interference

with occupational organisations could lead to inter-trade co-operation opposed to that interference. Craftsmen from different trades could also cooperate in pursuit of improvements in the legislation concerning trade organisations. Examples of this were the campaigns in the late 1820s in England to prevent alterations to the law governing Friendly Societies, resistance to the new Master and Servant Bill in 1844, and trade union political action at the 1874 general election due to disappointment with the Liberal legislation on trade unions passed in 1871. In France George Duchêne, a printer, helped organise an inter-trade campaign against an 1846 Bill on *livrets* (pass books), and a Paris ordinance of 1846 setting up new *conseils des Prud'hommes* which gave workers no vote in their election. In Hamburg an inter-trade organisation to promote the interests of the 'manufacturing estate' [*Gewerbestandes*] was founded in 1846 and campaigned for legislative improvements. The Brotherhood of German Workers and other artisan associations in Germany between 1848 and 1851 put forward elaborate industrial legal codes designed to serve artisan interests.[36] This sort of action was more important in England than in either France or Germany, and has a lot to do with the nature of the political and legal system.[37] Furthermore, action of this type was usually undertaken for specific purposes at certain times and it was difficult for it to generate more continuous forms of collective action.

It is sometimes argued that workers turned to politics when economic action proved ineffective. This idea is not very useful for an understanding of the artisan labour movement. First, it implies a deliberate choice of action which seems unlikely. Second, it tends to conflate a number of different phenomena under the heading of 'politics' such as food riots, strikes, demonstrations, etc. Many of these forms of action are collective but not organised and only acquire a continual organised form by virtue of leadership from organised groups. Once that leadership disappears the whole movement quickly fades away. Thus the general workers' associations set up in Cologne in 1848 under radical leadership quickly acquired a four-figure membership on paper, but had as quickly shrunk to nothing a year later.[38] This is very different from the type of artisan cooperation which sustained London Chartism in the 1840s, or the work of the Luxembourg Commission in Paris in 1848, or the centres of the Brotherhood of German Workers in Berlin, Hamburg and Leipzig.[39] It was not so much short-term crises giving rise to 'hunger politics' which underpinned these movements, but rather a collective response to a longer-term problem.

To explain how this happened one could combine the 'intertrade cooperation' and 'hunger politics' interpretations. The types of changes already mentioned — overcrowding, increased competition for jobs, limited de-skilling, penetration of merchant capital — weakened existing occupational activity without destroying it and reduced living standards. The problem was one which developed over a period of time rather than taking the form of a sudden and terminal crisis. It presented itself to a number of occupations at the same time. This provided the basis for co-operation amongst members of these various trades seeking to buttress occupational resistance with a more broad-based resistance.

This did not necessarily lead to overt political action; there might be cooperation through support in a number of trades for a strike. This seems to have grown in importance in London in the 1820s and 1830s and contributed to the establishment of general unions.[40] This in turn could promote certain types of class-consciousness and language, though only of an intermittent kind. Again, a comparison of strikes in late eighteenth-century Germany and in the 1860s suggests that support from other trades, as well as the reduced involvement of small masters on the side of the strikers, were the most important changes. Again this could easily go along with an increased class perception of conflict.[41]

Which comes first — class-consciousness or class politics? Clearly there is no simple answer, and one cannot crudely separate ideas from actions. Nevertheless, it is worth asking how artisan ideology could be transformed in ways which promoted a class perception of the artisan situation and then to relate that to the development of new sorts of political activity.

V. Ideology

Economic situations and changes can be described in fairly general terms which apply across national frontiers. It is much more difficult to do this with ideology. Ideas are expressed in language and it is not easy to move from one language to another. Ideology is generated in an intellectual and political context which makes comparison difficult. In order to avoid being too abstract I shall try to illustrate my general argument with examples from Germany to show how certain basic issues are translated into a particular set of ideas. I shall then relate these points more briefly to the French and English cases.

A useful point of departure is to note the interest in general social thought in artisan circles during this period. Owen and Owenism, certain early theories of labour value, and a tradition of radical thought are all important within artisan circles in London and various provincial towns. Radical political ideas had a fairly long tradition, but interest in attempts at general social understanding was rather newer.[42] Utopian and other types of socialist thought had a great influence within artisan clubs in Paris and Lyons in the 1830s.[43] These ideas were in turn communicated to German emigré artisan groups in Paris, and found their way back into Germany.[44] For example, the phrase about a harmonious relationship between rights and desires, the individual and the whole, and work and pleasure quoted earlier from the statutes of the *Arbeiterverbrüderung* stands in a line of thought which can be traced back via Wilhelm Weitling, the socialist tailor, to Fourier.[45]

These ideas can be related more specifically to artisans. Thus the notion of the 'organisation of work' was not just a popular slogan associated with Louis Blanc, but was closely related to elaborate schemes and demands worked out in the Luxembourg Commission which in turn were linked to artisan trade unions.[46] Owenism and the involvement of committed Owenites in the London tailors' strike of 1834 was closely linked to the establishment of producer cooperatives which helped reduce the pressure upon strike funds.[47] The German emigré artisans established support for journals and books, and collective eating arrangements which directly reflected some of the ideas about enlightenment and cooperation which became so popular within those circles.[48] Social thinkers like Owen, Cabet, Weitling, Blanc, Marx and Engels were directly involved in collective artisan action.

In part, one can account for this in ways that have little to do with specific artisan concerns. This was the period when these sorts of ideas first began to be properly aired and were taken up by a variety of groups. One could argue that this was a time of general uncertainty and anxiety about the nature and direction of social change. Many ideas critical of the emergent capitalism, itself only dimly understood, appeared attractive, even within middle-class circles. This may account for the temporary popularity of men like Owen and Marx in such circles. Generally, one can point to a fading-away of this type of intellectual anxiety around the 1850s and correspondingly of an interest in systematic social thought.

Such ideas received particular support within artisan circles. What is more, this reception emphasised some ideas rather than others, and in doing so adapted the original ideas to specifically artisan concerns. It is not enough to see this in terms of a desperate escape into a world of fantasy, a common way of interpreting artisanal interest in 'utopian' socialism. But it would also be crude to see the ideas as simply providing legitimacy and help in the pursuit of practical concerns such as producers' cooperatives and soup kitchens. It was not a coincidence that these ideas had a practical application. The ideas and the problems of artisans had certain common roots.

During the tailors' strike in London low start-up costs and the dominance of small units of production made temporary co-operative production a possibility which could in turn help the strike. This was also the case in other trades. The idea of producers' cooperatives was attractive because they seemed to be within the bounds of possibility. The next step was to ask — given that production was possible by small units of production under a substantial degree of control by their skilled workforce — why was it that these workers faced severe problems? Why did the capitalist play such a large part in many sections of these trades? The images of the capitalist as intermediary, monopolist of links to the market, able to control producers through this position, and earning his income by underpaying the producer and overcharging the customer — all this could appear very plausible and attractive in such circumstances.[49] Certain utopian thinkers went further by recognising that the new, extensive forms of production and distribution could not be met through a simple return to petty commodity production on a local basis. These thinkers offered new solutions of a general kind by envisaging much more organised forms of production and distribution, even if the small workshop often figured as the central type of production unit. As the pressures of growth and capitalist transformation bore down upon the artisan, so ideas of this sort which were also a response to a fairly general form of development proved insistently attractive. Clearly these ideas were not derived from a simple experience of the problems. They need to be related to certain intellectual traditions and to the strenuous attempts by particular thinkers to master puzzles and problems posed to them by unprecedented social change. One also needs to pay close attention to the ways in which these ideas were appropriated by artisans. But the basic condition for the reception of these ideas into artisan circles is that these thinkers confronted generally the problems also faced by artisans.

Utopian socialist ideas in particular went beyond the limits of a purely negative criticism of 'parasites' which was so popular in artisan circles. They also suggested new identities and actions to artisans which played an important part in the early artisan labour movement. These general points can be illustrated in relation to the German case. I shall begin by considering the role of Wilhelm Weitling in the early German labour movement.

Wilhelm Weitling (1808-71) was the most important utopian socialist thinker within the early German labour movement. This movement developed abroad amongst artisans in Paris, London and towns in the German-speaking cantons of Switzerland. A major reason for the growth of the German artisan communities in which this movement developed was a crisis induced by expansion, overcrowding and merchant capitalist transformation of the kind already outlined.[50] Exile favoured a move towards supra-occupational organisation. Artisans from different occupations came together in clubs and soon discovered that they suffered from similar problems. They were further exposed to the exhilarating experience of living in relatively free political systems. They came into contact with German political exiles, with Parisian artisans, radical and early socialist groups, with the mass and radical politics of London in the late 1830s and early 1840s, and with the political tensions in the Swiss cantons and the concerns with making a reality of various forms of direct as well as representative democracy. A number of them moved from one centre to another so that there were communications between centres and attempts to synthesise the conclusions drawn from the different experiences. Weitling was a typical figure in that he was a tailor and he spent some time in all three centres. His work as an editor of journals and as a writer of various socialist tracts was sustained only through the artisan readership of the clubs to which he belonged, as well as to more direct financial support. Police files containing confiscated papers of artisans reveal that Weitling's works were, from the late 1830s right into the 1850s and beyond, amongst the most popular reading-matter of members of the artisan labour movement. Library collections of artisan associations show the same thing.[51]

Weitling was a utopian socialist. By this I mean that his central concern was to describe in detail an ideal socialist society. This description took priority over a consideration of actions in the present which were seen simply as methods for reaching the ideal goal. The vision was socialist in that he envisaged a society in which the means of production were in social ownership, and production and exchange were socially planned. His response to criticism was typical of the utopian thinker: he tried to iron out any apparent inconsistencies in the blueprint and piled up further detail of how the ideal society would work. Like all utopian thought, his system was closed to external criticism. One either found the general vision attractive or not, and the detailed arrangements plausible or not. But why should artisans in the sort of situation I have already described be attracted to such ideas? How, indeed, did their situation in part help produce such ideas?

A closer examination of Weitling's ideas shows them to be based completely upon a vision of craft production in small workshops; large-scale manufacturing, domestic production and farming hardly figure. The manner in which the workshops are subjected to social authority bears an uncanny resemblance to the procedures of guilds, only these have become general and democratic institutions rather than occupational and local corporations largely under master control. For example, Weitling recognised that it would be necessary to plan the supply of labour to different branches of production. To do this he recommended that the standards of examination used to establish people's qualifications to carry out certain types of work should be varied in accordance to the number of people required. Guilds themselves used this as one method to regulate the labour supply. Artisan associations both before and during 1848 demanded that this be done (though not by the existing guilds) for the same reasons. Weitling's utopianism can be seen as generalised transformation of existing artisan practice. It is this which both helps explain how he could come to construct such an imagined society and why that construction should appear so relevant and attractive to his artisan audience. It was also one way of making the move beyond the occupational boundary.

Yet one cannot reduce Weitling's utopia simply to such terms. He was influenced by ideas which had little directly to do with artisans. Nineteenth-century utopian thought owes much to an Enlightenment tradition of the perfectibility of man and the associated notions of progress, equality, and the capacity to use reason to organise society rationally. Utopianism represents the most literal application of such notions. More specifically, Weitling took his ideas about basic appetites and the need to satisfy these in a balanced way from Fourier. He was indebted to other French socialist writers for his views about the close relationship between private property and inequality. A crude form of the labour theory of value underpinned his violent hostility to money and his elaborate system of labour notes which are needed in the absence of money to facilitate the equitable exchange of products over and beyond socially necessary levels of output.

Nevertheless one can relate much of this back to artisan experiences. The artisan who experienced capitalism as control through credit, access to the market and manipulation of competition amongst direct producers, rather than as a productive function itself, was likely to share this hostility to money and the power it seemed to confer upon its unproductive holders. Socialisation of the kind outlined by Weitling could be seen as enabling the direct producers once more to enter into direct relations with one another. It would cut out the intermediaries and the manipulations and mystifications that accompanied their mediations. But it would not mean a simple restoration of the guild system. Given the way the guilds were seen by many artisans as corrupt and discriminatory institutions, such a restoration could hardly appear attractive.[52] So in a number of ways one can make connections between Weitling's utopianism, the situation of many artisans, and the shift of artisan ideology beyond occupational boundaries. Because of these connections Weitling was able to flavour his speculations about the future with telling details about the humiliations of the tramping artisan, the egotistical character of guilds, the cold-shouldering received from local communities, the harassment from state officials, and the exploitation practised by parasitic merchants. This increased the sense of indignation amongst his readers and the feeling that some general solution was needed. This in turn made the artisan audience more receptive to the utopian recommendations. In this way Weitling helped provide artisans who were joining supra-occupational associations with a range of supra-occupational identities and objectives. These could then inform practical activity in artisan associations in such areas as consumer cooperation, education and personal relationships, even if these were only diluted expressions of the values commended by Wietling.

From the early 1840s artisans were able to set up general associations in a number of German states. Although modelled in many ways upon the exiles' experiences, these associations had to confine themselves, at least publicly, to non-political matters. Most of the associations called themselves workers' or artisans' educational associations (*Arbeiter-* or *Handwerker Bildungsvereine*).[53] Although utopian socialist and radical democratic ideas circulated within these associations, both the pressures from the authorities and the real, if very limited, practical improvements which the associations could promote, led to a stress upon peaceful change, above all through education. The 'true socialist' idea of locating the 'true' inner man and bringing him out into the social world by means of education could appear attractive in these circumstances.[54] These ideas, though more abstract than those of utopian socialism, can be connected to an image of the artisan as a truly respectable, independent, dignified person, degraded by external circumstances. The artisanal rather than class basis of this idea is revealed in the declaration of a Hamburg worker that 'The proletariat will start to vanish from the time when the self-knowledge of the worker begins to grow.' It is also expressed in the idea that education in this spirit can preserve the integrity of the *goldene Mittelstand.* The pressures of the economic crisis in the years 1845-47 meant that true socialist ideas, less specific to artisan interests than utopian socialist ideas, could evoke a response from a wide range of *petit bourgeois* groups. The political implications of the true socialist idea of educating individuals towards a better society and the utopian socialist idea of constructing an ideal society which will transform individuals are also very different. True socialism was less threatening to the existing order than utopian socialism. But both appealed to a class of small producers and retailers; both condemned capitalism perceived in mercantile terms; and both contributed to a type of populist politics which was central to the revolution of 1848.[55]

The stress on education had other implications. It shifted attention from power to enlightenment. This was a characteristic response of groups without power. It gave a special significance to the self-improvement efforts of artisan autodidacts and the propaganda work of intellectuals. It was accompanied by quite practical concerns with vocational education and repairing the deficiencies of elementary schooling. It could be used to mediate the culture of the 'educated classes' to artisans, though this was of very limited importance in this period. It is not very meaningful at this time to talk of any sort of bourgeois hegemony in these artisan associations.[56]

These ideas continue in very different forms and contexts. In 1848 discussion gave way to action. But many of those actions — as the quotation from the statutes of the Brotherhood of German Workers makes clear — were informed by ideas that had been taken up before 1848. In the brief era of a 'liberal labour movement' in the late 1850s and early 1860s, self-help projects were heavily impregnated with ideas about cooperatives and educational associations that can be traced back to Weitling. Schulze-Delitzsch, sometimes referred to as the Robert Owen of Germany, was popular amongst artisans less because of the liberal economic ideology to which he related his interest in cooperatives, and more because of his practical help to cooperative action amongst artisans which they invested with quite different meanings.[57] The appeal of Lassalle's emphasis in 1863 upon state funding of producers' cooperatives can also be related to this artisan tradition.[58] And even later, for example in the development of social democracy as an almost self-sufficient subculture organised around a network of associations, the tradition is carried on, even if now attached to notions of class and an official obeisance to Marxist ideas.[59]

Thus, right through the period 1830 to 1870, and even beyond, the ideas which attracted artisans who gathered in supra-occupational associations were those that related to the problems of expansion, overcrowding and merchant capitalist penetration. Utopian socialism, true socialism, liberalism and Lassalleanism were all linked to these central concerns which looked to general association and regulation as a solution. Ironically, even the ideas of Marx and Engels, which so trenchantly attacked these other ideas (and also shaped the way they were understood by posterity) were often appropriated by artisans in ways which linked them back to artisan rather than working-class concerns.[60] Furthermore, what Marx and Engels expressed was often shaped by these artisan concerns, either as a deliberate concession to gain artisan support, or as an assumption taken into their own understanding of the nature of the proletariat.[61] This continuity of concern which underlies many surface changes in artisan ideology, remained central to the labour movement as a whole because it was a response to certain central tendencies in the economic development of the period.

I have tried to illustrate the general arguments about the development of supra-occupational organisation and ideology with material from the German case. Clearly a full argument would have to expand on this case and also look at other national cases in detail. Some work on France and England has shown that it is possible to build a case of this kind. The arguments of Stedman-Jones concerning the language of Chartism, for example, can be connected to the artisan experience of capitalism as an external pressure rather than one located within the system of production.[62] Behagg has shown how an apparently 'traditional' small workshop sector can be transformed by forms of capitalist development, and how this linked to new types of associative effort amongst artisans.[63] Tholfsen, Crossick and Gray have shown — admittedly in very different ways — how an artisan tradition rather than the values of other social groups informs so much of the effort and ideology of the mid-century labour movement.[64] Prothero has demonstrated in detail the connections between the problems of London artisans in the first half of the nineteenth-century, and a range of ideas about cooperation, politics, respectability and socialism.[65] The links between the attractions of Owenism and the practical problems of London tailors in 1834, or the way in which artisan problems underpinned the moves to supra-occupational organisation in London in the National Charter Association in the early 1840s, can be analysed in broadly similar ways to those I have outlined for the German case. Again the work of Johnson on Cabet and the appeals of his utopianism in France, of Moss on the continuity of craft concerns in the French labour movement up to and beyond 1900, and of Hanagan on the centrality of artisans in the political and industrial labour movement in late nineteenth-century France, can support this kind of analysis.[66]

One must not overstate the similarities. The weight of such trades in the whole economy varied from one case to another. The time-lags between comparable problems in different trades could inhibit a supra-occupational response. The general social context varied. Thus artisan movements had a different character and importance in the city, the small town and the countryside. The points made here are particularly applicable to the city context. The institutional context is also very different — for example,

guilds are important in some cases but not in others. But nevertheless there is a general argument which can usefully be applied to
these different cases. The specifically political implications of these
arguments now need to be considered.

VI. Politics

If by politics is meant organised activity aimed at altering the
structure or policies of the state, then artisan politics in the period
under consideration was a discontinuous activity. Bodies such as
the National Charter Association, or the Brotherhood of German
Workers, or the Democratic-Socialist Party in the Second Republic
were temporary organisations. With developments such as the
establishment of a Political Committee of the TUC and an active
labour element in the Liberal Party, with the founding of the General German Workers' Association by Lassalle in 1863, and the
formation of socialist parties in France in the 1880s, one sees
developing a rather different conception of politics as a permanent
activity.

This discontinuity of political activity had implications for the
artisan understanding of politics. Politics was not seen in terms of
continuous bargaining between a variety of groups; rather politics
was seen as a temporary intervention which, if successful, would
remove the need for further political activity. At the limited practical level, politics was an interest-group activity taken up to remedy
some specific grievance. Once this had been achieved — for
example, the repeal of the Combination Acts in 1824 — the political interest-group could be dissolved, and one could return to a
range of non-political activities. This was, of course, true of
popular politics generally.

A second, broader but still negative view of politics was to see it
as a means of blocking intrusive action from above. Thus in part
the politics of the 1830s in England were intended to throw back
the new forms of state intervention in such areas as poor relief and
policing. What might be called 'old constitutionalism' was one
aspect of this defensive response. To some extent the demand for
the vote could be seen in a similar way: once there was a mass
electorate it would be impossible for the state to pursue such an
interventionist policy. Chartists do not seem to have worked out a
positive view of a new political process based upon universal

suffrage. This absence of a vision of a political process built upon a democratised state applies to France and Germany even more, where opportunities for continuous political participation in the existing state were much more limited. Interestingly, the case of Switzerland with a type of cantonal politics permitting broad participation also saw the development of a tradition of sustained practical democratic political thought which appealed to artisan groups.[67]

A third anti-political conception of politics was to see the political campaign as being about the implementation of social justice. Social justice itself was understood in terms of artisan ideas that have already been discussed. Once political action had achieved social justice — by abolishing the placemen, the parasites, the jobbers, etc. and by introducing the rule of the direct producer — then politics would be replaced by the organised activity of those direct producers who would have no serious conflicts amongst themselves. The purely radical democrats seemed to envisage that a limited range of political actions would suffice to create this happy state, whereas the social-democrats did see that some changes in the 'organisation of work' would also be required.[68]

There are two ways of accounting for this set of political attitudes. One approach would be to focus on the nature of the political system. If provision is not made for continuous political participation on the part of artisans; if there are not institutions such as enduring political parties, elections held on a broad franchise, and a broad-based structure of public opinion, then politics is bound to be discontinuous and to be seen as an abnormal activity. Equally, the political reforms which permit a continuous artisan presence to be articulated and organised in the political system will be seen as a sufficient condition for a shift to a view of politics as a normal enduring activity by which conflicting interests negotiate with one another. A second approach would emphasise the corporate nature of artisan life. Here the emphasis would be less upon the discontinous nature of politics, but rather upon the lack of specialisation in artisan life which would prevent a clear and distinct idea of politics developing.

The multi-purpose and often informal nature of artisan associations has already been mentioned. Politics was often just one of the areas in which an association intervened. Thus the Brotherhood of German Workers sought to bring an influence to bear upon voting in election campaigns and local branches were often the main vehicle for constructing political alliances between labour and middle-class groups. But the organisation continued simultaneously to pursue educational, cooperative, convivial, benefit fund and trade union purposes. Furthermore, like the Luxembourg Commission or the National Charter Assocation, it was organised on an occupational basis, though one should note that these latter two organisations were based only on Paris and London, respectively. People joined as members of the basic artisan unit, the occupation, and not as individuals. Yet, unlike a trade union federation, there was no conception of a specialised economic function for these organisations.

This had two implications. First, the emphasis upon one rather than another activity had less to do with a clear switch from one mode of action to another, but was rather a matter of what was appropriate in a given context. For example, the Brotherhood became increasingly 'non-political' in 1850 and 1851 and focused upon other areas. Some (mainly West German historians) have seen in this a form of reformism.[69] They argue that the move involved an abandonment of revolutionary illusions and a focus on practical work of the sort that would lead to pragmatic trade unionism. Others, (mainly East German historians) have seen it as no more than a public pose in the face of a hostile counter-revolution.[70] For them the League of Communists, now forced underground, continued to cultivate a revolutionary political attitude and was still central to the labour movement. Both approaches are anachronistic (the idea that the League of Communists was important is also absurd), projecting back on to the artisan movement of this time sets of contrasting terms such as reform and revolution, politics and trade unionism, which belong to a later age of specialised political and economic activity. Clearly the Brotherhood toned down its political concerns because of the dangers that became apparent from 1850, but equally clearly its emphases upon cooperation and education were not cosmetic or deceptive. Rather there was a shift in the balance of actions undertaken within this multi-purpose organisation according to changes in the situation in which the organisation found itself.

If one emphasises this aspect, it would not be political reform which would undermine the distinctively artisan view of politics, but rather the more general break-up of the artisan world. Thus many artisans objected to Lassalle's attempt to set up a specialised political party not because it was politically inappropriate, but because it broke with the whole character of artisan collective activity. One can go on to consider the penetration into artisan circles of new ideas which broke up the artisan emphasis. The penetration of liberal ideas appealing to people as citizens or as opponents of irrational or privileged religion; the appeal of class, whether in terms of a 'fourth estate' which needed to be accorded its place within the political order or as the instrument for the final abolition of class division; or the appeal of confessional or ethnic identities to minorities — these could all cut through the communal nature of the artisan world. The conditions under which political language of this kind penetrated artisan politics, and how far it could take up any connections with artisan traditions, needs careful analysis. For example, one might argue that the class perception of politics offered by Marx — which saw politics based upon a total, collective identity and which saw the ultimate end of politics in the classless society — that this perception of politics could more easily penetrate the artisan world than could the view of class politics which simply saw it in a permanent pluralist system. That in part can help account for why what was still very much an artisan labour movement in Germany could come to adopt an orthodox Marxist programme in 1891. But that goes beyond the concerns of this essay.

Two further points should be made about the general nature of artisan politics. First, it was often very imitative. Thus the oaths and cell structure of artisan societies under the July Monarchy and in the German exile associations owed something to the ritual of journeymen associations but much more to the secret societies of radical republicans. The educational associations established in Germany in the 1840s followed on closely from the setting-up of similar organisations amongst other social groups. Second, artisan politics often developed out of general crises which were first brought about largely independently of any artisan efforts: 1848 provides the best example of this.

Finally, the extent to which constructive political activity between artisans and non-artisans could be developed would influence how far specifically artisan concerns and attitudes were reflected in artisans' political activity. This is why it is perhaps harder to distinguish a specifically artisan mode in English politics compared with German or French politics of the period. The political systems in which artisans organised were very different and this had fundamental consequences for the overall character of the labour movement.

In the English case one needs to make a distinction between the period from 1830 to 1850 and that from 1850 to 1870. The first period is marked by a tightening-up of the political system and a number of innovations which threatened artisan interests. In many ways the political system was less open to artisan influence after 1832 than before, as the Reform Act standardised an exclusive franchise, as urban government reform diminished the importance of institutions such as vestries which had often been fairly open to popular pressure, and as changes in the methods of poor relief and policing appeared to threaten labour interests. In many ways one can see Chartism as a response to this political transformation rather than seeking an explanation in terms of industrial growth and crisis or the early emergence of a modern class society. This general political change led to links between artisan and non-artisan labour groups, even if the language of Chartism owed much to artisan perceptions of the divide between useful people and parasites.[71] But whereas many of these other labour groups (such as handloom weavers) ceased to act collectively from the mid-century, artisan groups were able to respond to changes in the political system which allowed limited participation by trade unions, political reform groups in urban politics and even, after 1867, in national politics. By this time, however, a range of other occupations were also involved in trade union and political activity — above all from the engineering and textile industries. The artisan contribution to politics is therefore sometimes difficult to distinguish as it develops within a broader-based labour movement.

In the French case one is dealing with a much more restrictive political system. From 1834 until the later 1840s these restrictions were intensified, though there was some relaxation prior to 1848. However, the July Revolution itself, and the role of radical republicanism in the underground politics of the 1830s and 1840s, meant that politics became specialised and at the same time transcended specifically artisan concerns. Nevertheless, by comparison with England, the labour movement itself was a much more narrowly artisan movement and those broader forms of politics, when responding to labour pressure, reflected specific artisan concerns much more clearly than in the English case. The role of someone like Louis Blanc in the early period of the Second Republic, and the urban base being developed from the early

1850s by a radical democratic movement that was no longer almost exclusively Parisian, illustrate this point. Blanc in particular was very clearly tied to the interests of artisan trades, as the work of the Luxembourg Commission demonstrates.

I have compared the development of German labour politics with that of England in the period 1850-75 elsewhere, and there is no need to go into this in detail here.[72] Instead I shall draw together a number of points on Germany in summary form. I have already pointed to a continuity of artisan concern underlying the interests in such various sets of ideas as utopian and true socialism, Marxism, liberal cooperation and Lassalleanism. One can relate the apparent shifts in ideological concerns to the shifts of emphasis in the actions of multi-purpose artisan associations as the context in which these operated changed. Thus the interest in liberalism in the late 1850s and early 1860s had a lot to do with the need to be cautious about open political activity and the value of operating under the umbrella of a broad liberal movement which furnished political leadership while the artisan associations could concentrate upon other activities. The shift to Lassalle (though only on the part of a small minority of organised artisans), as well as the rise of a conservative artisan movement amongst masters, arose out of a sense of frustration at the limited role offered to artisans within that broader liberal movement. But even in the Lassallean movement there was — at least amongst the artisan elements involved — a constant pressure to widen the scope of the association beyond specialised political activity. The more general moves of artisans to specialised politics came with three fundamental developments: first, the breakdown of the broad liberal movement in the face of unification in 1866-67 meant that the option of working within liberal politics suddenly became less attractive; second, unification led to the construction of political institutions such as a national Parliament elected on the basis of universal manhood suffrage which directly encouraged specialised political activity; and third, along with unification and political change went a series of economic changes — above all liberalisation and rapid growth — which pushed craftworkers into a wave of strikes and union formations. This both encouraged the use of the language of class and the making of a clearer distinction between political and economic forms of action. On the basis of these changes the traditional forms of artisan politics rapidly declined, although many of the broader artisan concerns remained influential.

It is possible, therefore, to discern a set of political attitudes and forms of political action in this period which might be regarded as typically artisan. One can also see what types of political change as well as broader changes could undermine that artisan politics. Finally, one can relate those general points to the different political contexts of the various countries in order to grasp both differences and similarities in the way artisans behaved politically.

VII. Conclusion

There is a distinctive set of artisan occupations which were both expanded and transformed by the development of capitalism in Western Europe in the mid-nineteenth century. These occupations were of central importance in both the economic development of the period and even more so within the labour movement. Their initial importance within the labour movement was because they could adapt existing ideas and forms of action to the pressures upon them in order to put up a collective resistance to those pressures. Their subsequent importance was because they played a significant part in the developing industrial capitalist economy and because they were responding to the impact of capitalism upon their own trades.

In responding to this impact these artisans appropriated, on their own terms, ideas which had been developed in an effort to make sense of the large-scale and unprecedented social changes of the period. These ideas went beyond occupational boundaries and the confines of artisan tradition, although artisan concerns re-emerge in a general form. The taking-up of these ideas was linked to the development of supra-occupational collective action on the part of artisans. These general ideas and forms of action in turn shaped artisan politics, although the specific forms taken by those politics depended upon the nature of the political system and the ways in which non-artisan groups related to artisans.

That briefly summarises the arguments of this essay. My main concern has been to show that artisans should neither be seen simply as 'pre-industrial' or 'pre-capitalist' figures, nor as skilled wage-earners. One approach stresses discontinuity within the labour movement too much; the other, continuity. What is needed is a general framework for analysis in which both change and continuity can be grasped and which makes it possible to compare and contrast the artisan role in the labour movements of different countries. The purpose of this essay has been to suggest the lines on which such a general framework might be constructed.

Notes

Unless otherwise stated, the place of publication is London.

1. J.H. Clapham, *An Economic History of Modern Britain: vol. II, Free Trade and Steel 1850-1886* (Cambridge, 1932), esp. Ch. IV. See also idem., *The Economic Development of France and Germany, 1815-1914* (4th edn, Cambridge, 1968).
2. K. Kumar, *Prophecy and Progress: The Sociology of Industrial and Post-Industrial Society* (Harmondsworth, 1978).
3. Quoted in I.J. Prothero, *Artisans and Politics in early 19th century London: John Gast and his Times* (Folkestone, 1979), p. 332.
4. Quoted in F. Balser, *Sozial-Demokratie 1848/49-1863: Die erste deutsche Arbeiterorganisation 'Allgemeine deutsche Arbeiterverbrüderung' nach der Revolution* (2 vols., Stuttgart, 1962), vol. 2, pp. 507-23.
5. *Populaire*, 30 January 1842. I am indebted to Iori Prothero for drawing my attention to this reference.
6. H. Weisser, *British Working-Class Movements and Europe 1815-1848* (Manchester, 1975); W. Schieder, *Anfänge der deutschen Arbeiterbewegung: Die Auslandsvereine im Jahrzehnt nach der Julirevolution von 1830* (Stuttgart, 1963).
7. A recent example is Barrington Moore, *Injustice: The Social Bases of Obedience and Revolt* (1978).
8. See A.E. Musson, *British Trade Unions 1800-1875* (1972) for this general view. It has been restated in a different way in recent work on craft control and sectionalism in the later nineteenth century. See, for examples, A. Reid, 'Politics and Economics in the Formation of the British Working Class: A Response to H. Moorhouse', *Social History* 3/3 (1978); R. Penn, 'Trade Union Organisation and Skill in the Cotton and Engineering Industries in Britain, 1850-1960', *Social History*, 8/1 (1983); R. Price, 'The Labour Process and Labour History', *Social History* 8/1 (1983); J. Zeitlin, 'Craft Control and the Division of Labour: Engineers and Compositors in Britain 1890-1930', *Cambridge Journal of Economics* 3 (1979).
9. J. Breuilly, 'The Labour Aristocracy in England and Germany: A Comparison', *Bulletin of the Society for the Study of Labour History* 48 (1984). For France the point has been made recently in M.P. Hanagan, *The Logic of Solidarity: Artisans and Industrial Workers in Three French Towns 1871-1914* (Urbana, Ill., 1980), though accompanied by the assumption that France is especially backward in this regard.
10. Clapham (1932), *op. cit.* A more recent argument on these lines, based on qualitative detail rather than quantitative evidence, is R. Samuel, 'The Workshop of the World: Steam Power and Hand Technology in Mid-Victorian Britain', *History Workshop Journal* 3 (1977).
11. See M. Berg, *et al.*, *Manufacture in Town and Country before the Factory* (Cambridge, 1983).
12. For the earlier period, see Balser, *op. cit.*; T. Offermann, *Arbeiterbewegung und liberales Bürgertum in Deutschland 1850-1863* (Bonn, 1979); U. Engelhardt, *'Nur vereinigt sind wir stark': Die Anfänge der deutschen*

Gewerkschaftsbewegung 1862/63 bis 1869/70 (2 vols., Stuttgart, 1977); W. Renzsch, *Handwerker und Lohnarbeiter in der frühe Arbeiterbewegung: Zur sozialen Basis von Gewerkschaften und Sozialdemokratie im Reichsgründungsjahrzehnt* (Göttingen, 1980). For examples from the period around the turn of the century, see E. Domansky-Davidsohn, *Arbeitskämpfe und Arbeitskampfstrategien des Deutschen Metallarbeiterverbandes von 1891 bis 1914* (Ph. D. thesis, Ruhr-Universitat Bochum, n.d., forthcoming); M. Nolan, *Social Democracy and Society: Working-class Radicalism in Düsseldorf, 1890-1920* (Cambridge, 1981); K. Schonhöven, *Expansion und Konzentration: Studien zur Entwicklung der Freien Gewerkschaften in Wilheminischen Deutschland 1890-1914* (Stuttgart, 1980).

13. T. Markovitch, 'The Dominant Sectors of French Industry', in *Essays in French Economic History*, ed. R. Cameron (Homewood, Ill., 1970). Generally, see R. Price, *An Economic History of Modern France* (2nd. edn, 1981). So far as the labour history is concerned, see in addition to work already cited B.H. Moss, *The Origins of the French Labor Movement: The Socialism of Skilled Workers, 1830-1906* (Berkeley London, 1976) for a general interpretation. More specifically see B. Moss, 'Parisian Producers' Associations (1830-1851)', and C.H. Johnson, 'Economic Change and Artisan Discontent: The Tailors' History 1800-1848', both in *Revolution and Reaction* ed. R. Price (1975).

14. Samuel, *loc. cit.*, indicates an economic continuity. A political continuity across the 1850 divide is indicated in P. Hollis and B. Harrison, 'Chartism, Liberalism and the Life of Robert Lowery', *English Historical Review* 82 (1967); and idem. (eds.), *Robert Lowery: Radical and Chartist* (selected writings) (1979).

15. Many of Fischer's articles which are used here, as well as others of relevance, are conveniently published in a collection of his writings, *Wirtschaft und Gesellschaft im Zeitalter der Industrialisierung* (Göttingen, 1971) in a section entitled 'Das deutsche Handwerk im Zeitalter der Industrialisierung'.

16. The major case-study is by a student of Fischer's, A. Noll, *Sozio-ökonomische Strukturwandel des Handwerks in der zweiten Phase der Industrialisierung unter besonderer Berucksichtigung Arnsberg und Münster* (Göttingen, 1975).

17. Clapham (1968) vol. 2, *op. cit.*

18. Samuel, *loc. cit.*

19. Markovitch, *loc. cit.* In a recent article H. Kaeble has argued the converse case that German industrialisation was not especially rapid or focused on heavy industry. 'Der Mythos von der rapide Industrialisierung in Deutschland', *Geschichte und Gesellschaft* 9/1 (1983).

20. An example is the argument about the role of the artisan in the June 1848 insurrection in Paris which threatened to become an assertion of the pre-industrial nature of the insurgents in order to contradict the contemporary interpretations of Marx and de Tocqueville that this was the first clear case of a modern class struggle. See R. Price, *The French Second Republic: A Social History* (1972) for a statement of the argument in these terms. A detailed consideration which indicates (though does not clearly argue) a different way of looking at the question is C. Tilly and L. Lees, 'Le peuple de juin 1848', *Annales Économies Sociétiés Civilisations* 29 (1974).

21. O. Crisp, 'Labour and Industrialisation in Russia', in *The Cambridge Economic History of Europe.* vol. II, Part 2, ed. P. Matthias and M.M. Postan (Cambridge, 1978).

22. For Germany, see W.H. Scroeder, *Arbeitergechichte und Arbeiterbewegung: Industriearbeit und Organisationsverhalten im 19. und frühe 20. Jahrhundert* (Frankfurt am Main/New York, 1978).

23. It is interesting that the continual role of skilled craftsmen from early to

later industrial times in Britain was most strongly emphasised by Musson, an historian of printers: *The Typographical Association* (1954); and that the leading advocate of a long enduring labour aristocracy in Germany was G.Beier, an historian of printers: 'Das Problem der Arbeiteraristokratie im 19, und 20. Jahrhundert', in G. Beier, *Geschichte und Gewerkschaften* (Cologne, 1981), and *Schwarzkunst und Klassenkampf* (Frankfurt am Main, 1966).

24. See the extended review of Foster's book on *Class Struggle and the Industrial Revolution* (1974) by G. Stedman-Jones, 'Class Struggle and the Industrial Revolution', *New Left Review*, 90 (1975), now reprinted in a collection of his essays, *Languages of Class: Studies in English Working-class History 1832-1982* (Cambridge, 1983).

25. On the tailoring trade see Renzsch, *op. cit.* for Germany; Johnson, *loc. cit.* for France; and T. Parssinen and I. Prothero, 'The London Tailors' Strike of 1848 and the Collapse of the Grand National Consolidated Trades Union', *International Review of Social History* XXII/1 (1971).

26. See Schroeder, *op. cit.* for Germany; and for a wide-ranging essay, E. Hobsbawm, 'Political Shoemakers', *Past and Present* 89 (1980).

27. For Paris tailoring, see Johnson, *loc. cit.*; and Moss, *loc. cit.*; and in 1848 R. Gossez, *Les Ouvriers de Paris*: vol. 1, L'Organisation 1848-1851 (Paris, 1967), esp. pp. 160-6.

28. The felt-hat industry in England in the early nineteenth-century offers an extreme example of regional concentration into one area — Lancashire and Cheshire, especially the firm Christys in Stockport — without any major technological changes taking place. See P.M. Giles, 'The Felt-Hatting Industry, c. 1500-1850 with Particular Reference to Lancashire and Cheshire', *Transactions of the Lancashire and Cheshire Antiquarian Society* LXIX (1959).

29. See P. Hudson, 'Protoindustrialisation: The Case of West Riding', *History Workshop Journal* 12 (1981) for the reasons why this type of economic activity could develop in different ways centred upon the direct producer or the merchant.

30. The small-scale nature of domestic house building is brought out in G. Crossick, *An Artisan Elite in Victorian Society: Kentish London, 1840-1880* (1978); and the development of the 'general contractor' in R. Price, *Masters, Unions and Men: Work Control in Building and the Rise of Labour* (Cambridge, 1980).

31. See M. Sonescher, 'Work and Wages in Paris in the 18th Century', in Berg, *op. cit.*, for a subtle account of the non-wage economic ties between craftworkers and masters.

32. On Germany, see R. Elkar, 'Wandernde Gesellen in und aus Oberdeutschland', in *Handwerker in der Industrialisierung* ed. U. Engelhardt (Stuttgart, 1984) who will soon be publishing a book on the subject. For Britain see E. Hobsbawm, 'The Tramping Artisan' in his *Labouring Men* (1968); P.H. Gosden, *The Friendly Societies in England 1815-1875* (Manchester, 1961); and R.A Leeson, *Travelling Brothers* (1979). For France see J. Briquet, *Agricole Perdiguier, compagnon du tour de France et representant du peuple, 1805-1875* (Paris, 1955).

33. This point has been well made recently by C. Behagg, 'Custom, Class and Change: The Trade Societies of Birmingham', *Social History* 4/3 (1979).

34. Official Handwerk statistics bear this out for Germany, as is shown in J. Breuilly and W. Sachse, *Joachim Friedrich Martens (1806-1877) und die Deutsche Arbeiterbewegung*, (Göttingen, 1984), Ch. 2.

35. See Behagg, *loc. cit.*

36. Prothero, *op. cit.* for the 1820s; and H. McCready, 'The British Election of 1874: Frederick Harrison and the Liberal–Labour Dilema', *Canadian Journal of Economic and Political Science* 20 (1954); G. Duchene, *Actualité, Livret et*

Prud'hommes (Paris, 1847). I am grateful to Iori Prothero for drawing my attention to this pamphlet and campaigners. On the Hamburg association, see Breuilly and Sachse, *op. cit.*, Ch. 4. For Germany between 1848 and 1851 see Balser, *op. cit.*; and P. Noyes, *Organisation and Revolution: Working-Class Associations in the German Revolutions of 1848-1849* (Princeton, N.J., 1966).

37. I argue this case at length in 'Bürgerliche Gesellschaft und Arbeiterbewegung, öffentliches Recht und Klassenverhältnisse. Ein Vergleich zwischen Deutschland und England', in *Arbeiter und Bürger im 19. Jahrhundert*, ed. J. Kocka (Munich, 1985). This article is in English.

38. S. Na'aman, *Demokratische und soziale Impulse in der Frühgeschichte der deutschen Arbeiterbewegung der Jahre 1862/63* (Wiesbaden, 1969).

39. Ibid., for comparisons between different areas in Germany. For Paris see Gossez, *op. cit.* For London see I. Prothero, 'London Chartism and the Trades', *Economic History Review* 24 (1971); idem., 'Chartism in London', *Past and Present* 44 (1969); and D. Goodway, *London Chartism 1838-1848* (Cambridge, 1982), Part IV.

40. Prothero, *op. cit.*; and R. Kirby and A.E. Musson, *The Voice of the People. John Doherty, 1798-1854: Trade Unionist, Radical and Factory Reformer* (Manchester, 1975).

41. J. Kocka, *Lohnarbeit und Klassenbildung: Arbeiter und Arbeiterbewegung 1800-1875* (Bonn, 1983), esp. pp. 154-62.

42. See G. Stedman-Jones, 'Re-Thinking Chartism', in *Languages of Class, op. cit.*

43. See C. Johnson, *Utopian Communism in France: Cabet and the Icarians* (Ithaca, Ill., 1970); and B. Moss, 'Parisian Workers and the Origins of Republican Socialism 1830-1833', in *1830 in France* ed. J. Merriman (New York, 1975).

44. Schieder, *op. cit.*

45. For Weitling, see below.

46. Gossez, *op. cit.*

47. Parssinen and Prothero, *loc. cit.*

48. Schieder, *op. cit.*; and for and East German study, see W. Kowalski, *Vorgeschichte und Entstehung des Bundes der Gerechten* (East Berlin, 1962).

49. For England see Stedman-Jones, *loc. cit.*; and I. Prothero, 'William Benbow and the concept of the "General Strike"', *Past and Present* 63 (1974). For France see Johnson, *op. cit.*; and W. Sewell, *Work and Revolution in France: The Language of Labor from the Old Regime to 1848* (Cambridge Mass., 1980). For Germany see Breuilly and Sachse, *op. cit.*, Ch. 2.

50. Ibid., Ch. 2.

51. Ibid., Ch. 2 for an extended treatment of Weitling along the lines sketched out here. The least important of Weitling's three main works is translated into English as *The Poor Sinner's Gospel* (1969). The German version of that along with his first utopian work *Die Menschheit wie sie ist und wie sie sein sollte* (1838) are published along with a useful introduction by W. Schafer (Reinbek bei Hamburg, 1971). The major work was *Garantien der Harmonie und Freiheit* (1842). *The Poor Sinners' Gospel* raises one issue of major importance in artisan ideology which I have had to omit for reasons of space — the abiding interest in a radical form of Christianity.

52. For the traumatic break between guilds (which often became instruments of territorial states) and journeymen around the beginning of the nineteenth-century, see A. Griessinger, *Das symbolishe Kapital der Ehre* (Frankfurt am Main, 1981).

53. K. Birker, *Die deutschen Arbeiterbildungsvereine 1840-1870* (West Berlin, 1973).

54. The labelling and critique of other forms of socialism was, of course, a major concern of *The Communist Manifesto* as well as *The German Ideology*.

Engels singled out 'true socialism' for attack in 'Die wahren Sozialisten', in *Marx-Engels Werke*, 3, pp. 248-90.
55. Breuilly and Sachse, *op. cit.*, for these details on Hamburg.
56. See R. Vierhaus, 'Bürgerliche Hegemonie oder Proletarische Emanzipation: der Beitrag der Bildung', in *Arbeiter und Bürger im 19. Jahrhundert, op. cit.*
57. See Breuilly, 'Liberalism or Social Democracy? A comparison of British and German labour politics, c. 1850-1875', *European History Quarterly* (January 1985); Offermann, *op. cit.*; and R. Aldenhoff, *Schulze-Delitzsch: Ein Beitrag zur Geschichte des Liberalismus zwischen Revolution und Reichsgründung* (Bonn, 1984).
58. Renzsch, *op. cit.*; and C. Stephan, *'Genossen, wir durfen uns nicht von der Geduld hinreissen lassen!' Aus der Urgeschichte der Sozialdemokratie 1862-1878* (Frankfurt am Main, 1977).
59. G. Roth, *The Social Democrats in Imperial Germany: A Study in Working-Class Isolation and National Integration* (Totowa, N.J., 1963).
60. The history of the League of the Communists could be written in terms of this relationship of mutual exploitation and incomprehension between Marx and Engels on the one hand and the artisan membership on the other. Unfortunately, that is not the form the fairly barren ideological histories of the League have taken.
61. For example when Engels wrote a communist catechism in 1847 and Marx the Inaugural Address of the International Working Men's Association in 1864, they had to modify their own position in order to appeal to artisans. The way in which a variety of experiences (the social question in Germany, Engels' work on the Manchester working class, and Marx's direct contacts with politically active artisans) shaped Marx's complex, even contradictory idea of the proletariat has still not received the treatment it merits. A step in that direction is H. Draper, 'The Concept of the *Lumpenproletariat* in Marx and Engels', *Économie et Société* (December 1972).
62. Stedman-Jones, *loc. cit.*
63. Behagg, *loc. cit.*
64. T. Tholfsen, *Working-Class Radicalism in Mid-Victorian Britain* (1978); Crossick, *op. cit.*; R.Q. Gray, *The Labour Aristocracy in Victorian Edinburgh* (Oxford, 1976) — though these three works argue somewhat different cases from different sorts of evidence. Much of this work is summed up in R. Gray, *The Aristocracy of Labour in 19th Century Britain, c. 1850-1914* (1981).
65. See the various works by Prothero already cited in these notes.
66. Johnson, *op. cit.*; Moss, *op. cit.*; Hanagan, *op. cit.*
67. See F. Wirth, *Johann Jakob Treichler und die soziale Bewegung im Kanton Zürich (1845/1846)* (Basle/Frankfurt am Main, 1981).
68. This argument surfaced in artisan circles in the mid-1830s and could also be seen as a source of tension within the Chartist movement.
69. Balser, *op. cit.*
70. H. von Berg, *Entstehung und Tätigkeit der Norddeutschen Arbeitervereinigung als Regionalorganisation der Deutschen Arbeiterverbrüderung nach der Niederschlagung der Revolution von 1848/49* (Bonn, 1981).
71. Stedman-Jones, *loc. cit.*
72. Breuilly, *loc. cit.*

BIBLIOGRAPHY OF GWYN A. WILLIAMS' WORK

Books

Medieval London: from Commune to Capital (Athlone, 1963).
Artisans and Sans-culottes: Popular Movements in Britain and France during the French Revolution (Edward Arnold, 1968).
Proletarian Order: Antonio Gramsci, Factory Councils and the Origins of Communism in Italy, 1911-21 (Pluto, 1975).
Paolo Spriano, *The Occupation of the Factories, Italy 1920* trans. and ed. G.A. Williams (Pluto, 1975).
Goya and the Impossible Revolution (Allen Lane, 1976; Peregrine edn, 1984; Spanish, Italian and German translations, 1977).
The Merthyr Rising (Croom Helm, 1978).
The Search for Beulah Land: The Welsh and the Atlantic Revolution (Croom Helm, 1980).
Madoc: The Making of a Myth (Eyre Methuen, 1980).
The Welsh in Their History (Croom Helm, 1982).
When Was Wales? A History of the Welsh (Black Raven, 1985; Pelican edn, 1985).

Booklets, Documentary Essays, etc.

Rowland Detrosier, A Working-class infidel 1800-1834 (Borthwick, York, 1965).
France 1848-51: Interpretations of the French Revolution: Karl Marx and Alexis de Tocqueville, Open University Course A321 Unit 7. (Milton Keynes, 1975).
'Proletarian Forms: Gramsci, Councils, Communism', *New Edinburgh Review*, Special Gramsci numbers I and II, ed. Chic Meisels, 1974.

Essays in Books

'Owain Glyn Dŵr', and 'The Emergence of a Working-Class Movement', both in *Wales Through the Ages*, 2 vols., ed. A.J.

Roderick (Christopher Davies, 1960, 3rd impression 1971).
'Hugh Owen', in *Pioneers of Welsh Education,* ed. C.E. Gittins (University College of Swansea, 1964).
'The Merthyr of Dic Penderyn', in *Merthyr Politics: The Making of a Working-class Tradition,* ed. Glanmor Williams (University of Wales, 1966).
Introductory essay to John Gorman, *Banner Bright: The Banners of the British Trade Union Movement* (Allen Lane, 1973; Penguin, 1976).
'Antonio Gramsci', in *The Founding Fathers of Social Science,* ed. Timothy Raison, a series from *New Society* (Scolar, 1979).
'Locating a Welsh Working Class: The Frontier Years', in *A People and A Proletariat: Essays in the History of Wales 1780-1980,* ed. David Smith, (Pluto and *Llafur,* The Society for the Study of Welsh Labour History, 1980).
'Druids and Democrats: Organic Intellectuals and the First Welsh Radicalism', in *Culture, Ideology and Politics: essays for Eric Hobsbawm,* ed. Raphael Samuel and Gareth Stedman Jones (Routledge & Kegan Paul, 1982).
'18ᵉBrumaire: Karl Marx and Defeat', in *Marx A Hundred Years On,* ed. Betty Matthews (Lawrence & Wishart, 1983).

Articles

'The Merthyr Riots: Settling the Account', *National Library of Wales Journal,* xi (1959).
'Friendly Societies in Glamorgan 1793-1832', *Bulletin of the Board of Celtic Studies,* xviii (1959).
'The Concept of *Egemonia* in the thought of Antonio Gramsci', *Journal of the History of Ideas,* xxi (1960).
'Edward I and London' (Alexander Prize Essay), *Transactions of the Royal Historical Society,* (1961).
'The Making of Radical Merthyr 1800-1836', *Welsh History Review,* i (1961).
'Morgan John Rhys and Volney's *Ruins of Empires*', *Bulletin of the Board of Celtic Studies,* xx (1962).
'The Succession to Gwynedd 1238-47', *Bulletin of the Board of Celtic Studies,* xx (1964).
'South Wales Radicalism: The First Phase', *Glamorgan Historian,* ed. S. Williams, ii (1965).

'Morgan John Rhees and his Beula', *Welsh History Review,* iii (1967).
'Merthyr 1831: Lord Melbourne and the Trade Unions', *Llafur* (Welsh Labour History Society), i (1972).
'The Making and Unmaking of Antonio Gramsci', *New Edinburgh Review,* special Gramsci number III, ed. Chic Meisels (1975).
'Welsh Indians: the Madoc Myth and the First Welsh Radicalism', *History Workshop,* i (1976).
'John Evans's Mission to the Madogwys, 1792-99', *Bulletin of the Board of Celtic Studies,* xxvii (1978).
'Dic Penderyn, the Making of a Welsh Working-class Martyr', *Llafur,* ii (1978).
'When was Wales?', BBC Wales Annual Radio Lecture (BBC, 1979).
'The Merthyr Election of 1835', *Welsh History Review,* x (1981).
'Mother Wales, get off me back?' *Marxism Today,* December 1981.
'Land of our Fathers', *Marxism Today,* August 1982.
'Women Workers in Wales, 1968-82', *Welsh History Review,* xi (1983).
'Karl Marx Journalist', *Journalism Studies Review,* Centre for Journalism Studies, University College Cardiff, viii (1983).
'Marcsydd o Sardiniwr ac Argyfwng Cymru' (Sardinian Marxist and Welsh Predicament), *Efrydiau Athronyddol* (Philosophical Studies, University of Wales) xlvii (1984).

Radio, Televison, Occasional Writings, etc.

Radio Scripts

Dowlais Story (*Iron Town* for BBC Home Service London), *Welsh Chartism, City Built on Sand* (Port Talbot) and *Tonypandy 1910,* produced by John Griffiths for BBC Wales, 1960-61.
Lady Charlotte Guest, produced by Herbert Williams for BBC Radio 3, 1984.
Numerous Schools broadcasts, talks, etc.

Television Script Writing and Presentation

Madoc, directed by Merfyn Williams (BBC Wales) for Chronicle,

BBC-2, 1977;

Merthyr Riots, St David's Day feature, directed by Merfyn Williams, BBC Wales, 1977, repeated 1979.

Ar Lan y Môr, mae Palas y Glo (on the centenary of the Coal Exchange, Cardiff) directed by Richard Pawelko (Teliesyn) for Sianel Pedwar Cymru, 1984.

The Dragon Has Two Tongues (with Wynford Vaughan Thomas), a 13-episode history of Wales, produced and directed by Colin Thomas, an HTV production for Channel 4, 1985.

Play

The View from Poppa's Head, performed by the Dramatic Society of University College of Wales Aberystwyth, and awarded the one-act plaque, at NUS Drama Festival, Bristol 1960.

Eye-Witness, the history page of the journal *Rebecca*, 1981-82.

Editorial Committee of the journal *Radical Wales* (Plaid Cymru), launched 1983.

Reviews, mostly for *The Guardian*, two of which (on the Marx family) were reprinted in a *Bedside Guardian*.

Fellowships, etc.

David Davies Open Scholarship, University College of Wales, Aberystwyth, 1943.

Dr Samuel Williams Studentship, University of Wales, 1950.

Fellowship of the University of Wales, 1952.

Goldsmiths' Company's Post-Graduate Research Studentship, University College London, 1952.

Alexis Aladin Russia Scholarship, University College of Wales, Aberystwyth, 1960.

Simon Research Fellowship, University of Manchester, 1961.

American Council of Learned Societies Fellowship, University of Pennsylvania, 1966.

John Carter Brown Library Fellowship, Brown University, 1966.

Visiting Fellowship, St Anthony's College, Oxford, 1970.

Prizes

Alun Lewis Memorial Essay Prize, University College of Wales, Aberystwyth, 1949.

Dr Joseph Hamwee Graduate Prize, University College of Wales, Aberystwyth, 1950.

Alexander Prize, Royal Historical Society, 1960.

Welsh Arts Council Prizes: for *Goya*, 1977; for *The Merthyr Rising*, 1979.

NOTES ON CONTRIBUTORS

JOHN BREUILLY is Senior Lecturer in History at the University of Manchester. He was taught by Gwyn Williams as an undergraduate at the University of York. His publications include *Nationalism and the State* (1982) and, with Wieland Sachse, *Joachim Friedrich Martens (1806-1877) und die deutschen Arbeiterbewegung* (1984), as well as a number of articles on comparative labour history in nineteenth-century Europe.

MICHAEL DUREY is Senior Lecturer in History at Murdoch University, Western Australia. He studied under Gwyn Williams as both an undergraduate and research student at the University of York. He is author of *Return of the Plague: British Society and the Cholera* (1979) and various articles on medical history in Britain and Australia. He is currently working on British political emigrants to the USA, 1790-1820.

CLIVE EMSLEY is Senior Lecturer in History at the Open University. He was taught as an undergraduate at York by Gwyn Williams. He has been visiting fellow at Griffith University, Queensland, and visiting professor at the University of Paris VIII. His publications include *British Society and the French Wars 1793-1815* (1979) and *Policing and its Context 1750-1870* (1983).

DAVID JONES is Senior Lecturer in History at the University College of Swansea. He is a graduate of the University of Wales and was taught by Gwyn Williams at Aberystwyth. He has published widely on British political and social history of the eighteenth and nineteenth centuries. His most recent book is *The Last Rising: The Newport Insurrection of 1839* (1985).

DAI SMITH is Senior Lecturer in the History of Wales at University College, Cardiff. He was educated at Balliol in History, and at Columbia in Literature. His research has been chiefly concerned with modern Wales. His publications include with Hywel Francis, *The Fed: A History of South Wales Miners in the Twentieth*

Century (1980) and *Wales! Wales!* (1984) which was linked with
his series for BBC television.

DAVID VINCENT is Lecturer in History at the University of
Keele. He was taught by Gwyn Williams as an undergraduate at
the University of York and went on to study for his doctorate at
Cambridge. His publications include *Bread, Knowledge and
Freedom* (1982) and, with John Burnett and David Mayall, *The
Autobiography of the Working Class* (1984). At present he is
writing a book on literacy and popular culture in England between
1750 and 1914.

JAMES WALVIN is Reader in History at the University of York.
He was educated at the Universities of Keele and McMaster; he
studied for his doctorate under Gwyn Williams at York. He has
published extensively on modern British social history and on the
history of slavery and the slave trade. His most recent publications
include *A Child's World* (1982) and *English Urban Life 1776-
1851* (1984)

ROGER WELLS is Senior Lecturer in Modern History at
Brighton Polytechnic. Another product of Gwyn William's period
at the University of York he has taught at the universities of
Exeter, Wales and York. He has published widely on late
eighteenth and early nineteenth-century British social history,
including *Insurrection: The British Experience 1795-1803* (1983).
He is currently preparing a study of famine in England during the
wars with Revolutionary France.

INDEX